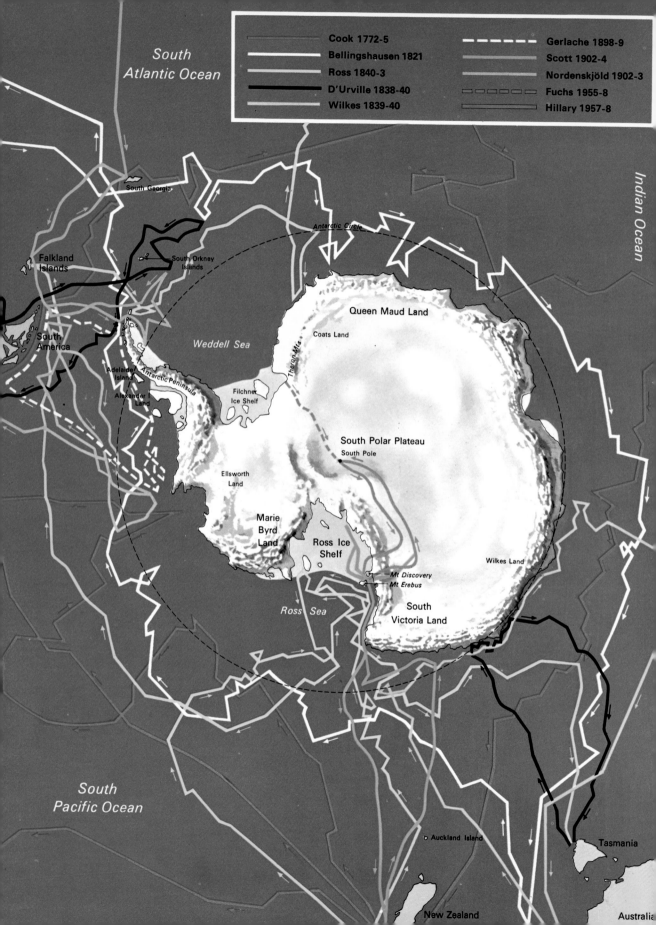

South
Atlantic Ocean

Indian Ocean

South Georgia

Antarctic Circle

Queen Maud Land

Coats Land

Falkland
Islands

South Orkney
Islands

Weddell Sea

South
America

Theron Mts

Adelaide
Island
Alexander I
Land

Antarctic Peninsula

Filchner
Ice Shelf

South Polar Plateau
South Pole

Ellsworth
Land

Marie
Byrd
Land

Ross Ice
Shelf

Wilkes Land

Mt Discovery
Mt Erebus

South
Victoria Land

Ross Sea

South
Pacific Ocean

Auckland Island

Tasmania

New Zealand

Australia

# Antarctica:
# The Last Continent

## Ian Cameron

**Cassell & Company Ltd   London**

CASSELL & COMPANY LTD

an imprint of
Cassell & Collier Macmillan Publishers Ltd
35 Red Lion Square, London WC1R 4SG
and at Sydney, Auckland, Toronto, Johannesburg

*and an affiliate of*
*The Macmillan Company Inc., New York*

This book was designed and produced by
George Rainbird Limited
Marble Arch House, 44 Edgware Road
London W2 2EH

House editor: Mary Anne Norbury
Designer: Jonathan Gill-Skelton
Maps: Tom Stalker-Miller
Coloured artwork: David Nockels
Index: E. F. Peeler

First published 1974

ISBN 0 304 29416 0

Colour plates originated by Westerham Press Ltd,
Westerham, Kent

Text set, printed and bound by
Jarrold & Sons Ltd, Norwich
F.474

*Reverse of frontispiece* Cape Kloostad taken
during Sir Edmund Hillary's expedition to
Antarctica in 1967

*Frontispiece* Map showing the routes taken
by the principal expeditions discussed in the
book

# Contents

# Illustrations and Acknowledgments

All maps are by Tom Stalker-Miller unless otherwise stated.

**(reverse of frontispiece)** Cape Kloostad taken during Sir Edmund Hillary's expedition to Antarctica in 1967. Daily Telegraph Colour Library, London

**(frontispiece)** Map showing the routes taken by the principal expeditions discussed in the book

**Page 11** The Antarctic seen from space. Copyright National Oceanic and Atmospheric Administration, Boulder, Colorado

**Page 13** The Earth as a flat ellipse enabling one to relate the Antarctic to other continents

**Page 14 (left)** Mean annual temperature. **(right)** Average annual accumulation

**Page 15** Tracks frequently/occasionally followed by cyclonic storms

**Page 16** Spray ridges of ice on Cape Evans – in the distance Inaccessible Island, photographed by H. G. Ponting, 8 March 1911. Royal Geographical Society, London. Copyright Paul Popper Ltd

**Page 19** Dawn over Adelaide Island showing consolidated pack ice. Photo Dr Ronald J. Lewis Smith

**Page 20** Detail of a romanticized depiction of James Clark Ross's ships *Erebus* and *Terror*, 1817, by J. W. Carmichael. National Maritime Museum, London. Photo Richard Jervis

**Page 22** Mela's map of the world, A.D. 1

**Page 23** Detail of a manuscript attributed to Macrobius in the Bibliothèque Nationale, Paris. Royal Geographical Society, London

**Page 24** Cordiform map of the world by Orontius Finaeus, 1566. Royal Geographical Society, London

**Page 27 (left)** Sir Francis Drake. **(right)** Ferdinand Magellan. Both Royal Geographical Society, London

**Page 29** Jean Bouvet de Lozier, engraved by Hubert after Dumontier. Bibliothèque Nationale, Paris

**Page 30 (above)** Yves-Joseph de Kerguélen-Trémarec. **(below)** The northern part of Kerguélen Island. Both Musée de la Marine, Paris

**Page 35 (above right)** Captain James Cook, engraved by J. Basire after William Hodges, 1777. **(below)** A pen and wash sketch showing the *Resolution en route* to the Antarctic, by William Hodges. Both National Maritime Museum, London

**Page 37** Captain James Cook, by Nathaniel Dance. National Maritime Museum, London

**Page 38** Detail of the *Resolution* beating through the ice, by J. Webber. National Maritime Museum, London

**Page 41** A plan of the *Resolution*. National Maritime Museum, London

**Page 44** Cook's voyage around the Antarctic continent

**Page 47** Detail of the *Journal* for 17 January 1773, in Cook's own hand. National Maritime Museum, London

**Page 52 (left)** Possession Bay in the island of South Georgia, engraved by S. Smith after William Hodges, from *A Voyage towards the South Pole and Round the World*, by James Cook, Vol. II, 1777. Royal Geographical Society, London. **(right)** View of the ice islands as seen by Cook on his second voyage. Radio Times Hulton Picture Library, London

**Page 55 (above)** Leopard seal (*Hydrurga leptonyx*). Photo Dr R. M. Laws. **(below)** Fur seals (*Arctocephalus gazella*) and gentoos (*Pygoscelis papua*), near Johnson Cove, Bird Island. Photo Dr Ronald J. Lewis Smith

**Page 56 (above)** Female Weddell seal *(Leptonychotes weddelli)* and pup. Photo Dr Ronald J. Lewis Smith. **(below)** Southern elephant seal *(Mirounga leonina)*. Photo W. L. N. Tickell

**Page 58 (above)** Distribution of leopard (*Hydrurga leptonyx*) and southern elephant (*Mirounga leonina*) seals. Copyright British Antarctic Survey, Monks Wood Experimental Station, Abbots Ripton, Huntingdon. **(below)** Southern elephant seals (*Mirounga leonina*). Photo Dr R. M. Laws

**Page 60 (above left)** A try pot in South Georgia. Photo Dr B. B. Roberts. **(above right)** Captain R. F. Scott's sealing knife. Scott Polar Research Institute, Cambridge. **(below)** Crabeater seals (*Lobodon carcinophagus*). British Antarctic Survey, London
**Page 63 (above)** Kerguélen (or 'white') fur seal (*Arctocephalus gazella*). Photo Dr R. M. Laws. **(below left)** Distribution of Weddell (*Leptonychotes weddelli*) and Kerguélen fur (*Arctocephalus gazella*) seals. **(below right)** Distribution of Ross (*Ommatophoca rossi*) and southern fur (*Arctocephalus australis*) seals. Both copyright British Antarctic Survey, Monks Wood Experimental Station, Abbots Ripton, Huntingdon
**Page 64 (above right)** Weddell seal (*Leptonychotes weddelli*). **(above left)** Kerguélen fur seal (*Arctocephalus gazella*). **(below)** Ross seal (*Ommatophoca rossi*). Photos Dr. R. M. Laws
**Page 70** Map of the South Shetland Islands and the adjacent Antarctic Peninsula with the outline of Edward Bransfield's chart superimposed
**Page 71** Nathaniel Palmer. American Geographical Society, New York
**Page 74 (above)** Thaddeus von Bellingshausen. **(below)** Bellingshausen's ships *Vostok* and *Mirnyi*. Both Scott Polar Research Institute, Cambridge
**Page 76** Map of Bellingshausen's route
**Page 78 (above left)** The *Vostok*. Central Naval Museum, Leningrad. **(above right)** Mikhail Lazarev, Captain of the *Mirnyi*. Scott Polar Research Institute, Cambridge
**Page 86 (above)** Peter I Island, off the southern end of the Antarctic Peninsula. **(centre)** Lyeskov and Visokoi, two of the South Sandwich Islands. **(below)** Candlemas and Vindication, two of the South Sandwich Islands. All redrawn by Tom Stalker-Miller from sketches illustrated in *The Voyage of Captain Bellingshausen to the Antarctic Seas, 1819–1821*, edited by Frank Debenham, 1945
**Page 91** Map showing John Davis's possible route in the *Cecilia*, 31 January to 10 February 1821, redrawn from American Geographical Society Special Publication, No. 39, 1971
**Page 93** Map of J. S. C. Dumont D'Urville's route
**Page 94 (above)** Dumont D'Urville, by D. Maurin, 1840. National Maritime Museum, London. Photo Rodney Todd-White. **(below)** One of the many engravings in Dumont D'Urville's *Atlas* illustrating various aspects of the *Astrolabe*'s and *Zelée*'s expedition to the South Pacific and Antarctic waters. Royal Geographical Society, London. Photo J. R. Freeman
**Page 97 (above)** Mt Erebus on the beautiful Ross Island with James Clark Ross's *Erebus* and *Terror* in the foreground, 28 January 1841, by John Edward Davis, second master of the *Terror*. **(below)** *Erebus* passing through a chain of bergs, 13 March 1842, by John Edward Davis. Both National Maritime Museum, London. Photos Rodney Todd-White
**Pages 98 and 99** Dumont D'Urville's corvettes *Astrolabe* and *Zelée*, 25 January 1840, drawn and lithographed by Louis Le Breton and published by Auguste Bry, Paris. National Maritime Museum, London. Photo Rodney Todd-White
**Page 100 (above)** Celebrating New Year's Day 1842 on the ice floes in latitude 66° 32′ S, longitude 156° 28′ W, by John Edward Davis. **(below)** Watering *Terror* in the pack ice, 1842, by John Edward Davis. Both Scott Polar Research Institute, Cambridge. Photos Edward Leigh
**Page 103 (above left)** Charles Wilkes, by Alonzo Chappel after a photograph. Scott Polar Research Institute, Cambridge. **(below)** Wilkes's brig *Porpoise*, colour aquatint by W. J. Bennett. National Maritime Museum, London
**Page 104** Map of Wilkes's route
**Page 106** James Clark Ross, by J. R. Wildman. National Maritime Museum, London
**Page 109** Adélie penguin (*Pygoscelis adeliae*). Ardea Photographics. Photo Bernard Stonehouse
**Page 110** Giant petrel chick (*Macronectes*

*giganteus*). Photo Dr Ronald J. Lewis Smith
**Page 112** Map of Ross's route
**Page 113** 'False sea leopard (*Leptonyx Weddelli*)' – now called Weddell seal (*Leptonychotes weddelli*), plate V in *The Zoology of the Voyage of H.M.S. Erebus and Terror*, by the zoologist who accompanied Ross to the Antarctic, Joseph Dalton Hooker. Scott Polar Research Institute, Cambridge
**Page 117** An eighteenth-century engraving of a female whale showing the various implements employed to secure her capture. National Maritime Museum, London
**Page 119 (above)** Fin whale (*Balaenoptera physalus*), **(centre)** blue whale (*Balaenoptera musculus*), **(below)** sperm whale (*Physeter catodon*). Artwork David Nockels
**Pages 120 and 121** Flensing baleen (or whalebone) whales. Photo Charles Swithinbank
**Page 122 (above)** Southern right whale (*Eubalaena australis*), **(centre)** humpback whale (*Megaptera novaeangliae*), **(below)** killer whale (*Orcinus orca*). Artwork David Nockels
**Page 124** A killer whale (*Orcinus orca*). British Antarctic Survey, London
**Page 128** Whale catchers of former times in South Georgia. British Antarctic Survey, London
**Page 129** A now disused land-based whaling station at Leith Harbour, South Georgia. Antarctic whaling is now entirely carried out from floating factory ships as seen on pages 120 and 121. British Antarctic Survey, London
**Page 131** Layered cloud on Coronation Island, South Orkney Islands. Photo P. J. Tilbrook
**Page 132** Sunset on Coronation Island as seen from Berntsen Point, South Orkney Islands. Photo P. J. Tilbrook
**Page 134 (above right)** Adrien de Gerlache de Gomery. Royal Geographical Society, London. **(below)** The *Belgica*. Scott Polar Research Institute, Cambridge
**Page 136** Map of de Gerlache's route
**Page 143** Henryk Arctowski. American Geographical Society, New York

**Page 147 (above right)** Members of the Swedish South Polar Expedition on their departure from Gothenburg: (standing left to right) Bodman, Skottsberg, K. A. Andersson; (sitting left to right) Ohlin, Nordenskjöld, Larsen, Ekelöf **(centre left)** Bodman working at the dining table. On the wall the barograph, evaporimeter, the registering apparatus of the anemometer and the paper of the sunshine recorder. **(below)** 'We were, on the whole, well satisfied with our dwelling-house'. All from *Antarctica*, by Dr N. Otto G. Nordenskjöld and J. G. Andersson, 1905. Royal Geographical Society, London
**Page 152** Map of Nordenskjöld's route
**Page 159 (above)** Sastrugi on Barne Glacier, by H. G. Ponting, 21 February 1911. (**(below)** Young ice forming, by H. G. Ponting, 7 March 1911. Both Royal Geographical Society, London. Copyright Paul Popper Ltd
**Page 161** Map showing Amundsen's and Scott's routes to the South Pole
**Page 162 (left)** Captain Robert Falcon Scott, leader of the 1901–4 expedition to Antarctica, aboard the frozen-in and snowed-up *Discovery* in McMurdo Sound. The ship broke free from the ice and sailed for home on 16 February 1904. Photo Paul Popper Ltd **(right)** Scott just before leaving for the South Pole, by H. G. Ponting, 26 January 1911. Royal Geographical Society, London. Copyright Paul Popper Ltd
**Page 163** Roald Amundsen. Roald Amundsens Museum, Borge, Norway. Photo Odd F. Lindberg
**Page 165** *Discovery* with parhelia, by Edward Wilson (SPRI 521). Scott Polar Research Institute, Cambridge. Photo Edward Leigh
**Page 166** Emperor penguins (*Aptenodytes forsteri*), by Edward Wilson (SPRI 491). Scott Polar Research Institute, Cambridge. Photo Edward Leigh
**Page 167 (left)** In order to free the *Discovery* from her ice prison in 1904, successful blasting operations were carried out. **(right)** The two relief ships *Morning* and

*Terra Nova* which were not needed when *Discovery* broke out of the ice. Photos Paul Popper Ltd

**Page 168** Evening in Amundsen's winter quarters: (left to right) Bjaaland, Hassel, Wisting, Helmer Hanssen, Amundsen, Johansen, Prestrud and Stubberud. Roald Amundsens Museum, Borge, Norway. Photo Odd F. Lindberg

**Page 169 (left)** Amundsen's ship the *Fram*. Radio Times Hulton Picture Library, London. **(right)** Members of Amundsen's team with dogs and sledges. Roald Amundsens Museum, Borge, Norway. Photo Odd F. Lindberg

**Page 175** Auroral corona with two figures, by Edward Wilson (SPRI 1386). Scott Polar Research Institute, Cambridge. Photo Edward Leigh

**Pages 176 and 177** Hut Point, McMurdo Sound, by Edward Wilson (SPRI 423). Scott Polar Research Institute, Cambridge. Photo Edward Leigh

**Page 178** Snow petrel (*Pagodroma nivea*), by Edward Wilson (SPRI 1932). Scott Polar Research Institute, Cambridge. Photo Edward Leigh

**Page 179** Amundsen at the South Pole. Royal Geographical Society, London

**Page 181 (above left)** Clissold the cook making bread, by H. G. Ponting, 26 March 1911. **(above right)** Captain Oates and some of his ponies, by H. G. Ponting. **(centre left)** Officers' living quarters: (left to right) Cherry-Garrard, Lieutenant Bowers, Captain Oates, Meares and Dr Atkinson, by H. G. Ponting, 9 October 1911. **(centre right)** In the wardroom of the *Terra Nova*, by H. G. Ponting. **(below left)** H. G. Ponting lecturing on Japan, 16 October 1911. **(below right)** Dr Atkinson in his laboratory, by H. G. Ponting, 15 September 1911. All Royal Geographical Society, London. Copyright Paul Popper Ltd

**Page 182** The *Terra Nova* held up in the pack ice, by H. G. Ponting, 13 December 1910. Royal Geographical Society, London. Copyright Paul Popper Ltd

**Page 183 (left)** Leopard seal (*Hydrurga leptonyx*), by Edward Wilson (SPRI 67/4/3). Scott Polar Research Institute, Cambridge. **(right)** Emperor penguins (*Aptenodytes forsteri*). British Antarctic Survey, London

**Page 184** Captain Scott working on his diary. Photo Paul Popper Ltd

**Page 185 (left)** Pitching a tent in a high wind, by Edward Wilson (SPRI 1343). **(centre)** Three men inside a pyramid tent, by Edward Wilson (SPRI 1396). **(right)** A bad-weather sketching box from the manuscript of *The South Polar Times*, by Edward Wilson (SPRI ms 231/1). All Scott Polar Research Institute, Cambridge

**Page 187 (above)** Opalescent alto stratus and a snowdrift 1–2 pm, 17 August 1903, looking north towards McMurdo Sound, by Edward Wilson (SPRI 1245). **(below)** Sledge hauling on skis on a grey day on the Great Ice Barrier, by Edward Wilson (SPRI 530). Both Scott Polar Research Institute, Cambridge. Photos Edward Leigh

**Page 188** Wandering albatross and chick (*Diomedea exulans*). Photo Dr Ronald J. Lewis Smith

**Page 191 (above)** Byrd wearing arctic kit with a sundial compass, 1926. Radio Times Hulton Picture Library, London. **(below left)** Map of Byrd's flight

**Page 194** Dog teams of the geological party crossing the Great Ice Shelf on the way to the Queen Maud Range. Royal Geographical Society, London

**Page 195** Admiral R. E. Byrd. Radio Times Hulton Picture Library, London

**Page 199** Aerial view of the foothills of the Queen Maud Range taken by Byrd. Royal Geographical Society, London

**Page 200** An aerial photograph by Byrd captioned 'The land of eternal snow'. Royal Geographical Society, London

**Page 205 (above left)** Sir Ernest Shackleton. **(below left)** *Endurance*. Photos Paul Popper Ltd. **(below right)** Map of Shackleton's journey

**Page 207 (above left)** Frank Hurley and Shackleton at Patience Camp, by Frank Hurley. **(above right)** Ice flowers in early spring, by Frank Hurley. Both Scott Polar Research Institute, Cambridge

**Page 209** Frank Wild examining the wreckage of the *Endurance*, by Frank Hurley. Scott Polar Research Institute, Cambridge

**Page 214 (top left)** Tracks of the *Endurance* and her boats. **(top right)** Drying clothes on Elephant Island, by Frank Hurley. Both Royal Geographical Society, London. **(above left)** The arrival at Elephant Island, by Frank Hurley. Scott Polar Research Institute, Cambridge. **(above right)** The living quarters on Elephant Island, by Frank Hurley and George Marston. **(below right)** Shackleton and his companions setting off for help. Possibly executed by George Marston from memory. Both Royal Geographical Society, London

**Page 220** Sir Edmund Hillary, Dr Vivian Fuchs and Rear Admiral George Dufek (American Task Force Commander) at the South Pole, 19 January 1958. British Antarctic Survey, London

**Page 223 (left)** The Ferguson tractor and 'caboose' in which Sir Edmund Hillary drove to the South Pole. **(right)** A Sno-cat being checked and loaded before leaving South Ice on Christmas Day. Both British Antarctic Survey, London

**Page 227 (above)** Aluminium bridges in position underneath Sno-cat *Able* to enable her to be hauled out of her predicament. **(below)** Sno-cat *Rock 'n Roll* down a crevasse. British Antarctic Survey, London
*Page 229 (above)* Moon halo (Mt Erebus behind) and a vertical beam, 12 June 1905, by George Marston. Photo Edward Leigh. **(below)** The coast of Elephant Island on one of the few bright evenings experienced by the men left behind, by George Marston. Both Scott Polar Research Institute, Cambridge

**Pages 230 and 231** Twin-Otter aircraft on the ice, Adelaide Island, 15 February 1973. British Antarctic Survey, London

**Page 232** Dr Michael Gill, in 1967, was the first man to climb Mt Herschel. Daily Telegraph Colour Library, London

**Page 235 (left)** The Crossing Party at the South Pole, 19 January 1958. Fuchs (front row left). **(right)** Coal seams in the Theron Mountains which correspond to the main coal horizons of Australia and South Africa. Both British Antarctic Survey, London

**Page 237 (below left)** A diver preparing to go through sea ice. Photo Dr R. M. Laws. **(below right)** R. H. Ragle, the leader of a 'deep-drilling' project at Little America, the headquarters of Operation Deep Freeze IV, checks the core brought up from more than 500 ft. Photo Paul Popper Ltd

**Page 239 (above)** The American base at Hut Point, McMurdo Sound. Beyond on the runway of the Sound's ice surface are some of the ski-equipped planes attached to Operation Deep Freeze. In the distance Mt Discovery. **(left)** The helicopter from the icebreaker U.S.S. *Glacier* unloads stores on to the ice. Photos Paul Popper

**Page 242** The British base Foxtrot on the Antarctic peninsula is one of the six scientific bases visited by the *John Biscoe*. Photo Paul Popper Ltd

**Page 247** The base by moonlight, Signy Island, South Orkney Islands. Photo P. J. Tilbrook

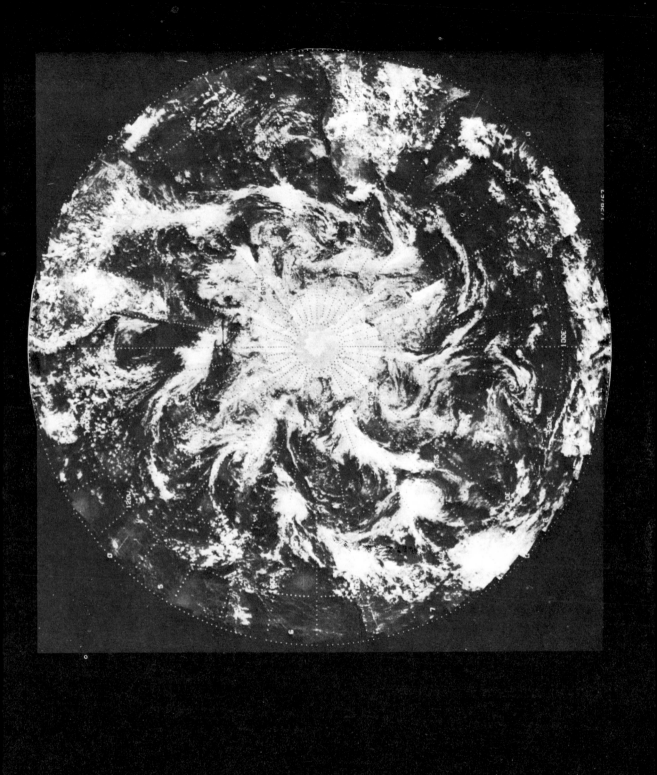

# Prologue: THE LAND GOD GAVE TO CAIN

SEEN FROM SPACE, the astronauts tell us, the most distinctive feature of our planet is the ice sheet of Antarctica, which 'radiates light like a great white lantern across the bottom of the world'. This ice sheet covers 5,500,000 square miles (an area greater than the United States and Central America combined); it averages more than 7,000 feet in thickness; it contains more than 90 per cent of the world's ice and snow, and if it suddenly melted the oceans would rise to such a height that every other person on earth would be drowned. Antarctica in fact is our planet's largest and most spectacular natural phenomenon.

Yet 160 years ago no one had ever set eyes on this vast continent, let alone set foot on it; and even today man's tenure of it is precarious and his knowledge comparatively slight. To understand why, we need to appreciate the sort of place Antarctica is.

People used to regard the Arctic and the Antarctic as much alike. In fact their differences outweigh their similarities. For whereas the Arctic is a depression filled with sea, the Antarctic is a protuberance – the world's highest continent – of ice-covered land. Another difference can be seen from the map opposite. The Arctic is closely hemmed in by the populated landmasses of Europe, America and Asia; the Antarctic in contrast is set in splendid isolation, divided from the nearest land by vast reaches of the most tempestuous seas on earth. Another big difference is the climate. We are so inclined to think of both the Arctic and Antarctic as cold, that we tend to forget how much more inclement the latter is. North of the Arctic Circle tens of thousands of families live in comfort all the year round; thousands of plants and animals (many of them are high on the evolutionary ladder) are able to survive; hundreds of children are born every year. South of the Antarctic Circle, in contrast, there is no habitation that a man can describe as home; the only plants are a handful of mosses and lichens; the only forms of indigenous landlife are one-celled protozoa and wingless flies; no human child has ever been born there.

It is not hard to see why. The basic essentials to life are rainfall, warmth and a degree of stillness. The Arctic, at times, provides all three; the Antarctic seldom provides any – witness the descriptions of those who have been there:

> As regards precipitation the Southern Continent is a desert, with an annual fall no greater than the outback of Australia. The exact accumulation is difficult to measure because of the high frequency of blown snow, but the central plateau certainly receives less than 5 cm per year; and there may well be places close to the Pole where snow has never fallen. (US Weather Bureau)

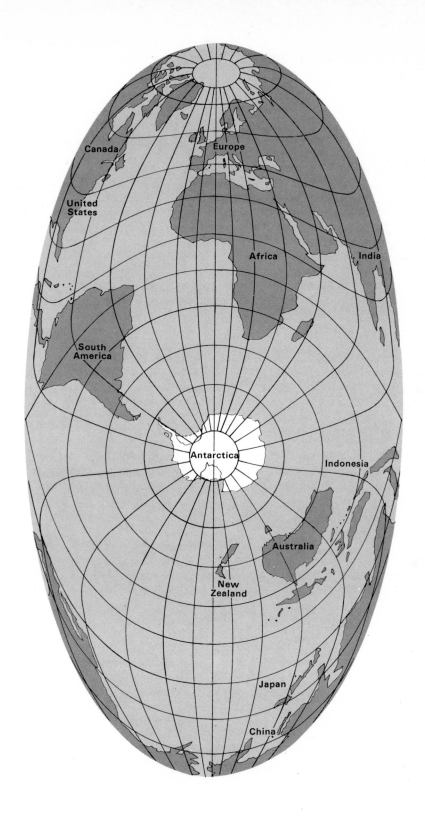

The Earth as a flat ellipse enabling one to relate the Antarctic to other continents

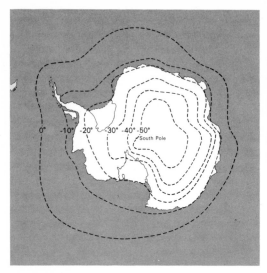 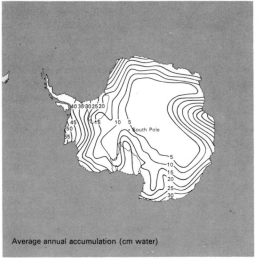

Average annual accumulation (cm water)

Antarctica is by far the coldest place on earth; weather stations have reported temperatures of $-88°$ C, more than $20°$ below those recorded anywhere else. In this sort of cold if you try to burn a candle the flame becomes obscured by a cylindrical hood of wax, if you drop a steel bar it is likely to shatter like glass, tin disintegrates into loose granules, mercury freezes into a solid metal, and if you haul up a fish through a hole in the ice within five seconds it is frozen so solid that it has to be cut with a saw. (John Bechervaise)

All who have set foot in Antarctica agree that its predominant and most malevolent characteristic is wind. When we wintered in Adélie Land the wind on 5th July blew non-stop for eight hours at an *average* speed of 107 mph; gusts were recorded of over 150 mph, and the average wind velocity for the month was 63·3. In these conditions it was possible to stand for no more than a few seconds, and then only by leaning forward at an angle of $45°$! (Douglas Mawson)

It is worth remembering that wind is as injurious to human health as cold; for by disrupting the cushion of warmth which is trapped by pores and hairs of the skin, each knot of wind has an effect on life commensurate to a drop of one degree in temperature. Thus whereas a man can live quite happily at $-20°$ in the still air, when the temperature is $-20$ and the wind 60 knots he will very quickly die. Small wonder that whereas in the eighteenth and early nineteenth centuries man swiftly explored and occupied the rest of his planet, the southernmost continent remained inviolate. Even present-day scientists, with the aid of a sophisticated technology, have difficulty in surviving in such conditions. How much more difficult must survival have been for the early explorers.

Yet climate by itself was not the principal deterrent to the unveiling of Antarctica; an even greater deterrent, at least initially, was the nature of the sea – the Southern Ocean – which surrounds it.

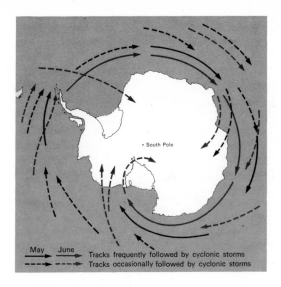

May   June     Tracks frequently followed by cyclonic storms
               Tracks occasionally followed by cyclonic storms

The Southern Ocean lies between the 50th and 70th parallels, where the Atlantic, Pacific and Indian Oceans converge to form a continuous belt of windswept water that encircles the earth. A glance at the map will confirm the obvious: that these are waters far removed from the trade routes and cities of the civilized world. If this is true today, it was even more true in the eighteenth century when the greater part of the southern hemisphere was unknown, and ports such as Buenos Aires, Sydney and Wellington did not exist. The early explorers had therefore to travel the better part of 10,000 miles before they reached even the approaches to Antarctica; all too frequently they arrived with their ships in poor repair and their crews in poor health.

The few vessels that did manage to penetrate to these southern waters found the worst sailing conditions in the world. Between 50° and 70° S there is no land, apart from the tip of Tierra del Fuego and a scattering of unbelievably bleak little islands. Winds and waves in these latitudes are therefore able to build up into a continuous stormbelt that blows non-stop around the earth. Even on relatively calm days there is a 15-foot swell in the Southern Ocean; and in days of storm great rollers surge endlessly over the horizon, three-quarters of a mile from crest to crest, 50 feet from trough to summit. Modern freighters have been known to founder under their bludgeoning.

The force that drives these gargantuan seas is the wind. The average windspeed of the 'Filthy Fifties' is 37·7 knots: that is to say day in and day out there is a constant Force 8 gale, and gusts of over 100 knots are recorded on average several times a month. In these conditions the wonder is not that sailing ships were sometimes dismasted and lost, but that they survived at all.

Fog is not a phenomenon that is usually associated with wind; but astride the 60th parallel it is both dense and ubiquitous – as seamen from the Ancient

16     Spray ridges of ice on Cape Evans – in the distance Inaccessible Island, photographed by
H. G. Ponting, 8 March 1911

Mariner to the captain of a present-day icebreaker have testified. It would be hard to overestimate the malign influence of this unexpected barrier, caused by the confluence of temperate wind and ice-cold sea. It made navigation hazardous; it made surveying difficult; and it delayed for many years the sighting of the mainland, the logs of the early explorers being full of such entries as 'Supposed Land: Lost in Fog', 'An Appearance of Land to S.W., obscur'd by Fog'.

The Southern Ocean's final and most formidable deterrent was something more tangible than fog and more difficult to penetrate: ice. Antarctica is ringed by a continuous girdle of pack ice, a girdle that may be anything from one inch to twelve feet in height and a thousand miles in width, effective chastity belt to a virgin continent. This pack ice is never still; it drifts this way and that under the influence of currents and winds, expanding and contracting according to temperature and season; so that whereas in summer its size may be no greater than that of the British Isles, in winter it covers an area larger than that of the United States and Canada combined. For ten months out of twelve it is impenetrable. In bad weather it is one of the most terrifying places on earth; ships caught in it are crushed or pounded to destruction – witness Ross's account of the tribulations of the *Erebus* and *Terror*:

> Our ships rolled and groaned amidst the blocks of ice, over which the ocean rolled its mountainous waves, throwing huge masses one upon another then burying them deep beneath its foaming waters, the while dashing and grinding them together with fearful violence. The awful grandeur of such a scene can be neither imagined nor described.

Yet in the height of summer, on rare days of calm, great lanes of ice-free water will open up in the pack, so that a man is able to paddle through it quite easily in a canoe.

Which highlights what is perhaps the most fascinating characteristic of the Antarctic. It is a land of extreme and spectacular contrast.

So far we have emphasized its bleakness. And rightly so. For on nineteen days out of twenty it is a terrain as frozen and desolate as the land God gave to Cain. Yet it can be transformed within minutes to an Eden of ethereal beauty. Quite suddenly the wind will drop, the sky will clear, the light will strengthen until mountains 300 miles away can be seen by the naked eye, and the ice will glow with colours so brilliant and be encompassed by a stillness so absolute that they have to be experienced to be believed. At such moments the Antarctic offers a pageant of beauty unequalled anywhere in the world.

It is because of these sudden and fundamental changes that a would-be explorer may sail one day over a certain area and sight nothing, whereas a second explorer may sail over the same area a few days later and sight a great range of snow-capped mountains. This explains – but does not altogether excuse – the controversy that has arisen over who sighted the mainland first. The truth is that we can not answer with certainty even such a fundamental question about Antarctica as who discovered it. American historians award the accolade to a New England sealer, Nathaniel Palmer; British historians to a master of the Royal Navy, Edward Bransfield; and armchair geographers from either side of the Atlantic have championed the cause of their respective claimants with such acerbity that for many years the Antarctic peninsula, which projects northward towards Cape Horn, was marked on American maps as Palmer Land and on British maps as Graham Land (the name given it by Bransfield). Ironically enough, neither British seaman nor American sealer has anything like as good a claim to be the first to sight the mainland as Russia's von Bellingshausen! And if today the whole question seems academic and hardly worth the rivers of ink that have been spilt in arguing it, one should remember that 'firstness' has always been a hallmark of discovery in the Antarctic.

When Dias rounded the Cape of Good Hope he was simply achieving what the Phoenicians had achieved 2,000 years before him; Columbus was preceded in the New World by several hundred (if not several thousand) Vikings; Roman merchants were running a white slave trade with the Malabar coast a millennium before the Portuguese. Without wishing in any way to denigrate the discoveries of the fifteenth and sixteenth centuries, the fact is that most of them were *rediscoveries*; they were also merely transferring Europeans to another and already populated part of the globe. Nineteenth-century seamen who penetrated the Antarctic, on the other hand, were the first men to set foot in territory that was truly virgin. No human being, since the dawn of creation, had preceded them.

Which brings us to a final point about the unveiling of Antarctica. In other continents explorers, generally speaking, have had to face the hostility of an existing population or have been hampered by commercial and nationalistic rivalries. In Antarctica these *divertissements* were, by and large, avoided; there was no indigenous population, and little rivalry – perhaps because the terrain seemed hardly worth fighting over. For this reason the story of exploration in the Antarctic has a classical simplicity. It is the story of a straight fight between two powerful and evenly matched protagonists: man at his most inquisitive and persistent, and nature at her most awe-inspiring and obdurate.

When giants such as these join in battle it is not to be wondered at that their conflict has something of the surge and thunder of the *Odyssey*.

Dawn over Adelaide Island showing consolidated pack ice

## CHAPTER I

# TERRA AUSTRALIS INCOGNITA

THE WORD ANTARCTIC owes its origin to Greek mythology. For it was the ancient Greeks who named the constellation that rotates above the North Pole *arktos* (the bear); and with the passing of time *arktos*, now modified to arctic, came to be used not only as the name of the group of stars but as the name of the polar regions on which it shines. Antarctic is a shortening of anti-Arctic: ie those regions which lie 'anti' or directly opposite the constellation of *arktos*.

The Greeks not only named Antarctica, they put it on their maps. The man who initiated this concept of a great southern continent was Aristotle, who might therefore be termed the first Antarctic explorer – though his discoveries, of course, were purely theoretical. Aristotle put forward the then revolutionary idea of a spherical globe. The earth must be a sphere, he argued, because all matter tends to fall together to a common centre, because during an eclipse the earth throws a circular shadow on the moon, and because no shape except a sphere could account for the ever-shifting horizon and the disappearing, as a man travels north or south, of familiar stars. This was inspired logic. And Aristotle's school of philosophers took his concept of the world a stage further; they put forward the theory of a great southern continent – a theory that was to influence men's thoughts and actions for 2,000 years. This theory was based on the principle of symmetry. The Greeks were a logical people; and it seemed to them a *sine qua non* that if the earth was a sphere, there must be a landmass in the south of it to counter-balance the landmass of Eurasia in the north. We can see from Mela's map how a cultured Greek or Roman of the first century pictured the world he lived in: an orderly, logical (and in view of what came later) surprisingly accurate conception.

A more sophisticated view of the world in general and the great southern continent in particular is provided by Macrobius's map. We have here the same orderly layout of land and sea, plus the addition of a number of parallel zones of climate. The ancients regarded these zones of climate not as supposition but as fact. They were convinced that to the north of their temperate and habitable Mediterranean lay a frigid zone where life was precluded by cold, and that to the south of it lay a torrid and quite impassable zone where life was precluded by heat; and it seemed to them self-evident that since the earth was a sphere these climatic zones of the northern hemisphere would be duplicated in the south. They believed, in other words, in the existence of a great southern continent that was populated but inaccessible, divided from the known world by a belt of equatorial heat, too great to be passed through.

Detail of a romanticized depiction of James Clark Ross's ships *Erebus* and *Terror*, 1817, by J. W. Carmichael. A picture which despite its obvious inaccuracies captures a certain admiration for Ross and the pioneering for which he was becoming famous

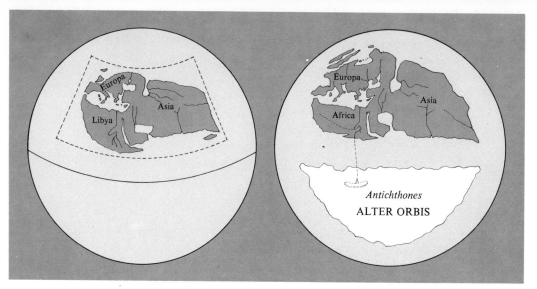

Mela's map of the world, A.D. 1

Not for a thousand years was man to have so clear a picture of his environment. For the rational thinking of Aristotle and his philosophers was superseded in Europe by the chaos of the barbarian invasions and the stultifying doctrines of the Christian Church.

The millennium between the collapse of the Roman Empire and the dawn of the Renaissance was in the field of cartography an era more of recession than of advancement. This recession can be seen at a glance by comparing the earth as visualized by Mela and Macrobius with the earth as visualized, four or five centuries later, by Rainaud and Indicopleustes. The grotesque creations of the latter were a direct result of the Christian Fathers' refusal to accept the idea of a populated Antipodes. For the concept of a southern landmass, inaccessible but inhabited, raised awkward theological questions. How, if such a land was divided from the known world by a belt of impassable heat, could the people who lived in it be descended through Noah from Adam? Had these people been vouchsafed a separate revelation? Could they be saved by a separate atonement? These, in the Middle Ages, were quite literally burning questions. It therefore seemed wisest to the Church to insist that the bottom half of the world was uninhabited, and one of the easiest ways to propagate this belief was to depict it as 100 per cent water – hence Rainaud's comical non-concentric globe without Antipodes. An even stranger creation was that of the monk Indicopleustes, who, determined to do away altogether with the southern hemisphere, constructed an Earth modelled on the Jewish tabernacle, with a great conical mountain in the middle for the sun to rise from and set behind. When theories such as these, not surprisingly, failed to gain credence, the Church played their trump card. Belief in a spherical globe, and hence in the Antipodes, was condemned as heresy. With the stroke of a quill the wisdom of the ancient civilizations was set aside, and for the better part of a thousand years the great southern continent was wiped not only off the maps of the world but out of the minds of men. A handful of dissidents, it is true, continued to speculate during the

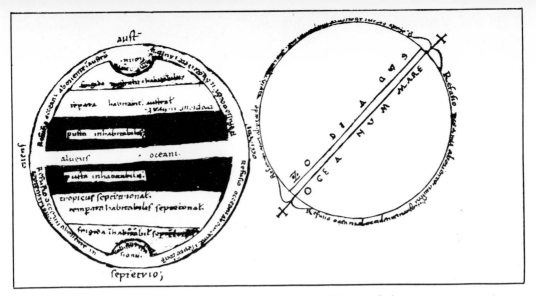

Detail of a manuscript attributed to Macrobius in the Bibliothèque Nationale, Paris

next few centuries by extending the world, in their imagination, on wheel map or tapestry. But heresy in the Dark Ages was not to be indulged in lightly; the authority of the Church was infrangible and ubiquitous – in 741, for example, Pope Zacharias excommunicated an Irish priest for teaching the doctrine of the Antipodes, 'thereby admitting the existence of souls who shared neither the sin of Adam nor the redemption of Christ' – and it was not till the early years of the fifteenth century that man began once again to grope towards a realistic conception of the world he lived in.

This renaissance in cartography, when it at last got under way, was different in one fundamental respect from the golden age of Greek cartography. It was practical rather than theoretical. The men who inspired it were not philosophers like Aristotle, but down-to-earth travellers like Marco Polo and Columbus; and what the ancient Greeks had deduced a thousand years previously by logic, the men of the Renaissance now confirmed by experience. They pushed farther and farther out of Europe, south by west, until they proved the earth was a sphere by the most practical method imaginable – they sailed round it.

After Magellan in the *Victoria* had 'turned a furrow of blue water round the globe' it seemed to the mapmakers that since the Greeks had been right over their spherical earth, they might well be right also over their great southern continent. It was therefore at this point in history that the search for Antarctica got under way.

What the early explorers expected to find was an enormous landmass the size of which can be seen from Ortelius's map, where the land marked *Terra Australis nondum cognita* occupies almost a third of the globe. Dreams die hard. And for 200 years the seamen of a dozen nations were to probe the Southern Ocean convinced that every landfall they made was the tip of this *Terra Australis*, the legendary 'Land of Brazil Wood, Elephants and Gold'.

It might be thought that as these early explorers landed first in the Solomon

Cordiform map of the world by
Orontius Finaeus, 1566

Islands (1568), then the Falkland Islands (1592), then Espiritu Santo (1606) and finally in 1616 in Australia itself, their reports would have exploded the myth of a great southern landmass. On the contrary, they strengthened it. For cartographers seized on the landfalls the seamen made, transcribed them onto their maps, then joined them together to form a continuous coastline: a classic example of the wish being father to the thought. And if today it seems almost incredible that so fundamental an error should have been made at all let alone perpetuated for so long, we should remember two facts. Firstly, that when someone has been at sea for a long time in a small ship almost *any* coastline appears extensive; and secondly, that in the sixteenth and seventeenth centuries navigation was very much by rule of thumb, and that hydrography and surveying were far from being the exact sciences they are today.

The 200 years 1550–1750 which form a prelude to the unveiling of Antarctica were therefore a period of frustration and uncertainty. Seamen made determined efforts to locate the Great Southern Continent and place it on the map; but their efforts were thwarted by the enormous distances they had to travel, and by the fact that when they did make a landfall their navigation was nothing like good enough for them to fix their whereabouts accurately (their position north and south they could judge with some precision by the stars, but their position east and west they could do little better than guess at). The southern hemisphere, therefore, remained an enigma. Though it occupied half the globe, it contained in 1600 less than 10 per cent of its population – and few of these had attained a high degree of civilization; though it could boast half the coastlines in the world, it had less than 2 per cent of its ports; and no one could answer even such a fundamental question about it as did it consist principally of land or principally of water? – though it was generally assumed that land, to balance Eurasia, would be predominant. Indeed before 1750 no more than a handful of voyages had made a worthwhile contribution to man's knowledge of the Southern Ocean. The most important were those of Drake (1578), de la Roché (1675) and Bouvet (1739).

Many people today still believe that when Drake left England in 1577, bound for the Strait of Magellan, his objective was piracy – an attempt to singe not the king of Spain's beard but his less well-protected tail. This is not so. Recent research has shown that Drake's principal objective was exploration. His sailing orders are explicit on this point: 'You are to enter the South Sea [i.e. the Pacific] and to explore and claim suzerainty over all lands and territories not already in the possession of any Christian Prince.' The land referred to in these orders could hardly have been the coast of Chile, for this had already been claimed and colonized by Spain; it must therefore have been the ubiquitous *Terra Australis*, and in particular that part of it known as The Land of Beoch rich in Gold. This Land of Beoch, first reported by Marco Polo, was marked on all contemporary maps; the Spaniards indeed were so convinced of its existence that in 1546 they appointed a governor, Sancho de la Hoz, to be responsible for 'all those very Great Lands of Beoch which lie to the south and west of the Strait of Magellan'. Hoz, it seems, made no attempt to visit his domain: an omission which it was Drake's intention to remedy.

His armada left Plymouth on 15 November 1577, and so veiled in secrecy were his orders that the crew signed on in the belief they were bound for Alexandria. The revelation of their less attractive goal triggered off a mutiny in the South American port of St Julian, where Drake beheaded his second-in-command on the very spot where Magellan some sixty years previously had beheaded his. After wintering in these inauspicious surroundings, the fleet passed through the Strait of Magellan, pausing only to land on an island where they 'found great store of foule [almost certainly penguins] which could not flie, of the bignesse of geese, whereof we killed in lesse than one day 3,000 and victualled ourselves thoroughly therewith' – the first but by no means the last of the fauna of the Southern Ocean that man was to butcher with merciless efficiency. A couple of days after clearing the strait, Drake's vessels were scattered by a violent storm; the *Marigold* sank with all hands, the *Elizabeth* was driven back into the Atlantic, and the admiral himself in the *Golden Hind* was driven farther to the south than a man from Europe had ever been driven before. Drake and his nephew describe their experiences as follows:

> From the Bay we were driven back to the southward of the streights in 57 degrees and a terce: in which height we came to anker among Islands, having there fresh and very good water, with herbes of singular virtue. (Drake's account)

> Having weathered the storm we fell in with the uttermost part of the land towards the South Pole, which uttermost cape or headland of all these islands stands in the 56th degree, beyond which there is no main nor island to be seen to the Southwards; but the Atlantic Ocean and the South Sea meet in a large and free scope. (His nephew's account)

Drake named his islands The Elizabethiades, and calculated their position as being a little to the south and west of Tierra del Fuego. There is no doubt, however, that what he in fact discovered was Cape Horn, which is not part of the American main-land, but the most southerly bluff in an archipelago. The Elizabethiades were in due course added to the plethora of mythical islands that adorned contemporary charts. But it was Drake's nephew, Francis Fletcher, who put his finger on the key point in their discoveries when he wrote that beyond the Horn 'there is no main[land] nor island . . . to the Southwards, but the Atlantic and the South Sea meet . . .'. Fletcher, in other words, was the first man to realize that Tierra del Fuego was part of a relatively small cluster of islands and not, as was then widely assumed, the tip of the great southern continent. His interpretation of his discoveries, however, was too revolutionary for sixteenth-century cartographers, who continued to mark on their charts a vast landmass to the south of Cape Horn, merely altering its name from *Terra Incognita* to *Terra nunc bene Cognita*! – an example of the fact that there is seldom much enthusiasm for a theory that runs contrary to popular belief.

Another explorer who received scant recognition for his discoveries was Antonio de la Roché, the little-known London merchant who was first to sight land which might be regarded as part of Antarctica itself.

There is only one contemporary account of his voyage: that of the Spanish naval captain Don Francisco de Seixas y Lovera. In the autumn of 1673, the Spaniard tells us, de la Roché raised money from a syndicate of merchants to finance a trading expedition to Peru; he fitted out two vessels, signed on a crew of fifty-six, and set sail in the spring of the following year. We do not know how successful his trading was, but we do know that he was homeward bound when he made his discovery. Here is what Don Francisco says:

> And endeavouring to make the Passage of Le Marie [i.e. to round Cape Horn] in April 1675 they could not effect it because of the high winds and strong currents . . . which made them disconsolate, for it was the beginning of winter and they began to doubt if they would escape with their lives, especially as they had no knowledge whatsoever of the new land which they suddenly came upon in 54 and 55 degrees. Reconnoitring this land and using every diligence to approach it, they anchored close to a Cape or Point which stretched out to the S.E., where they had depths of 28, 30 and 40 fathoms, the bottom being of sand and stones: in which anchorage they had a prospect of great snow-covered mountains falling sheer into the sea. They remained here for 14 days in tempestuous weather at the end of which time, the wind having dropped and the cloud and mist somewhat lifted, they realized they were at the extremity of an island . . . and saw towards the S.E. and S. other high lands covered with snow: leaving which, with a gentle wind, they sailed up the coast. . . . And it appeared to them that from the one land to the other the opening was about ten leagues and the currents strong to the N.E. Soon they found themselves in the North Sea, having in the course of three glasses passed through the said passage which is short, indicating that the newly discovered island was not of great extent.

Only one island in the vicinity of Cape Horn lies between latitude 54° and 55°,

Sir Francis Drake

Ferdinand Magellan

runs from southeast to northwest, and has snow-covered mountains falling sheer to the sea: South Georgia. And to make identification doubly certain, South Georgia is flanked by a small group of islands, the Clerke Rocks, that lie exactly 30 miles off its southern tip, where there are soundings of 25 to 40 fathoms on a sea bed of gravel. It therefore seems clear that de la Roché must have sailed between South Georgia and the Clerke Rocks. The former he identified correctly as an island 'not of great extent'; the latter he seems to have mistaken for the tip of *Terra Australis*. And if today the inconspicuous cluster of the Clerke Rocks looks, on the map, to bear little resemblance to the extensive coast of a great new continent, we should bear in mind that when de la Roché saw the Rocks they were veiled in mist and cloud, and as likely as not surrounded by tabular icebergs. Such a line of cliffs, 800 feet high·and covered with snow, must have been an imposing sight; also they loomed up in exactly the place where contemporary maps depicted the coast of the mythical *Terra nunc bene Cognita*.

It would be unfair to deny de la Roché his major discovery because he misidentified his minor.

The finding of this first lonely outpost of Antarctica may not have been a particularly great feat of exploration. It does, however, deserve a niche in history, because it gave men for the first time an inkling of what the land they were searching for would be like when eventually they found it – windswept, barren, and desolate beyond the power of words to describe.

A voyage that did even more to increase man's knowledge of the Antarctic was that of the French naval officer Jean Bouvet de Lozier.

Bouvet, Janus-like, looks both backward to the past and forward to the future. His expedition could hardly have had a more archaic background; for it was conceived as a search for de Gonneville's mythical 'Cape of the Austral Islands', from which, according to legend, a native prince had been brought to France in the early seventeenth century. No one, not even the descendants of the prince concerned, was sure where this cape was situated, though it was generally believed that it lay to the south of Africa. (Its most probable location, I think, is Madagascar.) In the early years of the eighteenth century the French East India Company decided that de Gonneville's Cape might be a useful staging post for their vessels *en route* to India and China. They therefore commissioned two vessels, the *Aigle* and the *Marie*, signed on a specially selected crew, and placed the expedition in the hands of Bouvet de Lozier, a young and exceptionally able officer who had experience in commanding both warships and East Indiamen. Bouvet's orders were to 'locate the Southern Lands formerly known to de Gonneville, proceeding if need be as far as 55 degrees South; and thereafter to follow a zig-zag course, at the highest latitude you are able, towards the East.' These orders were commendably flexible; they included a promise of increased pay for every day the ships were within sight of new land, and they also included a proviso which, in humanity and sensibility, was far ahead of its times. In an age when slavery was seldom questioned and natives were all too frequently massacred on the slightest pretext, Bouvet was expressly forbidden to bring back to Europe 'any inhabitant whatsoever from the Lands you discover'.

The two ships sailed from Lorient on 19 July 1738, with provisions for eighteen months; and by early December Bouvet had pushed far enough to the south to be encountering ice. On 15 December he sighted the first of the great slab-sided icebergs, the vanguard of Antarctica's defences, and a couple of days later his vessels ran into fog. It would be hard to imagine a more dismal scene: heavy seas, high winds, sleet pouring out of a low-hung canopy of cloud, and drifting into every nook and cranny of sea, ship and sky the ubiquitous miasma of fog. Bouvet, however, was a fine seaman and a determined man. He pushed on, through ice that became progressively thicker and fog that grew ever denser, until on New Year's Day his perseverance was rewarded. Early in the second watch the *Aigle*'s lookout gave warning of breakers on the starboard bow, and a few minutes later there loomed out of the mist a great snow-capped headland, its striated cliffs falling sheer to the sea.

The events that followed give an indication of the appalling conditions which explorers in the Antarctic had to cope with. For twelve days the *Aigle* and the *Marie* beat to and fro, attempting to land. But the sea was so heavy, the wind so strong and visibility so poor that no landing party was able to set foot ashore, nor was Bouvet able to discover if the cape was part of an island or part of the more extensive coastline of a continent; it was all he could do to keep his landfall in sight,

Jean Bouvet de Lozier

*Bouvet de Lozier*

and survive. On the thirteenth day a storm, even more furious than those that had gone before, drove his vessels away to the southeast, and the cape, which he named Cape Circumcision, disappears from history for the better part of 200 years. Not till 1927 was a Norwegian team able to land and survey his island – now known as Bouvetøya (Bouvet Island), a single volcanic cone rising almost vertically to 3,068 feet out of a vast loneliness of sea. (Bouvetøya in fact has the distinction of being the most isolated island on earth; there is no other land within a thousand miles.)

By 20 January the *Aigle* and the *Marie* had reached 54° 40′ S, and the ice had thickened to such an extent that it was impenetrable. Bouvet, in any case, had now reached the southern limit laid down in his orders, and he therefore turned east and

(left) Yves-Joseph de Kerguélen-Trémarec

(below) The northern part of Kerguélen Island

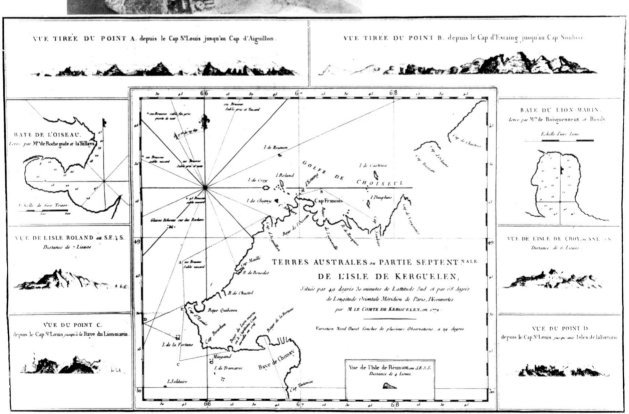

ran parallel to the edge of the pack ice, expecting any moment to sight the mythical *Terra Australis*. He skirted the pack ice, in appalling weather, for 1,500 miles; but he sighted nothing – nothing that is except icebergs, penguins and seals – and late in 1739, his crew debilitated by exposure and scurvy, he returned to France.

His expedition won him few accolades at the time. Yet it was a magnificent feat of seamanship, and it contributed a great deal to man's knowledge of the world. It should, in the first place, have removed *Terra Australis* once and for all from a vast segment of the Atlantic and Indian Oceans. (I say 'should have removed' rather than 'did remove' because cartographers again proved perversely loath to accept Bouvet's findings, and the mythical *Terra Australis* continued to feature in their maps right up to the 1770s.) In the second place, Bouvet brought back what might be termed the first truly scientific account of the approaches to Antarctica. It was he, for example, who was first to notice that the gargantuan icebergs were frequently streaked with bands of sand or deposits of rock, and must therefore have broken off from a not-too-distant mass of land. It was he too who was first to give a precise description of the penguins and seals that he encountered in vast numbers along the edge of the pack ice; he identified both these creatures as amphibian, and rightly construed their presence as yet another indication of the proximity of land. Bouvet, in fact, was the first man to visualize Antarctica as it actually is: an inaccessible continent girdled by pack ice; a land of wind and snow in harsh contrast to the green pastures promised by the cartographers of eighteenth-century Europe. In this he was a prophet, a man too far ahead of his time to win the recognition he deserved.

For in spite of Bouvet's voyage, and in spite of the voyages of trading vessels which in increasing numbers began in the eighteenth century to seek out the steady trade winds of the Forties on their way to India and Japan, the southern hemisphere was still believed in 1760 to be predominantly land. H. R. Mill in his book *The Siege of the South Pole* sums the situation up:

> In the middle of the eighteenth century the southern hemisphere figured upon all maps as the seat of a great continent awaiting discovery. The tenacity of the hold of this continent on the minds of geographers is remarkable, and probably no prepossession based on such inadequate data ever died a harder death.

Two of the last and most vociferous champions of this mythical continent were the able but unbalanced Dalrymple and the brave but over-optimistic Kerguélen.

Alexander Dalrymple's portrait gives an indication of his character: a massive brow, intolerant eyes and a florid complexion. He was a man of formidable intellect, a Fellow of the Royal Society and an astronomer of international repute; he was also, alas, self-opinionated, arrogant and contentious. In 1767 the Royal Society suggested he should be given command of the naval expedition that was about to sail to the South Pacific to observe the transit of Venus. Dalrymple, however, had few friends at the Admiralty – the First Sea Lord declared he would rather cut off his right hand than give him command of one of His Majesty's ships – and the appointment was offered instead to Cook. This sparked off a spate of acrimonious correspondence which has to be quoted to be believed. Dalrymple was determined to search for the southern continent, which, he was convinced, previous explorers had failed to find only through inefficiency. He bombarded the government with requests for a concession to exploit 'all those lands I shall discover between the equator and 60° S', and the following extract from his application demonstrates very clearly the sort of territory he expected to find:

> The American colonies are generally supposed to contain two millions of people. . . . The number of inhabitants in the Southern Continent is probably more than 50 millions, considering that their extent, from the eastern part discovered by Juan Fernandez to the western coast seen by Tasman is about 100 degrees of longitude, which in the latitude of 40 deg. amounts to 4,596 geographic or 5,323 statute miles. This is a greater extent than the whole civilized part of Asia, from Turkey to the eastern extremity of China. There is at present no trade from Europe thither, though the scraps from this table would be sufficient to maintain the power, dominion and sovereignty of Britain, by employing all its manufacturers and ships.

Dalrymple's concession was never granted. His expedition never sailed. And today, because he was wrong, we are tempted to smile at what has been termed his 'dogmatic absurdity'. Yet it is worth remembering that the whole civilized part of Asia *could* indeed have been fitted into the South Pacific, and if Dalrymple had been right in his supposition historians today would be showering him not with ridicule but praise.

The last, and perhaps the most tragic, of those who believed in an idyllic South-land was Yves-Joseph de Kerguélen-Trémarec, a Breton aristocrat who in 1771 was given command of yet another expedition with orders 'to search for the Very Great Land of de Gonneville which lies to the South of the Île de France'. Kerguélen in the *Fortune* and his second-in-command St-Allouarne in the *Gros Ventre* headed south from Mauritius in the early weeks of 1772. After a voyage of almost exactly a month they sighted a small island, and a day later, on 13 February 1772, Kerguélen's lookout reported a 'high and very extensive coastline to the S'. This coastline was clearly visible for five hours; but as they attempted to close with it, it disappeared in fog. The ships hove to. Next morning, with the visibility a little improved, Kerguélen ordered the *Gros Ventre*, which had a shallower draught than his flagship, to attempt a landing, and after a good deal of difficulty St-Allouarne managed to struggle ashore in Sea Lion Bay. He gave the new land the somewhat grandiose title of *La France Australe*, and calculated its latitude as being roughly that of Paris – 49° 40'. Before Kerguélen and St-Allouarne could confer, the fog closed in; and the following day their vessels were separated by a violent storm. There is little doubt as to what Kerguélen should have done next; he ought to have stayed in the vicinity of his landfall and attempted to make a more thorough survey. The weather, however, proved too much for him – tumultuous seas, hurricane winds and ever-shifting banks of fog – and anxious to take home the news of his success, he lost patience and returned to France. Back in Paris he made a report that was altogether unjustified in its enthusiasm:

> The lands which I have had the happiness to discover appear to form the central mass of the Antarctic continent. . . . This land which I have called South France is so situated as to command the route to India, China and the South Seas. . . . The latitude in which it lies promises all the crops of the Mother Country. . . . No doubt wood, minerals, diamonds, rubies and precious stones and marble will be found. . . . If men of a different species are not discovered at least there will be people living in a state of nature, knowing nothing of the artifices of civilized society. In short South France will furnish marvellous physical and moral spectacles.

It was a case, if ever there was one, of beauty being in the eye of the beholder.

Poor Kerguélen! He was soon made to eat his words. He was given new ships and a new crew and told to explore the lands he had discovered 'with more diligence. . . . To establish a trading post thereon, and to explore the coastline to the east, making observations'. But his second voyage was a fiasco. By the time he reached Mauritius his vessels were unseaworthy, having already been several times dismasted, and his crew so weak with scurvy they could scarce raise or lower sail; he continued, however, to head doggedly south, and managed to struggle through at last to *La France Australe*. It was midsummer. But when he landed he found the terrain sterile and uninviting; it rained continuously, the wind never dropped below a gale, and his crew were too debilitated to set up even a temporary camp; there was no trace of wood or minerals, much less the hoped-for precious stones. Kerguélen renamed his discovery Land of Desolation. He must have known, as he gazed at the snow-capped hills, that he had found a country very different from the 'Land of Brazil Wood, Elephants and Gold' of which he had dreamed. But his bitterest disillusion was still to come. Not till he returned to France did he learn that Cook, at the start of his great circumnavigation, had already sailed far to the south of the coast he had discovered, thus proving it not part of a new continent at all, but yet another cluster of islands: the last of the landfalls to be hailed with misplaced enthusiasm as the tip of *Terra Australis*.

Kerguélen's voyage was the last of those with their roots in the Greek conception of a Great Southern Continent. For his expedition was followed immediately by Cook's.

## CHAPTER 2

## DEATH OF A LEGEND

COOK'S CIRCUMNAVIGATION of Antarctica is considered by many practical seamen the greatest voyage ever made, and the question at once springs to mind – what sort of man was this middle-aged sea captain that he was able in the one stupendous voyage not only to sail through vast reaches of a previously unknown ocean but also to solve a problem which had puzzled geographers for more than 2,000 years?

He was born at Marton in Yorkshire on 27 October 1728, second child of a Scottish farm labourer. He may not even have set eyes on the sea before he was seventeen, when his parents took him to the fishing village of Staithes and apprenticed him to a grocer-cum-haberdasher. For eighteen months the tall, gangling young man sold potatoes and lengths of cloth in the village store – a more unlikely training for an embryo explorer it would be hard to imagine. The North Sea, however, lay almost at his doorstep, and in 1746 he decided to seek his fortune in the nearby port of Whitby. By the end of the year he was at sea: deckhand aboard the *Freelove*, a 450-ton brig carrying coal from Newcastle to London. It was now that Cook displayed the trait that was subsequently to take him to the farthest ends of the earth: determination. Having made up his mind that the sea was to be his calling, he set about mastering the many facets of seamanship with the zeal of a proselyte. There is no evidence that he had a particularly quick brain; but he was industrious, single-minded, and gifted with God's good common sense that is more than knowledge; he taught himself pilotage, navigation and the rudiments of astronomy, and in nine years, to quote his own words, 'dragged myself up through all the Stations from Prentice Boy to Commander'. In the spring of 1755 he was offered a vessel of his own, one of the latest Whitby coal snows in trade with the Baltic, and nothing seemed more certain than that another Yorkshireman was on the threshold of a successful career in commerce.

But now, to his friends' amazement, Cook made a decision that seemed at the time the height of folly. He enrolled as an able-bodied seaman in the Royal Navy.

It appeared to everyone a step backward rather than forward; for a master's cabin in those days was a very different place from the 14 inches of deck space allotted to seamen in a ship of the line, and Cook's initial impression of the Navy must have been one of unbelievable squalor. Here is Admiral Muir's account of conditions aboard his first ship, the *Eagle*.

> The only ventilation was by way of the gun-ports and hatches, which had to be closed in bad weather. The ship leaked badly, the bilge water stank with a nauseating odour which permeated the whole vessel, whilst suffocation from falling into the well was a common accident. The sanitary arrangements consisted of an open space about the

(above right) Captain James Cook, engraved by J. Basire, after William Hodges, 1777
(above) A pen and wash sketch showing the *Resolution en route* for the Antarctic,
by William Hodges

heel of the bowsprit, where the men were exposed to showers of spray, and excrement stuck to the bows until washed off in heavy weather. No wonder that cruising, even in home waters, was invariably accompanied by a shocking mortality.

It is hardly surprising that at the end of Cook's first voyage his captain's report made tragic reading: 'Put ashore at the hospital 130 men, most of which are extremely ill; buried the last month 22. The surgeon and four men died yesterday.' Yet conditions such as these were the rule rather than the exception in eighteenth-century vessels. Cook suffered them for years. And it is this, I think, that explains the almost fanatical measures he took, when he had a command of his own, to safeguard the health of his crew – not many naval captains in his day had 'enjoyed' first-hand experience of life on the lower deck.

It soon became apparent to the *Eagle*'s officers that their new A.B. was several cuts above the usual press-ganged landlubber, and Cook's promotions came rapidly: to petty officer, mate, and finally after no more than a couple of years to warrant officer. On 27 October 1757 (his twenty-ninth birthday) he was appointed to the *Pembroke*; almost at once the *Pembroke* was ordered to the St Lawrence; and it was here, on one of the trickiest waterways in the world, that Cook discovered his *métier*. Within a couple of years of his posting to Canada more than one admiral was referring to him as a 'genius', and the Royal Society had acknowledged him 'a man very expert in his particular business'. And the 'business' that brought him into the limelight was surveying.

His first piece of survey work led to Wolfe's capture of Quebec. The French defences of the city were based on the fact that part of the St Lawrence River known as the Traverse was thought to be impassable to shipping; in the weeks before the assault on the Heights of Abraham, however, Cook surveyed, sounded and buoyed the Traverse to such good effect that on the night of 24 June the British fleet passed through it without the loss of a man. This brought Cook to the attention of those in high places, and in particular of Lord Colville, who was so impressed with his work that he appointed him Master Surveyor to the North American fleet. For the next few years the not-so-young officer, now promoted to lieutenant, was occupied with mapping the St Lawrence and the coast of Newfoundland, which he did with a precision hitherto undreamed of – indeed his charts today are still the basis for local pilotage. The excellence of his work in this sphere is the more surprising when we remember the disadvantages he had to contend with. Many of his contemporaries had attended either the Mathematical School at Christ's Hospital (for masters and pilots) or the Naval Academy at Portsmouth (for officers); Cook on the other hand was entirely self-taught – witness the report of his captain: 'During the winter of 1758 Mr Cook first read Euclid and applied himself to the study of astronomy without any other assistance than what a few books and his own industry afforded him.' It has been suggested that the high quality of his work was due in part to the instruments he had the good fortune to use; and it is certainly true that about the

middle of the eighteenth century, surveying instruments did improve out of all recognition – Hadley's reflecting quadrant, Dr Knight's azimuth compass and Harrison's Number 4 chronometer, for example, were all capable of a precision which would have been considered miraculous in the early years of the century. Yet these instruments were available not only to Cook but also to his contemporaries; he alone made use of them to achieve superlative results; and the fairest assessment of his work is probably that of R. A. Skelton: '. . . although he invented nothing and originated nothing, Cook was a connoisseur of the instruments he used, and he used them with a meticulous accuracy which was in itself an innovation.'

One other aspect of his work in Canada is of particular significance. In 1766 he observed an eclipse of the sun, and this enabled him to calculate with unusual precision the longitude of a certain headland on the Newfoundland coast. His observations on this occasion were original enough to be sent to the Royal Society, together with a note from Colville to the effect that 'from my experience of Mr Cook's genius and capacity I think him well qualified for the (surveying) work he has performed, and for greater undertakings of the same kind'. It was this note and these observations that led to his being put in command of the expedition which, in 1768, set sail for the Pacific to observe the transit of Venus.

The antecedents of this expedition have been set out in some detail because they pinpoint very clearly Cook's two outstanding qualities: his unprecedented interest in the health of his crew, and his ability to survey and navigate with unparalleled precision.

Cook's expedition of 1768/9 added a great deal to knowledge of the Pacific; it did, however, leave a number of major questions unanswered – in particular that of the great southern continent. Cook was doubtful if such a landmass existed. But cartographers in general and the pugnacious and influential Dalrymple in particular were convinced that it did; and Dalrymple had high hopes of being given command of the second expedition which he knew the Admiralty were now planning to settle once and for all the enigma of *Terra Australis*. The sea lords, however, had the perspicacity to distinguish between an 'able but unbalanced braggart' and a 'right-headed unaffected man'; and Cook had barely paid off from his first expedition than he was promoted Commander and told to prepare for his second.

It is this second voyage, described by Alan Villiers as the greatest any man has ever made, which marks the dawn of exploration in the Antarctic.

The objective of the expedition is stated quite clearly in Cook's orders: 'you are to discover and take possession in the name of King George of convenient situations in the South Land'. This implies two motives: to extend cartographical knowledge, and to prevent other nations and in particular the French from building up an empire in the unknown south. It is doubtless because of this political connotation that the expedition was fitted out with a lavishness and care unprecedented at the time and seldom equalled since. Cook was given a free hand to select his ships, crew, equipment and stores. Nothing he asked for was denied him.

Detail of the *Resolution* beating through the ice, by J. Webber

The choice of a suitable vessel was of paramount importance. Cook was offered a newly commissioned sixty-gun ship of the line, but this he turned down; he had had a narrow escape on his previous voyage, when, sailing unaccompanied in the *Endeavour*, he had grounded on the Great Barrier Reef, and he was now determined to take two vessels rather than one. As to their type, he wrote:

> The ships must not be of great draught but of sufficient capacity to carry a proper quantity of provisions and stores for the crew, and of such construction that they will bear to take the ground, and of such size that they can be conveniently laid ashore if necessary for repairing any damage or defects . . . these qualities are to be found in North Country ships such as are built for the coal trade, and in none other.

He had his way, and two Whitby-built colliers were duly purchased; these vessels were initially rechristened the *Drake* and the *Raleigh*, but in deference to Spanish susceptibilities their names were later changed to *Resolution* and *Adventure*. The *Resolution* was Cook's flagship. As we can see from Webber's painting she was a full-rigged, three-masted snow, with a comfortable hull, a sweeping cutwater and a heavy, surprisingly ornate counter and stern. She was so clearly designed to carry well, sail adequately and run ashore if the need arose that she might have been built to Cook's specification – and indeed he describes her as 'the most proper ship for the service I ever saw'. Her dimensions were: length 110 feet, beam 35 feet, depth of hold 13 feet, burthen 462 tons; and her hull was sheathed not in copper, which tends to rub off in ice, but with a double skin of wood. The *Adventure* was 130 tons lighter: a stout nice-looking vessel, but not – at least under her commander Tobias Furneaux – a particularly good sailer.

There was no difficulty in selecting a crew. Both officers and men volunteered in such numbers that Cook was able to pick and choose. He wrote:

> I had all the reason in the world to be satisfied with my officers. The second and third lieutenants, the lieutenant of marines, two of the Warrant Officers and several of the Petty Officers had been with me on my former voyage. The others were men of known abilities, and all of them on every occasion showed zeal for the service in which they were employed.

Of the seamen, thirteen had served in the *Endeavour* – an unprecedented number to sign on for a second voyage in days when the recruiting officer was usually hard pressed to scrape together a full ship's company. Indeed the only people in his complement whom Cook had reason to be less than happy with were his supernumerary scientists, John and George Forster, a gloomy and complaining pair foisted on him in place of his friend Joseph Banks, who had withdrawn at the last moment because he did not fancy the *Resolution*'s accommodation. Cook's biographer, J. C. Beaglehole, is especially critical of the father, George Forster: 'Dogmatic, humourless, suspicious, contentious, censorious, demanding and rheumatic, he was a problem from any angle. One hesitates, in fact, to lay out his

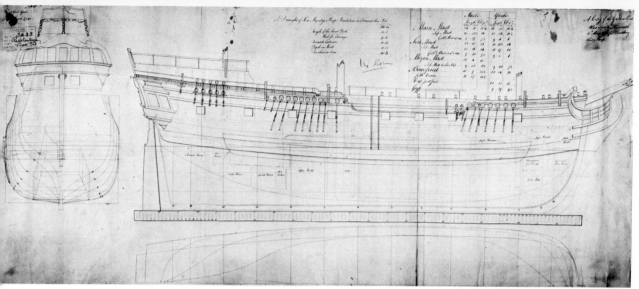

A plan of the *Resolution*

characteristics lest the portrait seem caricature.' Historians over the last 200 years have given these scientists so much stick that it is pleasant to recall one small incident that reflects to their credit. At a time when Cook was desperately ill in the South Pacific, the Forsters owned the only fresh meat in either vessel, and this they gave willingly to be made into broth for their Commander who was thought to be dying – their pet dog.

A list of the *Resolution*'s stores is given in Cook's *Journal*. In addition to the usual items – '59,531 lbs of biscuit, 7,637 pieces of salt beef, 14,214 pieces of salt pork, 1,900 lbs of suet, 19 tons of beer and 1,398 gallons of spirits' – we find an unprecedented quantity of vegetables: 'worts, robs, salops, Inspicated Juce of Beer, Sour Krout of Cabbage and Mermalade of Carrots', all of which were carried as antiscorbutics.

It was, perhaps, Cook's greatest achievement as an explorer that he succeeded, where all his predecessors had failed, in conquering scurvy. Before his three great expeditions this debilitating and lethal disease had for years been the bane of long voyages; for ships' companies who strayed from the quickest and easiest sea route died – sometimes literally to the last man – their health being unable to withstand the strain of spending month after month at sea without reprovisioning. It is now known that the principal cause of scurvy is a deficiency of vitamin C: in particular of ascorbic acid; and some writers have suggested that Cook was able to keep the disease at bay because he carried with him an almost magical antidote – sauerkraut. It is certainly true that the *Resolution*'s diet sheet was better balanced than that of any previous ship, and that in her hold were '8,000 lbs of cabbage cut fine and cured in brine', as well as a whole pharmacy of lemon and orange preserves; it is also true that men who refused to eat this new-fangled food were flogged. Yet two factors reduced the effectiveness of Cook's revolutionary diet. First, he unwittingly nullified the value of his sauerkraut

41

by serving it boiled and diluted as soup, the boiling of course reducing its vitamin content. Second, owing to an error in the victualling yards' nomenclature West Indian limes (which contain little vitamin C) were shipped in place of the intended lemons, rich in vitamin content; the value of the *Resolution*'s 'wort and lemon conserve' was therefore considerably lessened. In other words, Cook's conquest of scurvy can not be wholly attributed to the vegetable diet he imposed on his crew; of at least equal importance was the attention he paid to hygiene.

The expedition sailed from Plymouth on 13 July 1772, last aboard being the astronomers Wales and Bayley who had spent the preceding week in the naval dockyard making a precise calculation of longitude, so that at the start of the voyage 'Cmdr Cook's watch machines' might be accurately set. Among these watch machines, or astronomical clocks as they were sometimes called, was Harrison's famous Number 4 chronometer – now in the National Maritime Museum at Greenwich and keeping time every bit as accurately as it did 200 years ago. This was the first timepiece ever built that was impervious to heat, cold, damp, change of pressure or the motion of a ship, and it was to prove of the greatest value in pinpoint navigation.

The first few weeks of the voyage were near-idyllic: fair winds, moderate seas and shore leave at Madeira and the Azores. At the latter, fresh fruit and vegetables, including 'one thousand string of antiscorbutic onions' were taken aboard; also fresh water, for it was found that the livestock drank almost as much as the ship's company. These animals – bullocks, sheep, pigs and poultry – huddled in open pens on deck were carried partly to provide fresh meat and partly to provide the basis for herds which it was hoped to establish in the Great Southern Continent. Cook was in no hurry; and the 109 days from Plymouth to the Cape were in the nature of a shakedown cruise, with the crew becoming gradually accustomed to their new rules and regulations. These regulations were imposed with a strictness which has occasioned some of Cook's biographers to depict him as 'a disciplinarian, stern and cold'. The truth, however, is quite the reverse. Cook cared for his men: cared for them in a practical, unsentimental manner which was, at the time, unique in the annals of exploration. He was determined that no ship under his command should ever suffer the appalling incidence of sickness and death that had turned the *Eagle* into a charnelhouse. To ensure that his crew remained mentally and physically fit he insisted they kept three watches instead of the usual two. He insisted that every man had at least one cold bath a day, even in the Antarctic. Hammocks, clothing and bedding were brought on deck every three days for airing. Once a week the *Resolution* was either 'cured with fires' or 'smoked clean with a mixture of vinegar and gunpowder'. The well was regularly fumigated. Coppers were scoured daily. A carefully worked-out programme ensured there was no idleness; and Cook himself made frequent inspections of every part of his ship and every member of his crew. There was some discontent at first at so overpowering a routine – 'every day is

Sunday [i.e. a captain's rounds day] with Mr Cook!' one of the crew was heard to complain. But the precautions and inspections were to be justified by events.

The *Resolution* and *Adventure* arrived off Cape Town on 30 October, having for the last three weeks endured heavy rains and violent storms. The crew were given shore leave, fresh provisions were taken aboard, and the chronometers were corrected – it being found that Harrison's alone was keeping accurate time. It was during this stay at the Cape that Cook heard for the first time of Kerguélen's discoveries in the Indian Ocean. This gave him two 'tips of the Great Southern Continent' to search for – Bouvetøya and Kerguélen's *La France Australe*; and on 23 November 1772 the *Resolution* and *Adventure* stood south into unknown seas.

For the first time in history Antarctica's defences were about to be probed by a well-found expedition led by a supremely competent seaman who was determined, in his own words, 'to go as far as it is possible for man to go'.

Cook was to spend three years searching for the Great Southern Continent. He did not of course spend the whole of this time in the Antarctic; instead, he made three great probes to the southward – termed by Beaglehole 'the three ice-edge cruises' – and in between times wintered in either New Zealand or among the islands of the South Pacific. His discoveries in the latter were extensive; but it is the ice cruises we are concerned with: the Indian Ocean cruise of December 1772–March 1773; the Pacific cruise of November 1773–February 1774; and finally the Atlantic cruise of December 1774–February 1775.

A large number of books and articles have been written about these ice cruises. All are based on the *Journal* which Cook kept in his cabin aboard the *Resolution*, writing up the events of each day in his angular script and awkward style. The first two days' entries pinpoint the *Journal*'s merits and deficiencies.

MONDAY 23rd. Winds NBW to NWBW. Course S 44° W. Distce sail'd 56 miles. Latd in South 34° 36'. Longd in East of Greenwich 17° 34'. Longd made from the Cape of Good Hope 0° 49' W. First part moderate and Clowdy, remainder fresh gales and squally with rain. At 3 p.m. weighed and came to sail with the Adventure in Company. . . . Made several trips to get out of the Bay which we accomplished by 7 o'Clock at which time the Town bore SE. Distant 4 miles. Stood to the Westw'd all night to get an offing having the Wind at NNW and NW blowing in Squalls with rain which obliged us to reef our Top-sails; after having got clear of the land I directed my Course for Cape Circumcision.

TUESDAY 24th. Winds NW, SW to SE. Course S12°E. Distce sail'd 50 miles. Latd in South 35° 25', Longd in East of Greenwich 17° 44. Longd made from the Cape of Good Hope 0° 39'W. Moderate gales and Clowdy weather with a large swell from Southward. In the PM, judging that we should soon come into cold weather, I order'd Slops to be served to such as were in want, and gave to each man a Fearnought Jacket and a pair of Trowers which were allowed by the Admiralty. Many Albatroses about the Ship, some of which we caught with Hook and line and were not thought dispiscable food even at a time when all hands were served fresh Mutton.

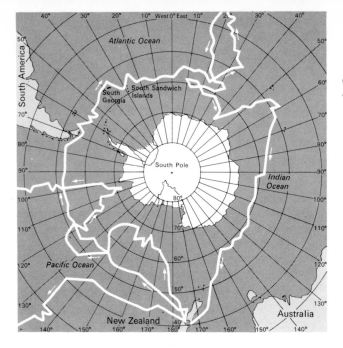

Cook's voyage around the
Antarctic continent

The merit of these entries is self-evident: a wealth of facts set down without
emotion in meticulous detail. If we want to know where the *Resolution* was on a
given day, the set of her sails, what sort of sea was running and what sort of
birds were in company, we have only to consult the *Journal*. And Cook's facts have
never been faulted. He was too scrupulous to make a careless error and too honest
to make a deliberate one. He is one of the very few explorers whose achievements
posterity has shown no inclination either to question or to denigrate. The weakness
of the *Journal* could be said to stem from its strength: it is so factual, so detailed
and so concerned with day-to-day trivia that its reader fails to get an overall
impression of what conditions were really like – a classic example of not being able
to see the wood for the trees. For Cook was too reserved in character to indulge in
even the occasional descriptive or purple passage; also he was no stylist; and it has to
be admitted that the *Journal*, taken in bulk, makes indigestible reading.

On leaving Cape Town the two vessels stood south through heavy seas. The wind
was strong and laced with sleet, and the barometer no higher than 28·5″. The
entry for Tuesday, 8 December gives a good idea of conditions in this early part
of the voyage:

Winds NW. Very hard gales and Hazey with rain. At 1 PM took in the Topsails and
brought to under the Mizen Staysail, Struck Topgt mast and got the Spritsail yard in
fore and aft. At 8 a.m. Wore and lay to on the other Tack, the gale something
Moderater but the Sea still high, and this together with the Weather which is very cold,
makes great distruction among our Hogs, Sheep and Poultry; not a night passes without
some dying.

Cook was now approaching the estimated position of Bouvet's Cape Circumcision.
Lookouts were doubled. And indeed on 11 December the *Adventure* did report

44

land – though as it turned out erroneously, her officer of the watch being, as far as we know, one of the first explorers to mistake a tabular iceberg for the coastline of Antarctica. During the night the icebergs increased in number; and next morning the two ships were brought up short by the barrier which was, time and again in the next three years, to bar their way south: the consolidated pack. This was in 51° 37' S (roughly the latitude of London), a fact which demonstrates very clearly the difference between the southern hemisphere and the northern. For in the northern hemisphere you can sail in ice-free water not only beyond the 50th parallel but beyond the 70th: that is to say a full 2,000 miles closer to the pole; and when Cook was halted that morning in 51° S he was brought up short by the sort of conditions you would expect to find in Novaya Zemlya or the north coast of Baffin Island.

The *Resolution* and *Adventure* skirted the edge of the ice, inching their way south whenever opportunity arose. But the ice in mid-December formed too compact a body to be breached. A month later Cook might perhaps have been able to force his way through to the Weddell Sea. As it was he had no option but to haul away to the east, and to start weaving his way through fog and floes along the perimeter of the ice pack.

The problems of such a voyage can be gleaned from the *Journal*.

TUESDAY 15th DECEMBER. Winds NW, North, N.E. Distce sail'd 23 miles. Steer'd SE along the edge of the ice till One o'Clock when we came to a point round which we hauled SSW, there appearing a Clear Sea in that direction. After running 4 Leagues upon this course (always along the edge of the Ice) we found ourselves in a manner surrounded by it, for it extended farther than the Eye could reach in one compact body, some few places excepted, where Water was to be seen like Ponds; in other places narrow creeks ran in about a Mile or less; high hills or rather Mountains of Ice were seen within this Field, and many Island of Ice without in the open sea, also Whales, Penguins and other Birds. At 5 o'Clock we hauld away in order to get clear of the Ice. We spent the night standing off under our Topsails [it being] so foggy that we could not see a ship's length. Betwixt 12 at night and 7 in the Morn 4 inches of Snow fell on the Decks, the Thermometer five degrees below Freezing point, so that our Rigging and sails were all decorated with Icikles. . . .

It is difficult to visualize from these unemotional entries the full extent of the perils by which Cook was beset. Even today vessels equipped with radar and echo sounders are loath to follow the edge of the Antarctic pack; for the weather here is as consistently bad as anywhere on earth – modern freighters have been known to accumulate so much ice on their decks they have turned turtle, merchantmen have been known to founder under the bludgeoning seas and warships to sink after being holed by the tabular icebergs. Even allowing for the fact that a wooden vessel is more ice-worthy than a metal one, it must in these conditions have been difficult for an eighteenth-century sailing ship to survive. The fact that the *Resolution* and *Adventure* not only survived but managed to follow the line of the pack ice week after week, month after month, for the better part of 10,000 miles is a tribute to the robustness of their construction, the determination of their commander, and the seamanship of their crews.

For the rest of December and the early weeks of January the two vessels followed the edge of the pack. They were far to the south now of Bouvet's and Kerguélen's landfalls, but there was still no sign of the hoped-for continent. On 17 January 1773, however, there occurred one of the great moments in the history of exploration, a moment described laconically by Cook: 'In the AM had hazey weather with Snow Showers. At about ¼ past 11 o'Clock we cross'd the Antarctic Circle [66° 30′ S]. At noon we were by observation four Miles and a half South of it, and are undoubtedly the first and only Ship that ever cross'd this line.' By nightfall the *Resolution* and *Adventure* had pushed as far south as the 67th parallel. They were at the same latitude now as many parts of the coast of Antarctica; indeed had they been able to stand a mere 80 miles to the east they would have sighted the mainland. But they were again brought up short by the consolidated pack which 'stretched away to the S and E without the least appearance of partition'. Cook recognized the inevitable: that he could penetrate no further. For a couple of days the *Resolution* and *Adventure* beat to and fro, searching for the slightest sign of a flaw in the ice's defences. But it was impenetrable; even a twentieth-century icebreaker would have been halted; the ships were in constant hazard from the enormous number of drifting floes; and on 19 January Cook hauled away to the northwest. He had decided, in his own words, 'that it was no longer prudent for me to persevere in going south, and that I would be better employ'd in a search for the land to W'ward [Kerguélen Island] recently discovered by the French'.

In the course of the next two months Cook crossed the Indian Ocean in a gigantic zigzag between the 50th and 60th parallels. He passed well to the south of Kerguélen's *France Australe*, thus establishing the fact that it was not the tip of a continent. And nowhere did he come across the slightest indication of land.

A negative discovery lacks the popular appeal of a positive one, but it may well be equally important; and in this the longest and most arduous of his ice-edge cruises Cook succeeded in removing the mythical *Terra Australis* once and for all from a third of the southern hemisphere.

At the approach of winter the *Resolution* headed for New Zealand, which she sighted on 25 March, having sailed 11,000 miles in 117 days through seas that were entirely unknown. No previous vessel had ever made so long a voyage out of sight of land – let alone in uncharted waters – and the fact that Cook ended with a perfect landfall is evidence of his skill as a navigator; the fact that he had 'only one man aboard that is ill of scurvy' is evidence of the unprecedented care he took of his crew.

The *Resolution*'s landfall was Dusky Sound, and the creek where she now nosed ashore must have seemed to her ship's company a veritable Eden – a setting of

Detail of the *Journal* for 17 January 1773, in Cook's own hand. Notice how it varies from the published version from which the passage opposite was taken.

superb scenic beauty, enhanced by an abundance of fresh water, timber and game. The forge and the sawpit were set up in a convenient clearing, the livestock which had survived were turned loose to pasture, and beer was brewed from the leaves of the local spruce trees. Of the animals they hunted, one in particular struck Cook as being 'of the greatest value, since its skin made chafing gear for our rigging; its fat could be render'd into oil for our lamps, and its meat was tasty as beef steak': the seal (*Arctocephalus forsteri*). It is a sad postscript to the idyll of Dusky Sound that as a consequence of Cook's report, the New Zealand fur seal was soon hunted to extinction.

After so arduous a voyage most commanders would have been happy to spend the summer careening and reprovisioning at leisure; but within six weeks Cook was again at sea, embarking on the first of his forays into the Pacific which form a languorous *divertissement* to the harsher theme of the ice cruises. His exploits in Fiji, Tahiti and Tonga have little bearing on his search for *Terra Australis* – except that the *Adventure* became parted from the *Resolution* in a storm, and since she failed also to keep the rendezvous which had been agreed in New Zealand, when it was time for Cook once again to head south he was obliged to sail without her.

He left New Zealand on 27 November 1773, his objective being to explore the southern rim of the Pacific Ocean as thoroughly as the year before he had explored the rim of the Indian.

This second ice cruise was similar in many respects to the first; for the *Resolution* was beset by the same perils – high winds, heavy seas, fog and, above all, ice. It was ice that was the common denominator in all Cook's tribulations. It fell from the sky, clinging to the *Resolution*'s sails and rigging and making her difficult to handle; it broke away in tabular bergs from the pack, threatening to hole her and sink her; it formed into a vast impenetrable barrier which again and again barred her way south. Each of these three facets of the ice is described in Cook's *Journal*.

> THURSDAY 16th DECEMBER. Weather dark, gloomy and very cold; our sails and rigging hung with ice and icicles these past two days. . . . SATURDAY 18th DECEMBER. Moderate breezes, thick foggy weather with snow and sleet which froze to the Rigging as it fell, so that every thing was cased with ice. . . . TUESDAY 21st DECEMBER. A strong gale attended with a thick fogg, sleet and rain which constitutes the worst of weather; our Rigging so loaded with ice that we could scarce get our Top-sails down to double reef. . . . FRIDAY 24th DECEMBER. Wind northerly, a strong gale attended with a thick fogg, sleet and Snow, which froze to the Rigging as it fell and decorated the whole Ship with Icicles. Our ropes were like wire, our sails like plates of metal and the sheaves froze fast in the blocks. . . . I have never seen so much ice.

These conditions would be unpleasant for the crew of a twentieth-century freighter. They were a great deal more unpleasant for the crew of the *Resolution*, who had to be continually aloft working their ship. Alan Villiers, who is a practical seaman, describes the situation very clearly.

> Ships like the *Resolution* and *Adventure*, as square-rigged ships, could be sailed only from their exposed deck (where all the sails' gear led) and in their exposed rigging. Their sails were planes, set and trimmed to catch the wind and convert its force to forward speed; and to set them, reef them and 'hand' them it was essential for men to go aloft, often in large numbers. The rigging froze, with snow and sleet coagulated into its fibres. The sails froze into stiffened statues touched to marble. It was as easy to 'hand' them as to furl pressed steel. To touch the rigging was to risk frost burn which sears like flame; and to fight the iron-hard sails aloft meant blooded hands, minced fingers and nails torn out by the roots. For this work could not be done in gloves; a sailing-ship sailor must have his 'feel' to work.

In such conditions the *Resolution* might have been expected to lose a fair number of her crew. The fact that she did not lose one is a tribute to the seamanship of both her ship's company and her commander.

An even greater hazard than the ice in the *Resolution*'s rigging was the ice in the sea. Cook, as ever, underplays his hand when describing the tabular icebergs, merely remarking that 'great as the dangers [from them] are they are now become so familiar to us that our apprehensions are never of long duration and are compencated by the very Curious and Romantik Views these ice islands frequently exhibit'. The truth is, however, that a collision with a tabular berg would almost certainly have been fatal; and it was little short of miraculous that the *Resolution* was able to follow the edge of the pack, month after month, without being seriously damaged.

But the most malign characteristic of the ice was its propensity to coagulate into an impenetrable mass. Cook's *Journal* is full of descriptions of this pack or field ice, the most evocative, I think, being that of 30 January 1774 – the day Cook both achieved his 'farthest south' and wrote one of the earliest descriptions of the ice blink and the false land, two phenomena that, during the early years of the next century, were to cause no little confusion among both sealers and explorers as they pushed south in search of the mainland. It was the day too on which he gives us an all too rare glimpse of his private thoughts.

A gentle gale from the NE with clear pleasant Weather. . . . At 10 o'Clock we pass'd a very large Ice Island which was not less than 3 miles in circuit, and presently after were encompass'd by a thick fog which made it unsafe to stand on, especially as we had seen more Ice Islands ahead. . . . At 4 o'Clock (the fog having somewhat dissipated) we perceived the Clouds over the Horizon in the South to be of an unusual Snow-white brightness, which we knew denounced our approach to field Ice; soon after it was seen from the Topmast head, and by 8 o'Clock we were close to the edge of it. It extended east and west far beyond the reach of our sight, while the southern half of the horizon was illuminated by rays of light which were reflected from the Ice to a considerable height. Ninety-seven Ice Hills were distinctly seen within this field, many of them very large and looking like a ridge of Mountains rising one above another till they were lost in the Clouds. The outer or Northern edge of this immense field was composed of loose or broken ice, packed together so that it was not possible for any thing to enter it; this was about a mile broad; and inside was solid ice in one continual compact body; it was rather low and flat, but seemed to increase in height as you traced it to the south in which direction it extended beyound our sight. Such Mountains of Ice as these, were, I believe, never seen in the Greenland Seas. I will not say it was impossible anywhere to get farther to the South, but the attempting of it would have been a rash enterprise and one I believe no man in my situation would have thought of. It was indeed my opinion, as well as the opinion of most on board, that this Ice extends quite to the Pole, or perhaps joins to some land to which it has been fixed since the creation. As we drew near the Ice some Penguins were heard but none seen, and there were few other birds nor any other thing that could induce us to think land was near. Indeed if there was land beyond this Ice, it could afford no better retreat for bird or animal than the Ice itself, with which it must be wholly covered. Even I who had Ambition not only to go farther than any one had done before but as far as it was possible for man to go, was not sorry at meeting this interruption since it shortened the hardships of our Navigation. Seeing therefore we could not proceed one Inch farther to the South, no other reason need be assigned for my Standing back to the North, being at this time in the Latitude of 71° 10′ S, Longitude 106° 54′ W.

Small wonder that by the end of this second summer in the Antarctic Cook was heartily sick of the Southern Ocean in general and the ice in particular. He had now sailed for more than 20,000 miles through seas in which no man had ever sailed before and had come across not the slightest indication of land. He had, however, made yet another major (if negative) contribution to geographical knowledge: he had eliminated *Terra Australis* from the Pacific.

Most men would have been content, after so arduous a voyage, to rest on their laurels. Cook, however, was loath to spend the coming winter in idleness, and almost at once he set out to survey the subtropical islands of the South Pacific. He completed this survey with precision and without the loss of a man; and it is worth noting that wherever he went, from New Zealand to the Bering Strait and from Nootka Sound to Macao, he won not only the respect of the people whose lands he visited but their affection. When we remember the disputes and killings which had attended the landings of previous explorers (and which indeed attended those of his second-in-command Tobias Furneaux) we realize that Cook must have had a unique talent for getting on with his fellow men. He had few enemies but many friends – a fact which was to have some bearing on the pattern of subsequent exploration in the Antarctic.

The last of the ice-edge cruises got under way in November 1774, with the *Resolution* again heading east from New Zealand. It was Cook's intention to cross the Pacific, to land at Cape Horn, and then to explore briefly the only segment of the Southern Ocean he had not yet ventured into: the southwest extremity of the Atlantic.

The voyage from New Zealand to the Horn took a little over five weeks, and ended on 17 December with the *Resolution* sighting the west coast of Tierra del Fuego. It was a dull, uneventful – but not unimportant – voyage of which Cook wrote:

> Since this was the first run that had been made directly a cross this Ocean in so high a latitude, I have been particular in noteing every circumstance that appear'd at all interesting; but I must observe that I never was makeing a passage where so few interesting circumstance(s) occurred. . . . However, I have now done with this SOUTHERN PACIFIC OCEAN, and flatter myself no one will think I have left it unexplor'd.

We have only to glance at Cook's sailing tracks that cross and recross 15,000,000 square miles of hitherto uncharted sea, to appreciate that this boast was no idle one: that after his voyages of 1773 and 1774 no place was left in the Pacific in which a Great Southern Continent could possibly hide.

The *Resolution* spent a fortnight off the coast of Tierra del Fuego. Cook was not impressed. 'This', he wrote, 'is the most desolate coast I ever saw, intirely composed of Rocky Mountains which terminate in horroable precipices whose craggy summits spire up to a vast height; nothing in Nature could have a more barren and savage aspect'. He managed nonetheless to land, and to spend several days ashore in Christmas Sound, where he took aboard 'fresh water of great sweatness as well as wild celery as good as any I ever tasted'. He also had a brief encounter with the natives, the Yaghans, whom he describes with a compassion which might be commonplace today but was rare in the eighteenth century. 'Of all the nations I have seen these people are the most wretched, doomed to live in one of the most inhospitable climates in the world without having sagacity enough to provide themselves with such necessities as might render life convenient.' It is interesting to note that this judgment of the Yaghans was endorsed a century later by Darwin.

The *Resolution* left South America on 3 January 1775 and headed northeast into the Atlantic, it being Cook's intention to search briefly for the legendary 'Gulph of St Sebastian' – which cartographers for generations had been placing on their charts off the coast of Argentina – then head for home. His crew by now had been away from England for two and a half years: both they and Cook were exhausted and eager to return to their families. This is understandable, but ironic. Cook had surveyed five-sixths of the Southern Ocean with unprecedented thoroughness, combing half the southern rim of the Atlantic Ocean, the entire southern rim of the Indian Ocean and the entire southern rim of the Pacific Ocean, without finding the slightest trace of the land that everyone had told him would exist. Now in the last remaining sixth of the southern hemisphere, the southwest reaches of the Atlantic, he carried out little more than a cursory survey. Yet it was here, and here alone, that he might have discovered not only skein after skein of sub-Antarctic islands but the continent of Antarctica itself.

If his exploration had started in the southwest Atlantic instead of finishing in it, Cook today would almost certainly be known as the man who discovered Antarctica. As it was, the *Resolution* stood not southeast from Cape Horn but northeast. The weather was appalling – high winds, heavy seas, fog and the thermometer at zero. Everyone was looking forward to a quick passage home when, unexpectedly, they sighted land: the first indication Cook had had in two and a half years that *Terra Australis* might, albeit in a very truncated form, exist. We can sense his surprise in the *Journal*:

FRIDAY 13th JANUARY. Calm attended by a thick Fogg. In the afternoon Wind veered SE and blew fresh to gale. At 9 o'Clock we saw an Island of Ice, as we then thought, but by noon were doubtful wether it was Ice or Land. At this time it bore E ¾ S, 13 Leagues; our Latitude was 53° 56½'S, Longitude 39° 24'W. Several Penguins, small divers, a snow Petrel and a vast number of Blue Petrels about the Ship. We had little wind all morning, and at 2 p.m. it fell calm. It was now no longer doubted but it was Land not Ice we had in sight, though it was wholly covered with snow.

Cook's first thought was that he might have stumbled at last on the Great Southern Continent. But he was soon disillusioned. He spent a week exploring, triangulating, and taking possession of his discovery, which turned out to be not the hoped-for mainland, but 'an island of no very great extent: a land doomed by nature to perpetual frigidity': South Georgia. He managed in three places to struggle ashore. The coast he describes as 'like the face of an ice isle, a perpendicular cliff of considerable height'. The interior struck him as being – if possible – even more forbidding: 'a terrain savage and horroable, the Wild rocks raising their lofty summits till they were lost in the Clouds, the Vallies buried in everlasting Snow . . .

Possession Bay in the island of South Georgia, engraved by S. Smith after William Hodges

View of the ice islands as seen by Cook on his second voyage

not a tree nor a shrub was to be seen: no not even big enough to make a tooth-pick'. And if this description strikes us as almost too grim to be true, we should remember that Cook was a man who set down the unadorned facts; he did not exaggerate.

On the day he left South Georgia Cook made an entry in the *Journal* which is of particular interest:

> Who would have thought that an Island situated between 54° and 55° S [i.e. the latitude of Northern England] should in the very height of summer be wholly cover'd many fathoms deep with frozen Snow. Not only [are] the very sides and summits of its Mountains cased with Ice, but the quantity which lies in the Vallies is incredible. . . . Yet this island alone could not have produced the ten-thousandth part of the ice which we met with during the previous years of our voyage. THEREFORE THERE MUST IN THE FAR SOUTH BE MORE LAND, to which this vast quantity of ice adheres.

We have here an observation that pinpoints the principal characteristic of the southern hemisphere, and a supposition which events were to prove correct. For there was indeed a landmass in the extreme south: Antarctica. And it is the ice cap of Antarctica which predetermines the climate of the southern hemisphere and is therefore responsible for the fact (observed by Cook) that polar conditions in the south extend some 2,000 miles closer to the equator than they do in the north.

In the hope that South Georgia might prove an offshore island, Cook altered course to the southeast. For the better part of a week the *Resolution* pitched into the teeth of a succession of violent storms, the malevolence of which defies description: thick fog, winds gusting to over 100 knots, heavy falls of snow, and seas as wicked as any the ship had encountered – three times she rolled to 43°, that is to say to within a hairsbreadth of turning turtle. But there was no sign of the hoped-for continent. And by the end of the month even Cook had had enough. His diary for 27 January reads:

> Had so thick a fogg we could not see the ship's length. We were now in Latitude 60, and farther I did not intend to go, for it would not have been prudent for me to spend my time trying to penetrate to the south when it was at least as possible that a large tract of land might be found near Cape Circumcision in the West. . . . Besides [he adds, with an

honesty we cannot help but sympathize with] I was now tired of these Southern Latitudes where nothing was to be found but Ice and Fogg.

The fact is that both ship and crew were by this time close to the limit of their endurance. No vessel apart from Magellan's *Victoria* had ever been so long continuously at sea, and no vessel had ever endured so prolonged a battering not only from wind and wave but also from snow and ice. Cook altered course to the north.

Almost at once he sighted part of the South Sandwich archipelago. And the unbelievable desolation of this grim little skein of islands confirmed the opinion that had, for some time, been building up in his mind: namely that even if a landmass was to be found in the extreme south, it would turn out to be so desolate and icebound as to be of no practical value. Here is the first description ever written of the South Sandwich Islands from the diary of Cook's Second Lieutenant, Charles Clerke.

> This land is as wretched a Country as Nature can possibly form. The shores consist of Icy Cliffs and precipices – we've not yet seen a Hole we could shove a Boat in. Here and there [are indentations] . . . which might form bays, but the intermediate spaces are quite chok'd up with Ice. When the Haze clears we can see Mountains of immense bulk and height Inland, but totally cover'd with Snow, as is the whole of this wretched country throughout.

An even more graphic description of these islands of the Southern Ocean is that of the nineteenth-century sealer Robert Fildes, who wrote of the South Shetlands: 'When She fashion'd this place, methinks Madam Nature had been drinking too much!' Yet these, it is worth remembering, were only sub-Antarctic islands. Antarctica itself, as Cook suspected, was to prove even bleaker. On Monday, 6 February the *Resolution* hauled away from the ice for the last time and headed for home.

It has sometimes been implied that Cook gave up the search for Antarctica because he doubted its existence. This is not so. The entry he made that night in his *Journal* is quite explicit.

> We continued to the SE till noon at which time we were in Latitude 58° 15'S, Longitude 21° 34'W, and seeing neither land nor sign of any I concluded that what we had seen (which I named Sandwich Land) was a group of islands. . . . Yet I firmly believe there IS a tract of land near the Pole, which is the source of all the ice spread over this vast Southern Ocean. It is, however, true that the greater part of such a continent (if indeed it exists) must lie within the Polar Circile, where the sea is so pestered with Ice that the land is inaccessible. The risk one runs in exploring a coast in these unknown and Icey Seas is so very great that I doubt if the land which lies to the South will ever be explored. Thick foggs, Snow storms, Intense Cold and every other thing that can render Navigation dangerous one has to encounter, and these difficulties are heightened by the enexpressable horrid aspect of the Country, a Country doomed

by Nature to lie buried under everlasting ice and snow. . . . It would have been rashness in me to have risked all which had been done in [our] Voyage, in finding and exploring a Coast which, when done, would have answer'd no end whatsoever. These reasons induced me to alter course to the north.

By midsummer the *Resolution* was back in England. Her voyage had spanned 1,114 days and 67,500 miles. She had not lost a single man from scurvy.

Cook had failed to find *Terra Australis*; he had taken possession of no 'convenient situations in the South Land'. Yet his voyage could not, by the wildest stretch of imagination, be dubbed a failure. It is true that it failed at the time to produce any great wave of popular enthusiasm, and it has failed subsequently to grip men's imagination in the manner, say, of Columbus's voyage, Vasco da Gama's or Magellan's. This is because it had no climax and because its discoveries and conclusions were negative rather than positive. Yet the contribution it made to our knowledge of the earth has not been surpassed by any voyage in history. Cook, who was nothing if not a realist, gives a very fair summing up of his own achievements:

> I had now made the circuit of the Southern Ocean in a high Latitude and traversed it in such a manner as to leave not the least room for the Possibility of there being a continent, unless very near the Pole. Thus the Southern hemisphere [has been] explored and a final end put to the searching after that Great Southern Continent which had engrossed the attention of the Maritime Powers for the past two centuries and the Geographers of all ages.

If Cook had been less highly thought of, his conclusions might have been challenged; other explorers might have pushed south in the *Resolution*'s wake, and Antarctica might well have been sighted in the latter years of the eighteenth century. As it was, he was universally held in such esteem that the attitude of explorers of all nationalities might be summed up as: 'Cook says there's nothing worth while discovering in the Antarctic so why go there?' Exploration shifted back to the northern hemisphere – in particular to the search for a North West and a North East passage – and the Southern Ocean reverted once again to its primordial solitude.

The voyage of the *Resolution* was, however, to have an unexpected aftermath: an aftermath involving the slaughter of wildlife on a larger scale than ever before. Cook's *Journal* is full of references to the mammals of the Southern Ocean: to the 'great number of whales disporting themselves about the ship' and 'the multitude of seals observ'd on the offshore rocks'. These references were not lost on the British and American seamen whose traditional hunting grounds in the northern hemisphere were becoming depleted. In the early years of the nineteenth century a new type of vessel began to nose into the Southern Ocean: the sloops of the New England sealers and the brigs of the North Sea whaling fleets. Commercial rivalry was soon to provide an astringent spur to exploration.

(above) Leopard seal (*Hydrurga leptonyx*)
(below) Fur seals (*Arctocephalus gazella*) and gentoos (*Pygoscelis papua*), near Johnson Cove, Bird Island

## CHAPTER 3

## SEEN DIMLY BEFORE DAWN?

FROM TIME IMMEMORIAL man has hunted the seal. In the Arctic the ecology of a whole race, the Eskimos, was until recently largely dependent on this creature, whose flesh provided food, whose fur was made into clothing, whose blubber was rendered into oil, and whose bones were fashioned into weapons and tools. In the Antarctic, however, where there is no indigenous population, sealing did not get under way until late in the eighteenth century.

That it got under way at all was due to the industrial revolution.

The vast and ever-growing army of machines needed oil for lubrication. Vegetable oils in the eighteenth century were expensive to process, and mineral oils were as yet untapped; animal oil, on the other hand, could be readily obtained from the vast herds of mammals (whales, seals, sea lions and walruses) that roamed the northern reaches of the Atlantic and the Pacific. These creatures were defenceless; they were hunted with merciless efficiency; their numbers dwindled, and it was not long before the demand began to exceed the supply. This was especially true of the seal. For in the 1760s a furrier in Canton perfected a method of separating these animals' coarse outer fur from their smooth and valuable underfur. The result was the sealskin – uniquely warm and perennially fashionable. A market for fur was now added to the market for oil; the price of a seal pelt rocketed from 50 cents to 5 dollars, and the sealing brigs descended like vultures on the rookeries (or breeding grounds) of the north. Within a decade the beaches of the Aleutian and Pribilof Islands were transformed from nursery to charnelhouse; and by 1780 the northern fur seal (*Callorhinos ursinus*) had been hunted to within a hairsbreadth of extermination.

It was about this time that Cook returned from the Antarctic with stories of the 'great numbers of [southern fur] seals [*Arctocephalus*] observ'd on the offshore rocks'. It was obvious that here, for those with sufficient courage and endurance, was an alternate source of supply, and in the last years of the century a succession of expeditions headed south.

Because America was at peace while Europe was deep in the Napoleonic Wars, the majority of these expeditions were launched initially from New England: from the ports of Boston, Nantucket, New Haven or Stonington. Hunter Christie describes the men who took part in them:

> These sealers were probably the toughest crews who ever put to sea. They followed a brutal calling in high latitudes, and soon became inured to the danger of navigation in ice-filled waters and among rocks veiled by mist and snow. Risking their lives in uncharted seas, undergoing appalling hardships and working caked with grease and

(above) Female Weddell seal (*Leptonychotes weddelli*) and pup.
(below) Southern elephant seal (*Mirounga leonina*)

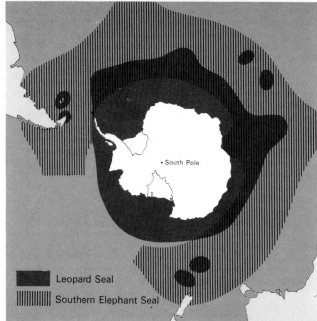

Leopard Seal

|||||| Southern Elephant Seal

(below) Southern elephant seals
(*Mirounga leonina*)

literally up to their waists in blood, it is no wonder they were hard. It can only be said to their credit that they were as careless of their own suffering as they were indifferent to the cruelties they inflicted on their victims.

Some British historians have embroidered on the sealers' toughness and have depicted them as 'soaked in rum and ever eager to pick a fight'. But this is nonsense. The bulk of the New England seamen were God-fearing Puritans, men whose dogma encouraged them to combine commercial acumen with stern morality; their ships were 'dry', their sole ambition was to load a full cargo, and they were far too busy fighting the elements to want to fight anyone else. In search of new breeding grounds – where they could make their kill at leisure and their fortunes in a single voyage – their brigs pushed ever deeper into the icy periphery of the Antarctic.

The quest for new hunting or fishing grounds has, throughout history, frequently led to geographical discovery. The sealers, however, were to prove coy and uncommonly reticent discoverers; for they kept the whereabouts of any new lands they sighted to themselves. To understand why, we need to know something of the habits of their quarry, the seal.

There are some thirty different species of seal, ranging from the ponderous $4\frac{1}{2}$-ton elephant bulls of South Georgia to the diminutive 60-lb sea lions of the Galapagos. The New Englanders, however, were interested only in two – the fur seal for its pelt and the elephant seal for its oil.

The fur seal *Arctocephalus* is found throughout the Southern Ocean, as far north as the Cape of Good Hope and as far south as the coast of Antarctica. It is a harmless, gregarious creature spending some three-quarters of its life at sea and one-quarter on land. At sea it is all power and grace, and well able to look after itself; on land, however, while breeding, it is vulnerable. Each year towards the end of November the big bull seals haul up onto the shore of one of the lonely sub-Antarctic islands. Here, with much bellowing and tussling, they stake out their territory, the larger and more powerful achieving a strategic position at the water's edge, while the weaker are driven inland or precluded altogether from the shore. They wait. And after they have waited a couple of weeks the cows come up from the sea. The cows are less than half the size of the bulls, a lissom four-foot-six, with glossy grey-green coats and a distinctive collar of white encircling their throat. They are herded into harems, nine or ten to each of the bulls – and woe betide the flibbertigibbet who attempts to leave her master's domain, or the marauding male who attempts to enter it! Within three or four days of their arrival, the cows give birth, always to a single pup; and by the end of December the beach is a close-packed bedlam, with birth, feeding and weaning being followed in rapid succession by mating and moulting. By mid-February the harem bulls are emaciated and exhausted, having had no food and very little rest for upwards of ten weeks. They abandon their territory and take to the sea, being followed four or five weeks later by the females

59

60        (top left) A try pot in South Georgia
(top right) Captain R. F. Scott's sealing knife
(above) Crabeater seals (*Lobodon carcinophagus*)

and young. Nine months later they are back again, and the cycle of procreation begins anew.

Recent research has confirmed that the same seal, obedient to a behaviour pattern followed for millennia, will return to the same breeding ground year after year. It is this which explains the sealers' preoccupation with secrecy. For a captain who discovered a new island discovered as often as not a new breeding ground; and, provided he kept his discovery to himself, he had every expectation of scooping an exceedingly rich pool. J. C. Furnas puts the case very clearly in his *Anatomy of Paradise*: 'Whalers could afford to swap information about their quarry. But sealing was wholesale massacre on a deserted shore; and a newly discovered rookery was like a vein of precious metal, too easily exhausted to tell rivals about.'

It is not therefore surprising that the New England captains kept their own counsel, burned their records and made few entries in their logs. Nor is it surprising that we have today a great deal more information on the technique of sealing than we have on the precise whereabouts of individual sealers.

Their technique was simple, brutal and effective. The ships they sailed in were small (seldom more than 250 to 300 tons) but meticulously coppered and caulked; they were rigged as brigs, and usually carried on deck a shallop or small cutter which was useful for working in shallow water. The parent vessel would seek out a rookery, drop anchor offshore and use her shallop to land the better part of her crew; she would then try to find a sheltered anchorage (no easy job in the Southern Ocean) where she could lie snugged down under a skeleton watch. For the men put ashore, sealing was not so much a hunt as a massacre. The British captain, Robert Fildes, describes the beaches of the sub-Antarctic islands as 'fur lined: so close-packed it is impossible to haul up a boat without killing your way ashore. . . . And when one has landed,' he adds, 'it is impossible to push through the creatures unless one has a weapon with which to clear a path.' The sealers did not lack weapons – 14-inch stabbing knives and long specially weighted clubs – and with these they made short work of their victims. The seals made little effort to escape; for centuries of immunity to any form of predator had atrophied their suspicions. A bull in his harem might occasionally rear up and bellow in defiance; but the mild-eyed cows simply watched the slaughter with incurious passivity, lying and even mating among the carnage until it was their turn to be clubbed, stabbed and flayed to death. An expert, it was reckoned, could kill and skin fifty seals an hour; at the end of which, if he was working on rock, he would be literally knee-deep in blubber and blood.

To start with, the sealers' callousness was directed solely against their quarry. It was found that the bulls, in the early stages of the *pogrom*, were more useful alive than dead, for they prevented their harems from wandering off the rocks; on the other hand they would sometimes make a nuisance of themselves by attempting clumsy and ineffectual charges at their assailants. To stop this they were blinded in one eye. 'It was laughable,' writes Fildes, 'to see these old goats, planted at intervals along the beach, keeping their remaining peeper continually fixed on their seraglio of clapmatches [cows] while we went about our business on their blind side.' It was not long before the same callousness was reflected in the men's relations with one another. As their quarry grew scarcer they took to leaving parties ashore for weeks or even months at a stretch. Conditions were bleak – rough stone huts, snow or mist on nine days out of ten, and no warmth except from the burning of blubber – and to add to their troubles many of these shore parties were deliberately marooned. Captain Althearn of Nantucket is quite explicit about this: 'If,' he wrote, 'I got out to a rookery early and found a great show of seals, I would get as many aboard as I could. I would then leave on the rocks all the men I thought might blab, go to the most convenient port and sell my skins. This way I should expect to have another season without company.' One wonders how many potential blabbers died of exposure and starvation, waiting in vain on some desolate outcrop of rock for a skipper who valued his profits more highly than the lives of his crew.

One wonders too just how many seals were killed. Estimates vary from 3 million to $5\frac{1}{2}$ million. Whichever figure is more accurate, the southern fur seal – like its counterpart in the north – was butchered to within a hairsbreadth of extinction. 'The harvest of the seas has been so effectively reaped', reported Webster in 1829, 'that not a single seal was seen, although it is only a few years since countless multitudes covered these selfsame beaches.' Williams, writing a generation later, was even more pessimistic. 'Our hunters gleaned every beach', he wrote, 'and searched every rock, but not a remnant of the species was found. Thus in wretched and wanton destruction has gone for ever from the Southern Ocean a whole race of animals useful to man.' Williams in fact was over-pessimistic. A small number of seals managed to survive; these were rigorously protected, and there are signs today that their numbers are increasing steadily enough to save the species from extinction.

The elephant seal, being less valuable, was not sought out with such rapaciousness at first; but once the bearers of fur had been hunted to exhaustion, the predators turned their attention to the bearers of oil.

The smooth-skinned *Mirounga leonina* is a less attractive creature than its fur-coated cousin. Two hundred years ago the Swedish naturalist Linnaeus wrote the classic description of them: 'This is a dirty, curious, quarrelsome tribe: polygamous and gross.' The bulls indeed are not only gross but gigantic, averaging some 19 feet in length and 3 tons in weight. They have an inflatable proboscis, like a trunk, which normally hangs over their mouth but which can be erected in battle to act as both a cushion against attack and an amplifier for their ear-splitting roar. Their life cycle is similar to that of the fur seal, except that their battles for dominance are bloodier and their harems larger. They too were defenceless against the sealers. The huge creatures were herded as close as possible to the water's edge, so as to save the labour of moving their carcasses, then stabbed or clubbed to death. Bulls reluctant to die were dispatched by a musket ball fired through their palate as they reared up – 'but only one shot since powder is expensive'. Their blubber was stripped off, hacked into 'horse-pieces' and roughly minced; the mince was then

(above) Kerguélen (or 'white') fur seal (*Arctocephalus gazella*)

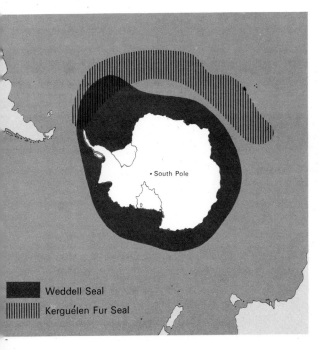

Weddell Seal

Kerguélen Fur Seal

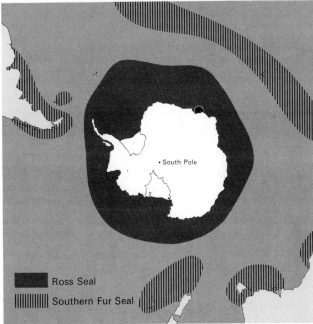

Ross Seal

Southern Fur Seal

(right) Weddell seal (*Leptonychotes weddelli*)
(below) Fur seal (*Arctocephalus gazella*)
(bottom) Ross seal (*Ommatophoca rossi*)

boiled in a huge iron pot or try, rendered into oil and poured while still hot into 100-gallon casks. The trys were kept burning not with wood – because there is none on most Antarctic islands – but with fresh blubber and penguin skins. The stench, the fumes, the piled-up carcasses and the sea birds darting in and out of the carnage like a macabre *corps de ballet* of the air, combined to make the sealing beaches like some stage set for Dante's *Inferno*.

Sealing, in brief, was not for the squeamish; and the brutality of the New Englanders precludes our affection. It should not, however, preclude our admiration. For their fortitude and endurance were truly heroic; and when they had hunted the beaches of Chile and the Argentine to exhaustion they pushed doggedly south, working their way from island to island in conditions as hazardous as any on earth, until they came at last to the *Terra Incognita* which had eluded man for 2,000 years, the Great Southern Continent itself.

Which of them sighted it first?

American historians champion the cause of Nathaniel B. Palmer, British historians that of Edward Bransfield; and it is sad to relate that the first-sighting claims of these two explorers have sparked off a bitter controversy. This controversy has been raging for 150 years, and has been conducted by armchair historians on either side of the Atlantic with an acerbity that would have horrified Palmer and Bransfield – both of whom were reasonable men, devoid of jingoism. Words such as 'fake', 'forgery', 'liar' and 'cheat' have been used freely by writers who have never been within a thousand miles of the Antarctic, and whose dogmatic assertions prove only that they have little understanding of the problems involved.

These problems are principally two: the weather, and the fragmentary nature of the sealers' reports.

Heavy seas, gale-force winds, snow squalls and mist are not the easiest conditions for accurately plotting the position of an unknown coast, and it is hardly surprising that many of the sealers' fixes were subsequently proved to be inaccurate. Nor is it surprising that when icefields were sighted fleetingly through mist and snow, the beholders had little means of telling if they were island, mainland or pack ice.

As for written reports, even if a captain succeeded in making an accurate landfall, there was no reason why he should record the fact in his log, since he was far more concerned with preserving the secret of new breeding grounds than with adding to cartographical knowledge. There is also the point that although the sealers were magnificent practical seamen, many of them were far from literate, and their logs are often none too easy to interpret.

The truth about the first sighting of the mainland may therefore be difficult to arrive at. But we shall, I think, get close to it if we chronicle the sealers' progress south in the manner in which they made it: year by storm-encompassed year, degree by hesitating degree.

The first Antarctic sealing vessel whose voyage is recorded in detail is the *States of Boston*, an enormous 1,000-ton brig which visited the Falkland Islands in 1784 and loaded a cargo of '13,000 sea otters'. The following year a smaller vessel from Stonington dropped anchor off South Georgia, and her captain wrote, 'the seals are so numerous I declare that if many thousand were killed overnight their loss would not be noticed in the morning'. By the turn of the century New England sealers had visited not only the principal offshore islands (the Falklands, South Georgia and Juan Fernandez) but also most of the mainland beaches from Buenos Aires to Valparaiso. Their depredations invariably followed the same pattern: elation at finding a new rookery, three or four seasons of indiscriminate slaughter, naïve surprise that 'our quarry seem to have deserted their former haunts', and finally the brigs again standing south in search of new hunting grounds. The number of fur seals killed was astronomic, and so were the profits. One brig alone, the *Betsy*, working one island, Mas Afuera, killed in a single season more than 100,000 seals; sold in New York their pelts fetched 680,000 dollars.

By the early years of the nineteenth century the sealers found themselves obliged to extend the range of their operations; for the beaches around South America had been hunted to exhaustion. New breeding grounds were found in Bass Strait (between Tasmania and South Australia), off the Cape of Good Hope and off the southwest tip of New Zealand. Then came a spate of discoveries in the extreme south of the Pacific: the Antipodes Islands in 1800, the Auckland Islands in 1806, Campbell and Macquarie Islands in 1810. All these were a cornucopia to the sealers – but for a few years only. What happened on Macquarie Island was typical: a tragedy repeated many times on many isolated outcrops of rock throughout the Southern Ocean. The first ships to drop anchor there found the beaches crowded with seals. Some 90,000 were butchered the first season, 60,000 the second and 20,000 the third; in the fourth season 'only a handful of seals were sighted', and within the decade a rare and beautiful subspecies had been butchered to extinction. All that remains of them today are a couple of skulls in a museum, and a handful of paintings made by a seaman aboard the *Perseverance* – the brig that first sighted the island.

After 1815 the plight of the seals became even more desperate. For with the end of the Napoleonic War a large number of seamen, discharged from men o' war, made their way south, intent on finding in trade the fortune which as likely as not had eluded them in war. In 1813 there had been no more than a couple of British vessels in the Southern Ocean; by 1819 there were over a hundred. Most of the sub-Antarctic islands, by this time, had been worked out; and both the established New Englanders and the newly arrived Europeans found themselves obliged to seek new rookeries in the extreme south, along the very perimeter of the Antarctic pack.

It was not long before rumours of 'huge snow-capped mountains seen dimly before dawn' began to reach South American ports. We are on the threshold now of a moment unique in recorded history: man's first sighting of a virgin continent.

It is certainly not impossible that an unknown sealing brig, driven south into the Ross or Weddell Sea, sighted the mainland of Antarctica before 1819; but if this is so her log has not been found and her achievement will probably never be recognized. By far the most likely time for a first sighting is the summer of 1819/20, and by far the most likely place the Antarctic peninsula – the thin finger of ice-clad mountains reaching towards South America, between the 60th and 70th meridians. The sequence of events seems to have been this.

In February 1819 the brig *Williams* was rounding Cape Horn on a routine trading voyage when she was blown far to the south by a succession of storms. On 19 February she sighted land. Here is the report of her captain, William Smith:

> On the 19th aforesaid at 7 a.m. Land or Ice was discovered bearing South-east by south – strong gales from the Southwest accompanied with Snow or Sleet. At 10 a.m. more moderate and clear, made sail for the land. At 11 rounded a large Ice Berg. At noon fine and pleasant weather – Latitude by Observation 62° 01′ West. At 4 p.m. made the land bearing from S.S.E. to S.E., distance about 10 miles, hove to, and having satisfied ourselves of land, headed to Westward and made sail on our voyage to Valparaiso.

This is a straightforward, unambiguous report. The log of the *Williams* is available for inspection, and the latitude given by Smith pinpoints his landfall as almost exactly in the middle of the South Shetlands, a cluster of ice-coated islands on the very threshold of the continent. Arriving in Valparaiso, Smith made his discovery known. He was offered considerable sums of money by a group of New England sealers, who, anxious to find new breeding grounds, pressed him to divulge the position of his landfall; but he refused, having, in his own words, 'the good of my country at heart'. The advent of winter precluded further exploration for the time being, but as soon as the weather improved Smith was again at sea, and on 16 October he sighted the South Shetlands a second time. He landed at Shirreff's Cove on Livingston Island, 'and took formal possession of the new discovered land in the name of His Majesty George the Third'.

There is no reason to doubt the validity of Smith's reports. Yet he was not, I think, the first man to set foot on the islands. Early in September 1819 the Spanish warships *San Telmo* and *Primerosa Mariana* were rounding Cape Horn. The *San Telmo* was crowded with troops – reinforcements for the Viceroy of Peru; she was a big vessel, a seventy-four-gun ship of the line; but in a series of violent storms she was dismasted, her rudder was wrenched off, and she fell helplessly away to the south. The *Mariana* tried unsuccessfully first to take her in tow, then to rescue her crew but she too was dismasted, and on 4 September in 'latitude 62° South, longitude uncertain' the luckless *San Telmo* was left to her fate. When Smith landed six weeks later in Shirreff's Cove, he found her anchor stocks together with a great pile of splintered timbers; and the chances are, I think, that some of the Spaniards survived the wreck and managed to struggle up the rocks only to die of cold, exposure and starvation on one of the most desolate shorelines on earth. Smith, who seems to have been a somewhat lugubrious character, took the *San Telmo*'s anchor back to England and had it made into his coffin!

After this second sighting by Smith the British authorities woke up to the fact that he had made a discovery of some importance; and the *Williams* was loaned to the Royal Navy, given a naval complement and put under the command of Edward Bransfield. Bransfield's orders were comprehensive: 'To chart and survey whatsoever coasts you may encounter, taking soundings, reporting on anchorages etc. . . . To ascertain whether there is indeed an uncommon abundance of whales, otters and seals in these waters. . . . To report on the natural resources of the land for supporting a colony, and to observe the character, habits and customs of the inhabitants, to whom you will display every friendly disposition.' These orders represent something of a watershed in Antarctic exploration. For they look both backward to the past and forward to the future: that is to say although they obviously have their roots in the Ancients' concept of a rich and populated Southern Continent awaiting exploitation, they also contain a hint of the twentieth-century concept of Antarctica as a place to be studied, a storehouse, as it were, of information. The quest for wealth was being gradually superseded by the quest for knowledge.

It would be wrong, however, to give Bransfield's expedition too laudatory a gloss – especially in view of its embarrassing anticlimax. For when, late in 1820, Bransfield submitted an account of his discoveries to the Admiralty, his report was promptly lost. It arrived in London, was marked 'for early attention', and has never been seen or heard of since! American historians have tended to read something sinister into this; they have viewed Bransfield with suspicion – some have even expressed the opinion that his voyage never took place – and one can sympathize with their mistrust. Two wrongs, however, do not make a right. And though the Admiralty deserve condemnation for a quite appalling piece of incompetence, there is no reason for us to extend our condemnation to Bransfield. His reputation should remain untarnished, since even without an official report enough material is available from which to reconstruct his voyage. For the charts of the *Williams* are extant; so also are eye-witness accounts from her surgeon Dr Young and her midshipman Thomas Bone.

We learn from the latter that the expedition left Valparaiso on 19 December 1819. They arrived in the South Shetlands on 16 January 1820, and spent the next ten days surveying and sounding, much hampered by fog. A landing was made on one of the larger islands, and the usual rigmarole of raising flags and burying coins was observed: also observed was the quite fantastic number of seals, 'stowed in bulk the length of the beaches'. On 27 January the *Williams* headed southwest into unknown waters, and early next morning sighted the volcanic horseshoe of Deception Island. The fog was troublesome, and Bransfield seems to have been uncertain if Deception was peninsula or island. For the next 48 hours the track of the brig is tantalizingly conjectural, but she appears to have tried to stand south through a sea encompassed by fog and sown with icebergs and reefs. Then comes the passage which has led to so much controversy. It first appeared in the London *Literary Gazette* in November 1821, and was written by Midshipman Bone, in the third person and under a pseudonym. This may sound devious; but Bone in fact was simply complying with the naval regulations of his day which forbade serving officers to publish accounts of their exploits. The inference is, I think, that the Admiralty were thoroughly embarrassed at having lost Bransfield's report and were prepared to turn a blind eye to the publication of Bone's, provided this was done discreetly. Here is what the midshipman tells us:

> January 30th. They [the *Williams*] now steered southward, and seemed to be running from the land [i.e. heading away from the South Shetlands and Deception Island]; but at three o'clock in the afternoon, after having their attention attracted by three immense icebergs, the haze clearing, they very unexpectedly saw land to the S.W. and at four o'clock were encompassed by islands spreading from NE to E. The whole of these formed a prospect the most gloomy that can be imagined, and the only cheer the sight afforded was in the idea that this might be the long-sought Southern Continent, as land was undoubtedly seen in latitude 64° and trending to the eastward. In this bay or gulph there was a multitude of whales, and a quantity of seaweed apparently fresh from the rocks. A round island was named Tower Island, and the land Trinity Land.

There are two diametrically opposed interpretations of this: one that it is a pack of lies, the other that 'the *Williams* deserves to go down in history with Columbus's *Santa Maria*, for without any question her crew that afternoon were the first to sight an unknown continent.' The truth lies half way in between. On 30 January the *Williams* was undoubtedly somewhere in the reach of water now known as Bransfield Strait. Even though the haze had cleared, visibility was far from perfect. To the westward, it looks from Bransfield's charts as though the strait must have been choked by ice, and this he mistook for land. To the southward, Trinity Island and Tower Island (now Hoseason) are delineated accurately enough, and they must therefore have been sighted. I do not, however, subscribe to the view held by most British historians that if the fog had cleared sufficiently for Bransfield to see Trinity Island he could hardly have avoided seeing the much larger extent of land behind it. For although Trinity Island looks an insignificant speck on the map, it is in fact nearly 100 miles in circumference and over 3,000 feet in height; it is divided from the mainland by ten miles of sea (Orléans Strait); and it strikes me as quite possible that Bransfield saw Trinity Island but that the 'land' he plotted behind it was in fact a jumble of icebergs caught up in the Orléans Strait. This part of his claim I would therefore regard as not proven.

The fog, we are told by Bone, closed in on the evening of 30 January, and the *Williams* stood northeast. A couple of days later, however, in a momentary clearance, Bransfield again sighted land to the south: 'two high mountains covered with snow'. He took bearings and estimated the mountains' position as approximately 63° 40′ S, 59° 50 W; he then inked them in on his chart, and connected them to his Trinity Land by a dotted line which he marked 'supposed Land, Lost in fog'. This was a lucky guess; for Bransfield's line of dots coincides closely with the actual coastline of Antarctica. What is more, his mountains coincide even more closely with the actual peaks Jacquinot (1,600 feet) and Bransfield (2,500 feet) on the tip of the

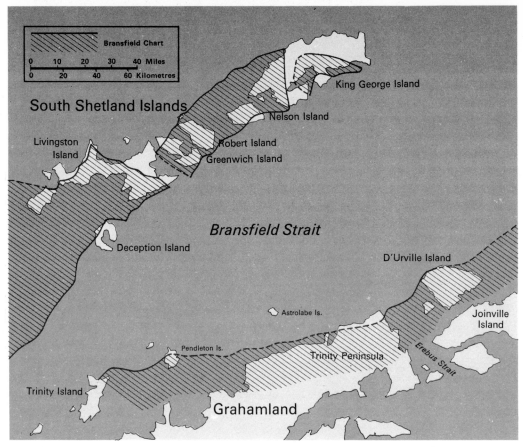

Antarctic peninsula. There are no other mountains in this area, and there are no offshore islands which contain anything remotely resembling a 'high mountain covered with snow'. On this occasion, therefore, the crew of the *Williams* must indeed have sighted the mainland of Antarctica; and we can only marvel that so much controversy has surrounded the Trinity sighting of 30 January when an indisputable sighting took place only a few miles to the north on 1 February!

Bransfield was no Cook nor even a Bellingshausen (one cannot imagine either of these great explorers sighting a virgin continent and not making determined efforts to land on it); he headed for the South Shetlands, and by mid-April was back in Valparaiso. If today his praise is seldom sung and his name little remembered, this is partly because of his failure to follow up his sighting by a landing, partly because of the loss of his reports, and partly because his discovery proved of little commercial value. He remains a shadowy, vaguely unheroic figure: a man who had greatness thrust upon him but lacked the calibre to grasp it. This, however, should not blind us to the fact that he did make a genuine discovery and was the first man to chart a portion of the Antarctic mainland.

The voyages of Smith and Bransfield form a British *divertissement* to the main theme of exploration by New England sealers. And it was the latter who now transformed Bransfield's half-discovered coastline into the last great killing ground of the fur seals. The most famous of these New Englanders was Palmer of the

(opposite) Map of the South Shetland Islands and the adjacent Antarctic Peninsula with the outline of Edward Bransfield's chart superimposed
(right) Nathaniel Palmer

*Hero*; the most deserving of fame was a character probably few people today have heard of, Davis of the *Cecilia* (who will be discussed in a later chapter).

Nathaniel Palmer is in some ways as shadowy a figure as Bransfield. Not as a man. As a man he leaps boldly from the pages of history: a fearless navigator, a born leader, a brilliant shipwright and a successful and respected businessman. As an explorer, however, he remains an enigma; for it is hard to know which of his exploits are fact and which fiction. This is because contemporary United States historians (Fanning in particular) went out of their way to build him up into a national hero. England and America, it should be remembered, had in 1819 just stopped fighting each other for the second time in a generation; and although Palmer himself was no flag-waving fanatic (he went on several voyages with British sealers – the most famous being that of 1821–2 when with George Powell he discovered the South Orkney Islands – and remained all his life on the best of terms with them), the same cannot be said of his biographers.

He first came to the Antarctic in the summer of 1819–20, having, according to some reports, tailed the *Williams* to the South Shetlands. The ship he was in took 9,000 seals in fifteen days – 'we could have had 90,000 but were lacking salt'. Not surprisingly the following season a veritable armada of New Englanders sailed south for the Shetlands, among them Palmer, aged barely twenty-one but already with a command of his own. His command was the *Hero*: a diminutive sloop – length

47 feet, beam 17 feet, one mast, one deck and a displacement of little more than 40 tons – and he must have been a magnificent seaman to take so small a vessel into the wildest seaways on earth. Exactly where he did take her is a matter of controversy; for fact now becomes interwoven with fancy.

According to Fanning, 'While the fleet lay at anchor in Yankee Harbour, Deception Island, during the season 1820 and 21 . . . during a very clear day Captain Pendleton sighted mountains (one a volcano in operation) in the South. To examine the newly discovered land Captain N. B. Palmer in the sloop *Hero* was despatched.' And it was, Fanning would have us believe, during this voyage that Palmer discovered Antarctica.

The trouble is that the New England fleet did not in fact lie at anchor off Deception Island during the season of 1820/21. It lay at anchor off Livingston Island, some twenty miles to the north. This is confirmed not only by the logs of the other sealing brigs concerned, but also by Fanning's own remark that one of the mountains sighted was a volcano in operation. For the sole volcano within 500 miles of the South Shetlands is Deception Island itself – which contains sulphur springs hot enough to boil an egg in, and is sporadically active. It is therefore beyond dispute that Captain Pendleton must have stood on Livingston Island, looked south, sighted Deception in eruption, and ordered the *Hero* to investigate. Here is Palmer's own account of his investigation.

> Nov. 15th. These 24 hours commences with Thick weather Light breese from N.W. at 2 P.M. clearing off got Underway on a cruise for Deception course East for the North head wind Light at N by W. at 8 Being close in with the Land tacked to the Northw'd. Middle part thick snow storm. . . . Reffd the mainsail Tacked to the E'wd at 5 made the Land stood along and Examined it but were Disappointed. stood along to the southward saw an Opening stood in found it to be a spacious harbour with very deep Water 50 to 60 fathoms. got out the boat to sound, found anchorage about a mile from the mouth. at 11 we came too in fifteen fathoms off the mouth of a lagoon went on shore and got some eggs. . . .
>
> Nov. 17th. These 24 hours commences with fresh Breese from SWest and Pleasant at 8 P.M. got over under the Land found the sea filled with immense Ice Bergs – at 12 hove too under the Jib Laid off and on until morning. at 4 a.m. made sail in shore and Discovered-a-strait – Tending SSW and NNE it was literaly filled with Ice and the shore inaccessible thought it not Prudent to Venture in we Bore away to the Northw'd and saw 2 small Islands and the shore every where Perpendicular. we stood across toward Freseland [Livingston Island] course NNW.

For many years American historians held the view that these entries described a passage from Deception Island to the continent, and on this assumption they hailed Palmer as the man who discovered Antarctica. However, it has recently been suggested by Edouard Stackpole (Curator of the Marine Historical Association of Mystic) that what the entries in fact describe is a passage from Livingston Island to Deception Island. Bearing in mind the *Hero*'s point of departure, this makes sense;

and indeed when one analyses the courses and descriptions and relates them to a chart, the evidence is overwhelming. Palmer's 'spacious harbour' with its south-facing entrance was obviously the flooded crater of Deception Island (an anchorage used the following season by both the British and American fleets), and his 'perpendicular shore' the southeast face of Livingston Island (a coast subsequently described by Bellingshausen as 'rocky and sheer'). The claim that Palmer sighted Antarctica in November 1820 is, to say the least, not proved.

Not that the question of who, by a few days, caught sight of the mainland first is all that important. What *is* important is that within a decade the New Englanders had worked the last retreat of the fur seals to exhaustion; more than a million were slaughtered, and by 1829 'on the rocks which only a few years ago had teemed with life not a creature was to be seen'. Many of these sealers undoubtedly sighted the continent; some landed on it – the first, in my opinion, being Davis of New Haven.

British sealers too were quick to exploit the new rookeries; and in 1822 one of them, James Weddell, embarked on one of the greatest of all Antarctic voyages. In the brig *Jane* and the diminutive cutter *Beaufoy*, he pushed south into the sea now bearing his name and in remarkably ice-free conditions managed to struggle to 74° 15′ S – more than 200 miles closer to the Pole than Cook. His voyage was part-commercial, part-scientific and wholly arduous. As L. P. Kirwan puts it, 'a whaleboat overboard; a rudder frozen into immobility; bulwarks, decks and rigging so heavily encrusted with ice that the ship could scarcely rise to the sea – such experiences were common in the brigs of the Antarctic sealers.'

As for Palmer, the next incident in his career is even more dramatic and controversial than his passage to Deception.

We are told that while the *Hero* was returning from the mainland – presumably on about 18/19 November 1820 – she became enveloped in thick fog. Palmer, it seems, was on watch himself that night, and when he struck one bell he was startled to hear an echo. 'I could not credit my ears', he wrote later. 'I thought I must be dreaming.' He told himself that the echo must be a trick of the fog; but when an hour later he struck two bells, exactly the same thing happened! Each hour, we are led to believe, when Palmer tolled the bell, there came a ghostlike toll in answer out of the night.

At dawn, as the light gained in intensity, we can picture the crew of the *Hero* peering with some apprehension into the gradually dispersing mist. Vague shapes began to materialize: first tall masts (more than double the height of the *Hero*'s), then a strange castellated hull with gun ports, and at last, as the sun rose palely over the horizon, Palmer realized that he was lying becalmed midway between a frigate and a ship of the line. Unable to identify their nationality, he hoisted the American flag. And the ships he had shared the night with ran up their colours in reply: about the last flag in the world that Palmer could have expected, the double-headed eagle of Imperial Russia.

73

(left) Thaddeus von Bellingshausen
(below) Bellingshausen's ships *Vostok* and *Mirnyi*

74

## CHAPTER 4

# THE FIRST SIGHTING

THE FRIGATE AND THE SHIP OF THE LINE had not arrived off the coast of Antarctica by chance; they were there with a mission.

Russia at the end of the eighteenth century consisted of two widely separated communities – the old or European kingdom centred around Moscow, St Petersburg and Kiev, and the new or Asiatic kingdom centred around Alaska, Kamchatka and the Bering Strait. These communities were divided by 4,500 miles of barren, largely uninhabited steppe; and communication between them by land was difficult. If a trapper in Cordova needed a musket or a seaman in Okhotsk an anchor, it had to be transported by wagon and packhorse, across great forests, swamps, rivers and plains for nearly twice the width of the Atlantic; and the same applied, of course, to bringing the wealth of the Pacific settlements (fur, timber, minerals and fish) to Europe. It is hardly surprising that the Russians soon looked into the possibility of fashioning a link by sea. There was, however, a problem. For a thousand years Russia's energies and interests had been orientated to the land; not till the eighteenth century did she even gain access to the sea – first to the Baltic, then to the Black Sea and finally to the Pacific – and in 1800 she had few ships, and fewer deepwater seamen. In 1803, however, von Kruzenstern, the father of the Russian Navy, circumnavigated the world in a remarkable three-year voyage; and the success of this circumnavigation (during which not a single man succumbed to scurvy) attracted the attention of the authorities in general and the Tsar in particular.

Tsar Alexander I was probably the most progressive and liberal-minded of the rulers of pre-Soviet Russia, and he was quick to see in the emergent Russian Navy a potential instrument of expansion. He proposed two expeditions: one to search for a North West Passage in the Arctic, and one to search for staging posts in the Antarctic. Both these expeditions were given a scientific veneer – 'to help extend the field of knowledge' – but both in fact were basically commercial, their objective being to facilitate the flow of trade between Russia-in-Europe and Russia-in-the-Pacific. Their sailing orders show this: '[You are] to make special endeavours to discover good harbours . . . which might be used to promote communication by sea and would be useful for the repair of ships.' And if routing goods from Kamchatka to Moscow via the Antarctic sounds an inordinately long way round, the fact is that by 1800 the other nations of Europe had appropriated virtually every coastline and island in the world except for those in the extreme north and the extreme south. Russia's late arrival in the field of maritime expansion gave her no option but to set her sights immediately on the farthest ends of the earth.

The success or otherwise of this sort of leap in the dark depends very largely

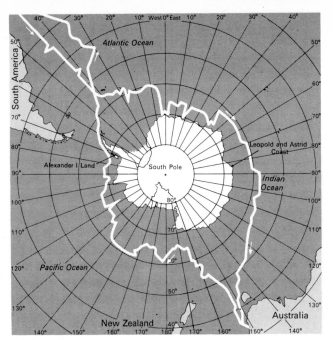

Map of Bellingshausen's route

on its leader, and the Tsar's choice fell on Thaddeus von Bellingshausen, a 39-year-old naval officer who had been Kruzenstern's fifth-lieutenant during his circumnavigation of the world.

Today there are probably not many people outside the Soviet Union who have heard of Bellingshausen or could identify the sea to which he has given his name. It is high time this ignorance was dispelled and due recognition accorded; for in the galaxy of great explorers this little-known Russian deserves to rank with Amundsen, da Gama and Columbus.

He was born in 1779 into the petty nobility of Estonia. The Navy was just becoming a fashionable career, and at an early age Bellingshausen was sent to the naval college in St Petersburg. Between 1803 and 1806 he served aboard the *Nadezhda* during her circumnavigation, being described by Kruzenstern as a 'skilful and well-informed officer'; then came a spell in the Black Sea in command of a frigate. His frigate was engaged in survey work, and it was in this field that Bellingshausen, like Cook, first made a name for himself; for his charts were models of painstaking accuracy. In April 1819 he was given command of the Tsar's much-heralded expedition to the Antarctic, with orders to 'approach as close as possible to the South Pole and to search diligently for land . . . you are only [the orders add] to abandon this undertaking in the face of insurmountable obstacles.' We know little about the personality of the man who was given this formidable assignment; but in this respect again he seems to have resembled Cook, being reserved, formal, humane and supremely efficient. He also shared – unfortunately perhaps – another of Cook's traits: a reluctance to indulge in his diary in even the occasional purple passage or personal aside. His narrative therefore is by no means light reading, though this may be due in part to the fact that before publication it was heavily and incompetently cut.

76

Bellingshausen arrived in Kronshtadt at the end of April. He was to spend the next three months supervising the preparing of his ships, the assembling of his crew and his stores, and the clarifying of his instructions.

His ships were the *Vostok* and *Mirnyi*. The former was a pinewood sloop of a little over 450 tons: length 130 feet, beam 33 feet and draught 9 feet 7 inches. She was carefully recaulked, her masts were shortened, her hull was sheathed in copper and strengthened with a network of iron stanchions, and her rudder, bulkheads and cathead were refashioned in oak; to quote Bellingshausen 'so great was the interest of the officers in this work that not a nail or a piece of timber was passed untested'. The *Mirnyi* (or *Peace*) was smaller and older. A frigate of 230 tons, length 120 feet and beam 30 feet, she too was given a thorough overhaul; but no amount of refurbishing could disguise the fact that she was a sluggish sailer, and her captain, Mikhail Lazarev, was hard pressed in the months to come to keep pace with his faster and more seaworthy consort.

The complement of the *Vostok* was 117, that of the *Mirnyi* 72. Both officers and men were hand picked. Among them were three surgeons, an artist (Paul Mikhailov of the Academy of Fine Arts) and an astronomer (Ivan Simanov, regius professor at Kazan University); there was, however, no naturalist, since the two German scientists who had been appointed by the Tsar withdrew at the last moment. In anticipation of the hardships to come and the long duration of the voyage, the crew were guaranteed eight times their normal pay. They were also fitted out most generously with clothing – four uniforms per man, with twelve spare trousers, four spare coats, eighteen shirts and eight pairs of thick woollen stockings. We have, unfortunately, no detailed list of their provisions, though we know they included 'salted beef stowed in good oak barrels . . . wheat and rye biscuits . . . sauerkraut which had been slightly oversalted to ensure preservation . . . and beef tea in the form of tablets.' Here again we can trace the influence of Cook, whom the Russian Admiralty held in high esteem. As well as these provisions and the usual items of spare equipment the *Vostok* also carried a curious variety of gifts for the natives – hussar jackets, tambourines, hunting horns, knitting needles, kaleidoscopes and bronze medallions of the Tsar.

As for Bellingshausen's instructions they can only be termed formidable, for they embraced objectives that were both traditional and forward looking: that is to say he was expected to report not only on fisheries, harbours and new lands to be exploited, he was expected also to report on geodesy, astronomy, magnetic variation, tides, meteorology, the *aurora australis* or Southern Lights, oceanography, ice formation, mineralogy and anthropology: a truly Herculean assignment. There is one other point worth noting about the Russians' instructions: 'Whenever you land in inhabited country the natives are to be treated with kindness and humanity. You must avoid giving offence or displeasure; on the contrary, you must make every effort to win their friendship by gentleness. You shall never resort to severe measures. . . .' Bellingshausen observed these orders.

(left) The *Vostok*
(above) Mikhail Lazarev

His expedition left Kronshtadt on 16 July 1819. (Bellingshausen gives the date as 4 July – by the Julian calendar, which remained in use in Russia throughout the nineteenth century and was twelve days behind the Gregorian.)

Their first port of call was Copenhagen; their second Portsmouth, where they took aboard charts, sextants and chronometers, together with a selection of 'soup and vegetable preserves' as a preventive against scurvy. They were obliged to spend longer than they anticipated in England, partly because of the difficulty of obtaining good navigational equipment, and partly because the local workmen they had employed in Portsmouth dockyard to alter the *Vostok*'s portholes staged a go-slow. 'We made the mistake', Bellingshausen writes, 'of hiring and paying these men by the day, and in order to line their own pockets they deliberately slowed down the rate of work.' By early September, however, the Russians were again at sea – equipment, stores and portholes to their satisfaction; by the middle of the month they were standing handsomely into the Atlantic.

As soon as his expedition was in blue water, Bellingshausen initiated a daily routine that was Spartan in its rigour. His crew were organized into three watches instead of the customary two; his ships were scrubbed down twice a week at sea and every day in port; linen was washed twice a week, hammocks once a fortnight. He did not approve of fumigating between decks; instead, whenever the weather was suitable, he ordered stoves to be lit in the messes; these 'dried and purified the atmosphere and left neither smuts nor grease'. Dinner each day was served punctually at 12 and supper at 6; and in the evenings the crew were encouraged 'to indulge in popular pastimes on deck, such as singing, story-telling, dancing and leap-frog'. Diet was strictly supervised, the daily ration of beef being hung each morning over the bowsprit till it was thoroughly impregnated with brine. And if some of these regulations seem to border on the pernickety, we should bear in mind that the dividing line between a clean bill of health and a crippling rate of mortality was razor fine. On voyages far less arduous than the *Vostok*'s, a 50 per cent death rate from scurvy was nothing unusual – Anson, for example, started his voyage round the world with 961 men; before he was halfway across the Pacific 620 had died. Bellingshausen was too humane to countenance laxity. The slovenly were flogged.

His ships had an easy run from Portsmouth to the Southern Ocean, calling only at Tenerife and Rio. By mid-December they were approaching the Antarctic Convergence; the temperature dropped, special clothing was issued, and aboard the *Vostok* stoves were kept permanently alight and hatches permanently battened down. On 23 December they caught their first glimpse of petrel and albatross; and a couple of days later the island of South Georgia appeared over the horizon, its mountains dark with cloud and its shoreline white with snow. It was a desolate, uninhabited land, but the sea surrounding it was vibrant with life: whales spouted, blue and white petrels circled the ships, and crested penguins, with cries of alarm, dived off the patches of floating ice. The *Vostok* and *Mirnyi* dropped anchor in Queen Maud Bay.

They were met by two British sealing vessels, the *Indispensable* and the *Mary-Ann*, whose crew gave Bellingshausen a description of their trade:

> They told us they had been in South Georgia for four months extracting blubber from the seals and elephant seals. Their work takes them onto all the beaches where it is possible to put ashore. At night, as a shelter, they turn their boats upsidedown and light fires beneath them. For melting the seals' blubber they use penguin skins as fuel. . . . I ordered our guests to be given grog, sugar and butter.

The Russians spent a mere three days in the vicinity of South Georgia. In this short time, however, Bellingshausen completed a survey of the south coast and its adjacent shoals: a masterly piece of work, which was subsequently incorporated into British Admiralty charts, and has only been superseded within the last twenty years.

On the last day of 1819 the *Vostok* and *Mirnyi* hauled off from South Georgia and sailed deeper into the Antarctic in search of Cook's 'Sandwich Land'. They were on the threshold now of the unknown, approaching a cluster of islands that had been sighted but never surveyed.

Cook had thought Sandwich Land to be 'either a group of islands or else the point of a continent'. Bellingshausen soon disproved the latter theory. For three days his vessels stood east-southeast from South Georgia. The weather was bad: heavy seas, high winds, and violent squalls of snow which cut visibility to 20 yards. They passed an iceberg $1\frac{1}{2}$ miles in length and 180 feet in height. Then, on 3 January, they sighted land. Bellingshausen has frequently been dubbed a dull writer, but the following description strikes me as decidedly evocative:

> January 3rd. We had strong winds that night which knocked up a high sea. The moon was bright, and the thermometer a little below zero. In the small hours of the morning we were brought up short by a line of drift ice, which stretched northeast by southwest in gargantuan floes. At dawn we had a fall of snow, and the thick weather forced us to turn into wind. This snow continued intermittently throughout the morning; but at 11 a.m., during a brief clearance, we sighted an unknown island about 13 miles to the north. We crowded on all the sail we dared, and headed towards it. . . .

This was Lyeskov Island, a mountain rising so sheer out of the water that no landing on it has ever been made. Next morning a second island was sighted.

> Thick black clouds were observed to the north; these seemed to remain in the same position, which led me to believe that there might be more land in the vicinity. Indeed after a couple of hours sailing we sighted an island from which a mushroom of evil-smelling vapour was continually rising – like smoke from the funnel of a steamer, only of much greater volume and density. . . .

This was Zavadovski Island, a volcano which is periodically active.

For more than a fortnight the *Vostok* and her consort picked their way through a skein of unknown and indescribably barren islands. The weather was appalling, and the ships, on several occasions, were within an ace of running aground; this is Bellingshausen's entry for 11 January:

> The snow continued all morning. We knew there were icebergs in the vicinity, and the crew were stationed along either side of the Vostok to listen for the sound of surf. A little after 5 p.m. we heard to leeward the sound of heavy breakers, and the officer of the watch expressed the opinion that we were closing with a shore on which the surf was breaking. The snow at this moment was falling so thickly that we could see no more than 30 yards ahead. I therefore turned onto another tack, the Mirnyi following, and we headed north-northwest. I hoped on this new course to draw clear of the ice and land, but at 10 p.m. we were brought up short by an impenetrable barrier of brash ice. This forced us to turn again. For the rest of the night we remained under topsails only, in order to reduce speed. But so heavy was the snow that the topsails became unmanageable, and we had to keep turning the ships sharply into wind to shake the snow off; while on deck it collected so thickly that the crew were hard pressed to shovel it away. . . . In the small hours the snow gave way to fog, the cries of the penguins echoing and re-echoing on all sides. A little after 5 a.m. we saw a line of icebergs. . . . Each time we turned into wind, icicles and frozen snow fell from the rigging; the ropes froze, and looked as though they were threaded through glass beads a full half-inch in diameter. . . .

In spite of these appalling conditions Bellingshausen managed to explore the whole of 'Sandwich Land'. He found that it consisted of two adjoining archipelagos. The more northerly he christened the Marquis de Traversey Islands (in honour of the Russian Minister of Marine) – a name subsequently corrupted on British charts to The Traverse Islands; the more southerly he christened the South Sandwich Group, because, in his own words, 'Cook saw these islands first and therefore the name which he gave them should remain unchanged.' Each island was not only placed accurately on the map, it was surveyed with care, and the artist Mikhailov made precise and elegant sketches of the coastal profiles – sketches which today still grace the pages of the *Antarctic Pilot*.

This was a major achievement. Bellingshausen, however, must have been disappointed by the utter desolation of the islands and their lack of harbours, and in the hope of more promising discoveries he headed east.

For a week the *Vostok* and *Mirnyi* skirted the pack in typical Antarctic weather: strong winds, high seas and a kaleidoscope of mist and snow. The ice was troublesome; and both vessels had to be steered by their officer of the watch, who stationed himself on the fo'c's'le and shouted orders to the helm. The last few days of the month witnessed two important events. Here is Bellingshausen's account for 26 January: 'We proceeded on a course of south by west. . . . A little after midday we passed three icebergs; we were then in Lat. 66° 53′ 42″ S, Long. 3° 03′ 54″ W. Thick weather, with snow and a high northwesterly wind continued for the rest of the day and well into the night.' The importance of this lies in what it *omits* to say. For on 26 January, Bellingshausen crossed the Antarctic Circle – being preceded in this only by Cook. He must have known what he had done; yet he did not apparently rate the event worth even a mention. Which brings us to a key point in Bellingshausen's character: he was diffident to a fault. All the indications are that he was a delightful man: efficient, humane, courteous and ever happy to acknowledge the feats of his fellow explorers; the sort of man who was likely not to boast of his discoveries but to play them down. And this has a very definite bearing on how we should interpret the events of the next few days. Here is the entry in Bellingshausen's diary for 27 January.

At 4 a.m. we saw a grey, smoke-coloured albatross. At 7 a.m. the wind shifted, the snow momentarily ceased and we had a fleeting glimpse of the sun. [The snow, however, obviously soon returned.] We proceeded south. . . . At midday in Lat. 69° 21′ 28″ S, Long 2° 14′ 50″ W we encountered icebergs which loomed up through the falling snow looking for all the world like white clouds. There was a moderate northeast wind and a heavy northwest swell at the time, and because of the snow we could see only a short distance. We had just hauled close to the wind on a course of south by east, when we observed in front of us a solid stretch of ice, running from east to west. Our course was taking us directly onto this icefield, which seemed to be covered with small hillocks. The barometer had recently fallen from 29.5 to 29, a warning of bad weather, and I therefore turned away to the northwest, hoping that in this direction we should find no ice.

A few days later (on 1 February) he sighted this icefield again.

Towards the south it grew lighter hour by hour. At 1 a.m. we saw ice ahead, and at 2 a.m. found ourselves virtually encompassed by it. Away to the south we could see some 50 icebergs or hummocks frozen into the field. As we surveyed the extent of this icefield we were unable to see its limits; but I judged it to be an extension of the field we had seen on the 27th but had been unable to examine properly. . . .

For 150 years the generally accepted interpretation of these entries has been that of Frank Debenham (Professor Emeritus of Geography at Cambridge) –

This day (January 27th) must be accounted an unfortunate one for the Russians for we now know that they must have been within a few miles, not more than 20 at the most, of Princess Martha Land, discovered in 1929/30 by the *Norvegia* expedition. A few hours of clear weather on this particular day would have antedated the discovery of this stretch of coast by more than a century. . . . And again (on February 1st) the Russian vessels must have been within 25 miles of the continent without apparently sighting it.

But the truth is, I think, that they *did* sight it.

Soviet scholars (in particular M. I. Belov of the Arctic and Antarctic Research Institute, Leningrad) have recently pointed out that Bellingshausen's passage about the 'icefield' is in fact an extremely accurate description of this particular stretch of the coast. If we bear this in mind, if we pinpoint the known position of the ships, and if we take into account Bellingshausen's subsequent references to 'an icy continent' (*materik l'da*) it seems beyond dispute that on 27 January 1820 the crews of the *Vostok* and *Mirnyi* became the first men in the world to set eyes on the mainland of Antarctica.

This was a major discovery; and one wonders why it has not, up to now, been universally recognized. The reason, I suggest, is twofold. In the first place I doubt if Bellingshausen himself, at the time of his sighting, appreciated the full significance of what he had seen; it was only gradually, as he circumnavigated the Antarctic and saw the same phenomenon again and again, that his idea of a 'continent of ice' took gradual shape; he was too honest to rephrase his entry for 27 January in the light of subsequent knowledge, and this entry is in consequence utterly devoid of dramatic impact or the sense of occasion which one normally expects to associate with a historic discovery. In the second place when Bellingshausen returned to Russia it was many years before even an expurgated version of his diary was published; his concept of an ice continent was neither liked nor understood by the Ministry of Marine who seem to have deleted almost every reference to it in the text. In other words it is only during the last decade that the Russians themselves have fully appreciated Bellingshausen's stature.

In comparison with the momentous events of these first few weeks the rest of his voyage was – as regards discovery – something of an anticlimax.

On 17/18 February he sighted land for the third time. His position was 69° 66 S, 15° 51 E: only a few miles off King Leopold and Queen Astrid Coast and not far from the site of the present Soviet base at Novolazarevskaya. His diary on this occasion is explicit.

> At 9 a.m. a dazzling brightness appeared in the south; this indicated our proximity to field ice. The weather was fine but cloudy, with neither mist nor snow. A little before midday ice was observed from the look-out. . . . by 3 p.m. we were passing through it, the waves abated, and as we proceeded the ice thickened. At about 3.15 p.m. we observed ahead of us a number of high flat-topped icebergs frozen into the field. The edge of the field was perpendicular and formed into little coves; its surface sloped upward towards the south, and even from our masthead we could see no end to it. . . . At 6 a.m. [on 18 February] the broken ice became so thick that it was quite impossible to force a way farther to the south. In the far distance we saw ice-covered mountains rising to a great height.

There are two points of particular interest here: the description of the edge of the ice being 'formed into little coves', which is in fact a formation peculiar to the King Leopold and Queen Astrid Coast; and the 'ice-covered mountains', which were undoubtedly part of the Sør-Rondane range (one of the highest in Antarctica). On this occasion therefore we can not only say that Bellingshausen sighted the continent, we can pinpoint his landfall with some precision.

For the next six weeks the *Vostok* and *Mirnyi* continued their circumnavigation, first skirting the edge of the pack ice, then, as the brief Antarctic summer drew to its close, slanting gradually away from the continent as they set course for Australia. This part of their voyage was similar to Cook's: the same wicked 'near perpendicular' seas, the same bludgeoning winds, the same blizzards, the same mists and the same hair-raising encounters with the ice: indeed a good deal of Bellingshausen's diary could be transposed to Cook's and vice versa. In mid-March, however, the Russians encountered a phenomenon about which their British predecessors had said little.

> The thermometer that night [15 March] stood at 27° F. The officers of the watch had just changed over when we noticed an intermittent flashing light, the cause of which we could only hazard a guess at. Round about 2 a.m., however, the clouds lifted, and we beheld one of nature's most beautiful and spectacular displays. There appeared in the south two columns of blue-white, like phosphorescent fire; these flashed across the horizon, from cloud to cloud, with the speed of rockets. Each column was about three times the width of the sun. The columns multiplied, until eventually the whole sky, from horizon to zenith, was covered with these bright pulsating pillars. The light was so strong that shadows were distinct, and we could read even quite small print without difficulty. . . . Next evening . . . the southern aurora appeared again in all its magnificence and brightness, though in a guise quite different from the night before. This time the whole vault of the heavens – except for some 12 to 15 degrees above the horizon – was covered with bands of rainbow hue, which, with the rapidity of lightning, traversed the sky in sinuous waves from south to north, shading off from colour to colour. This spectacle . . . very likely saved us from disaster. For as the sea was lit up by the aurora we saw we were heading straight for a large iceberg which

we might well, in darkness, have run into. . . . Many of the seamen were much moved by the magnificence of the aurora. One fell to his knees:

'The sky is on fire!' he shouted. 'Heaven is coming down to earth!'

Four weeks later the *Vostok* and *Mirnyi* dropped anchor in Sydney harbour. They had in the last three months sailed for more than 5,000 miles wholly within the Antarctic Convergence; and even the unemotional Bellingshausen was moved to joy at the sight of green trees and the warmth of the sun. As for his crew, they set up a steam bath ashore and 'sweated and stewed to their hearts' content'; they also, on their captain's orders, ate an abundance of citrus fruit and fresh green vegetables; for in spite of their well-balanced diet and meticulous hygiene several were showing symptoms of scurvy.

One might have expected Bellingshausen to spend the whole of the winter in repair and recuperation. Like Cook, however, he seemed happier afloat than ashore, and after only six weeks embarked on a cruise in the waters northeast of New Zealand. He doubtless hoped, during this part of his voyage, to discover the 'good harbours' whose importance had been stressed in his orders. But he was out of luck. He sighted seventeen new islands and a number of atolls; but none of them large enough to be used as a staging post for trade. In the scramble for oceanic bases the Russians had arrived half a century too late. Bellingshausen's Pacific cruise was, however, successful on another level. His contacts with the Polynesians were invariably friendly. In all his meetings with the South Sea Islanders not a shot was fired in anger – a happy contrast to the massacres of the previous century.

September and October were spent in Sydney, repairing, recaulking and reprovisioning the ships. Bellingshausen seems to have got on well with the Australians. 'Our stay', he wrote, 'was a happy one. We were constantly invited out to dinners and social gatherings, and parties and dances were often specially arranged for us. . . . We were treated with nothing but kindness.' It was as well for the Russians that they had this near-idyllic interlude at the halfway stage of their circumnavigation; for by mid-November they were back once more in the bludgeoning winds and juggernaut seas that guard the approaches to Antarctica.

On 29 November they hove to off Macquarie Island, an isolated outcrop of rock in the same latitude as South Georgia. They expected the island (like their previous landfalls at this latitude) to be covered with ice and snow; instead they found it 'beautifully green, with a wealth of tussock grass, moss and wild cabbage'; the climate, however, left much to be desired, for they had rain and mist on every single day of their visit and the wind never dropped below a gale. They were met by a party of sealers, and Bellingshausen went ashore to visit their huts. These, he tells us, were some 20 by 10 feet, lined on the outside with turf and on the inside with sealskins; a fire and a lamp were kept continually burning, and the interior was so dark and smoke filled that the Russians, their eyes unaccustomed to the gloom, had to be led by the hand. Bellingshausen gives one of the fullest descriptions extant of these men's macabre and lonely calling – one of them apparently had spent ten consecutive years on the island – and he ends with the words, 'the abundance of fur seals at one time caused many vessels to come to this island, but the unbounded greed of the sealers quickly exterminated their quarry, and today not one of the creatures is to be seen'.

The *Vostok* and *Mirnyi* left Macquarie Island in early December, and a few days later were brought up short by the inevitable ice. On 9 December they crossed the 60th degree of latitude, and started (to quote Hunter Christie) 'a voyage which is without parallel in the history of exploration. For two months and three days, through a distance of 145° of longitude, the two vessels remained to the south of the 60th parallel and within sight of the Antarctic pack-ice.' Their track was well to the south of Cook's, through some of the most tempestuous and ice-choked sea lanes on earth; and Bellingshausen's log becomes almost monotonous in its description of hazards faced and obstacles overcome.

Once, in a violent storm, the *Vostok*'s topsails, mizzensails and staysails suddenly and simultaneously split, and the vessel broached to under bare poles at the mercy of wind and wave. 'The seas', Bellingshausen wrote, 'were an extraordinary height, and appeared to mingle with the air. In order to try and keep our head into wind, I ordered the men to hoist hammocks into the shrouds.' On another occasion the vessels were trapped in fog in a moving icefield. They were unable to see the bergs, but could hear the waves pounding their sides and could judge their proximity by the sudden chill in the air and the droop of the *Vostok*'s sails as great walls of ice blocked off the wind. Bellingshausen ordered his crew to lower themselves from ropes and ladders all round the ship – 'for the lower one is the more easily the white of the bergs is picked up and the more easily the sound of waves is heard, because the fog is thinnest at sea level. . . . Many times', he tells us, 'the roar of great breakers was terrifyingly close, and we thought our last moment had come.'

It was an achievement for any vessel to survive two months in this latitude; for a seriously damaged vessel to survive was little short of a miracle; and it is perhaps the most amazing feature of Bellingshausen's voyage that for the last half of the circumnavigation the *Vostok* leaked like a sieve. For a week out of Sydney water had begun to pour in through her stem. 'It poured in with such force', we are told, 'that its gurgling could be heard all over the ship, and the leak was in so awkward a position it was impossible to bung it.' Stanchions were inserted, and stores and armaments were moved hurriedly aft; but for the rest of the voyage the pumps had to be continually manned and the *Vostok* was never able to carry full sail. This disability makes the latter part of her voyage an epic.

By the New Year the Russians were eighteen months out of Kronshtadt, and they could have been forgiven had they begun to lose heart. For they had circumnavigated five-sixths of the Southern Ocean and sighted nothing but cliffs of ice and desolate outcrops of rock. On 22 January, however, when they least expected it, their perseverance was rewarded.

Peter I Island, off the southern end of the Antarctic Peninsula

Lyeskov and Visokoi, two of the South Sandwich Islands

Candlemas and Vindication, two of the South Sandwich Islands

They had no premonition of discovery. There were no circling landbirds or drifting patches of kelp. But on the evening of 21 January a brilliant white reflection appeared on the southern horizon, and the air became suddenly colder. Next afternoon, at 3 p.m., 'a black patch' appeared briefly through the haze to the northeast. Bellingshausen got a good look at it through his telescope before the haze closed in and felt certain it was land; his officers were less sanguine, but an hour later their doubts were dispelled.

> The sun came out from behind the clouds and so lit up the scene that we could see quite clearly that our discovery was land covered with snow; the rocks and cliffs too steep for the ice to cling to showed up jet-black against the contrasting mantle of white. Words can not describe our delight as the cry 'Land! Land!' echoed from all parts of the ship. Nor was our joy surprising after so long, monotonous and dangerous a voyage.

Rum punch was served to all hands; a toast was drunk to the Emperor, and the *Vostok* and *Mirnyi* headed for the shore. They got to within 14 miles of the land, and were able to survey it with some precision before being brought up short by solid ice. They found, to their disappointment, that their discovery was not part of a continent but an island; they named it Peter I, and headed north in the hope of falling in with further land. And indeed a few days later, on 27 January, an extensive coastline was sighted to starboard. The weather, for once, was kind: a gentle breeze, no cloud and perfect visibility. Though the vessels were prevented from closing with the land because of ice, they were again able to survey it with reasonable accuracy. 'I named our discovery Alexander Land', Bellingshausen wrote, 'in memory of the Emperor. Monuments of stone erected to great men may in time be erased from the face of the earth, but the names Peter I and Alexander Land are indestructible monuments which will perpetuate the memory of our Emperors till the end of time.' Alexander Land has since been proved an island, some 300 miles in length, divided from the continent by a 40-mile-wide strait; but this in no way diminishes the importance of Bellingshausen's discovery. A segment of land of continental proportion lying well within the Antarctic Circle had been clearly sighted and surveyed, and Bellingshausen himself obviously felt that he had achieved a major breakthrough – that he had penetrated at last to the shore of the almost legendary *Terra Australis*. 'I refer to our discovery as land', he wrote, 'because its southern extent was beyond the range of our vision. The shore was deep in snow, but there was no snow on either the cliffs or the mountain faces. The change in colour of the sea led us to believe that the land is extensive, and does not consist of only the part we could see.'

If the weather had stayed fine the *Vostok* and *Mirnyi* would almost certainly have held course to the northeast, hugging the coast; they would then have sighted the extensive chain of islands off the Antarctic peninsula and the mainland itself. The weather, however, deteriorated. On 30 January a violent blizzard swept down from the north, and this was succeeded by dense banks of fog that cut visibility to

30 yards. Fearing he might become embayed on a lee shore, Bellingshausen set course for the South Shetlands – he had heard of Smith's discovery while refitting in Australia, and was anxious to find out if the land sighted by the *Williams* was a group of islands or part of the continent which he himself had just sighted.

After a week of groping blind through mist and snow, there was a sudden cry from the *Vostok*'s masthead: 'Land! Land above the clouds!' And the 6,000-foot cliffs of Smith Island loomed out of the mist, 'like a great black pedestal holding up the sky'.

In the course of the next six days Bellingshausen surveyed the whole of the South Shetland group with his usual precision, thus proving that none of the islands was connected to the continent. The names he gave – Smolensk, Beresina, Polotsk and Waterloo – have been superseded today; but the work of his expedition lives on in the sketches of Paul Mikhailov.

It was during this survey that there occurred one of the most controversial episodes in the history of exploration: Bellingshausen's meeting with Palmer.

The fact is that the account of this meeting given by Bellingshausen is very different from that given by Palmer's biographer Fanning. Here is Bellingshausen's account.

> February 5th 1821. In front of the low lying shore we saw 8 British and American vessels at anchor. . . . At 10 o'clock we entered the strait between Smolensk and Teille [i.e. between Livingston Island and Deception Island] and sighted a small American sealing vessel. The *Vostok* lay to, and I lowered a boat to invite the American captain aboard. The lead did not touch bottom at 115 fathoms. Soon after Mr Palmer [the American captain] arrived aboard. He told us he had been here for four months, engaged in killing and skinning the seals whose numbers were perceptibly diminishing. . . . According to Mr Palmer the bay in which we saw the 8 vessels lying at anchor is protected from all winds and has a depth of 18 fathoms in thin mud – though because of the peculiar nature of the bottom the vessels frequently drag their anchors. . . . Mr Palmer soon returned to his ship, and we proceeded along the shore. At noon we were in Lat 62° 49′ 32″ S, Long 60′ 18″ W.

Here is Fanning's account. The date of the meeting he gives as November 1820 (i.e. eleven weeks earlier than Bellingshausen), and the place not far from the coast of Antarctica (some 40 miles further to the south).

> [Palmer found the vessels between which he had anchored for the night] were two discovery ships sent out by the Emperor Alexander of Russia, on a voyage round the world. To the commodore's interrogatory if he had any knowledge of those islands then in sight, and what they were, Captain P replied he was well acquainted with them, and they were the South Shetlands, at the same time making a tender of his services to pilot the ships into a good harbour at Deception Island. . . . The commodore thanked him kindly: 'but previous to our being enveloped in the fog', said he, 'we had sight of those islands, and concluded we had made a discovery; but behold, when the fog lifts, to my great surprise, here is an American vessel, apparently

in as fine order as if it were but yesterday she had left the United States; not only this, but her master is ready to pilot my vessels into port; we must surrender the palm to you Americans'. . . . His astonishment was yet more increased when Captain Palmer informed him of the existence of an immense extent of land to the south, whose mountains might be seen from the masthead when the fog cleared. . . . Captain Palmer, while on board the frigate, was entertained in the most friendly manner, and the commodore was so forcibly struck with the circumstances of the case, that he named the coast then to the south Palmer's Land.

When these descriptions are considered side by side, it is clear that the latter – to put it mildly – has flaws. Leaving for a moment the question of time and place, Deception Island was not used by American sealers in November 1820, so it is unlikely that Palmer would have offered to pilot the Russians there; Bellingshausen would never have said we 'concluded we had made a discovery' of the South Shetland islands when he knew very well that Smith in the *Williams* had visited them the year before; as for his 'astonishment' at Palmer having sighted 'an immense extent of land to the south', this is clearly apocryphal; for if Palmer had indeed mentioned land, Bellingshausen would surely have noted the fact in his diary and gone to look for it – he had after all sailed literally the length and breadth of the world in the hope of making just such a landfall! It is also worth noting that in Bellingshausen's account their meeting is convincingly dated and located – the time and position he gives tying in exactly with Palmer's voyage from Livingston to Deception Island. The same can not be said of Fanning's account which, even allowing for the vagaries of time and translation, is short of verifiable facts.

American sealers played a major role in the unveiling of Antarctica. It is unfortunate that one of the greatest of them, Nathaniel Palmer, should have been ill served by his biographers, and that exaggerated claims should have been put forward on his behalf.

A couple of days after this encounter, the *Vostok* and *Mirnyi* set course for home.

Bellingshausen had found none of the 'good harbours' which, it had been hoped, would promote Russia's trade, and because of this his report when he landed in Kronshtadt was received with little enthusiasm. He had, however, been successful on two counts. By circumnavigating Antarctica on a track well to the south of Cook's, he enabled cartographers to limit still further the size of the continent; and by bringing back a mass of carefully observed facts he had added enormously to knowledge of the Antarctic. Some of his findings were relatively trivial – his observation, for example, that 'in daylight the pupils of a penguin's eyes are square but that as darkness falls they gradually become round'; some were conjectural – his theory, for example, now proven, that the South Sandwich Islands were part of a 'chain of drowned volcanoes forming an extension of the Andes'; some led to important discoveries by others – notably his data on magnetic variation which enabled Gauss, a generation later, to calculate the position of the South Magnetic Pole. But he did himself make one outstanding contribution to man's understanding of the world: he put forward the suggestion, hinted at by Cook but now stated categorically from first-hand experience, that Antarctica would prove to be *ledyanoy materik*, a continent of ice.

Bellingshausen and Lazarev both use this phrase 'icy continent' in their letters; and on 24 January 1821 the former wrote in his diary:

> On several occasions we saw compressed and continuous formations of ice stretching for more than 300 miles from east to west. Assuming that these stretched for the same distance from north to south, then the centre of the continent must be entirely firm, a sheet of ice, added to by falling snow and hail, and frozen into a solid block. . . . The massive formations of ice, which, as they approach the Pole become sloping hills, I would describe as continental [*materymi*]; for even on the warmest day our thermometer recorded 4° of frost, and this obviously does not diminish as one progresses south. I therefore conclude that a great and immovable sheet of ice stretches across the Pole, passing in some places over shallow areas and in other places over Islands like Peter I.

This is a not unreasonable description of Antarctica.

The idea of an 'icy continent' was, however, too far ahead of its time to be comprehended by the hierarchy at the Russian Ministry of Marine. Bellingshausen's report was filed away, and when it eventually appeared in print more than a decade later it had been heavily expurgated. The rest of his career was in a minor key compared to the heroic events of his circumnavigation; and his last post was that of Governor of Kronshtadt where he died in 1852.

It has been said that each explorer who ventures into the Antarctic takes with him his own particular world. Bellingshausen's world was one of diffidence; and as a result, his achievements have been underrated. It is pleasant to record that he is at last being recognized as one of the company of great explorers: the man who was not only first to sight Antarctica, but first also to make a reasonable assessment of its structure.

## CHAPTER 5

# THE FIRST LANDING

THE QUESTION OF WHO FIRST SET FOOT on the mainland of Antarctica is almost as controversial as that of who was first to sight it. The usual claimants are the cultured Dumont D'Urville, an admiral of the French Navy; the turbulent Charles Wilkes, a lieutenant of the United States Navy; and the dedicated James Clark Ross, a captain of the Royal Navy. None of these, however, has so convincing a claim as the little-known sealer John Davis of Connecticut.

If we look at the question dispassionately, the first person to set foot on Antarctica is very likely to have been a sealer; for these were men whose business took them year after year to the very threshold of the continent, and once the South Shetland Islands had been discovered it was bound to be only a matter of time

Map showing John Davis's possible route in the *Cecilia*, 31 January to 10 February 1821 before a sealing brig made the 60-mile crossing to the mainland. The first brig to do this that we know of was the *Cecilia*. Her log is extant, and her voyage is easy to reconstruct.

During the summer of 1820/1 there was a glut of sealing vessels in the South Shetlands. First to arrive were those of the Stonington fleet; they established themselves in the flooded crater of Deception Island and enjoyed a profitable season; by mid-January their holds were packed tight with pelts – the last golden harvest of the unfortunate fur seal. Next to arrive was a British contingent from Botany Bay; its members landed on Livingston Island and warned off their rivals 'with Guns, Pistoles & Swords'. Last to arrive were the New Haven men; they found the best beaches either worked out or occupied, and were forced to look farther afield. Captain Davis of the *Cecilia* sums up their predicament: 'Concluded it best to go on a cruse to find new lands, as the seal is done for here.' And on Tuesday, 30 January 1821 Davis sailed southwest from Deception Island into the ice-choked waters that guard the Antarctic peninsula.

Next afternoon he sighted a low 'new-discovered island' to the west-southwest, and after a good deal of difficulty from ice and underwater rocks, managed to put a boat ashore on the north coast. The sun made a brief but welcome appearance the following morning and Davis took a midday sight which enabled him to fix his latitude – 63° 25′ S; this places him, beyond doubt, on Low or Jameson Island. In the course of the next few days Jameson Island was systematically plundered, the better part of a thousand seals being clubbed to death. Then, on 6 February the *Cecilia* again headed into the unknown. For that evening, as the clouds rolled clear of a dying sun, more land was sighted to the southeast. This can only have been Hoseason Island, which is less than 30 miles from Jameson – less than 30 miles also from the mainland of Antarctica. Throughout the night the *Cecilia* held course to the southeast, and at dawn she might have been expected to be close under Hoseason. Davis's log, however – albeit in a very matter-of-fact manner – records something far more spectacular:

Wednesday 7th February 1821
Commences with open Cloudy Weather and Light winds a standing for a Large Body of Land in that direction S.E. At 10 A.M. close in with it, out Boat and Sent her on Shore to look for Seal. At 11 A.M. the Boat returned but [had] found no Seal. At noon our latitude was 64° 01 South. Stood up a Large Bay, the Land high and covered intirely with snow. . . . I think this Southern Land to be a continent.

This is an authentic extract from an authentic logbook; and bearing in mind that the *Cecilia*'s starting point is known to have been Jameson Island and that her course is known to have been southeast, there can be little doubt as to what the entry describes: a vessel standing into Hughes Bay (at the mouth of the Gerlache Strait) and landing a boat on the mainland of Antarctica in the vicinity of Cape Charles. What must have happened was this. The *Cecilia* must have sailed past

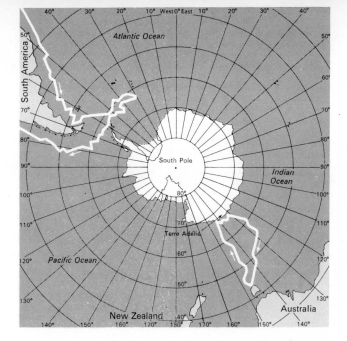

Map of J. S. C. Dumont D'Urville's
route

Hoseason during the night, and at dawn have been brought up short by the mainland itself. This is confirmed both by Davis's fix, which places him well to the south of Hoseason and within a couple of miles of the Antarctica coast, and also by his description of a large continental mass of land, high and covered entirely with snow – a description which he would never have made of the diminutive Hoseason.

There seems little doubt therefore that the honour of being first to set foot on the mainland belongs not to D'Urville, Wilkes or Ross, but to the little-known Davis of New Haven.

It has nonetheless been the big, nationally sponsored expeditions which have caught the attention of posterity. Nor is this surprising. For there is a world of difference between a secret landing of which no report is published for more than a century, and a great imperialistic-cum-scientific voyage of discovery, attended by a fanfare of publicity and followed by a spate of controversy. Of the three such expeditions which in the mid-nineteenth century headed for Antarctica, the first to get under way was the French.

Early in September 1837 a pair of unconverted corvettes, the *Astrolabe* and the *Zelée*, set sail from Toulon. The portents for a successful voyage were not auspicious. The two vessels were ill equipped – they were not even copper sheathed; the expedition was divided in its objective – for its patron Louis Philippe was anxious to surpass Cook's farthest south, whereas its commander Dumont D'Urville was anxious to carry out a magnetic survey; and D'Urville himself was past middle age and in poor health – 'Ah! ce bonhomme-là ne nous menera pas loin!' a seaman was heard to mutter as the admiral, who was plagued by gout, hobbled aboard. In fact D'Urville was to take his expedition a great deal farther than anyone had a right to expect, and at the end of his voyage was to produce one of the most beautiful and erudite books of exploration that has ever been published.

(left) Dumont D'Urville, by
D. Maurin, 1840
(below) One of the many
engravings in Dumont
D'Urville's *Atlas* illustrating
various aspects of the
*Astrolabe*'s and *Zelée*'s
expedition to the South
Pacific and Antarctic waters

Jules Sébastien César Dumont D'Urville is an entertaining character. It has been said – and said rightly – that he was 'brusque, intolerant and born to trouble as surely as sparks fly upward'; but on the reverse side of the coin he had courage, determination and a quality which may not always be associated with explorers – he was, in the classical sense of the word, a deeply cultured man. Indeed he is probably best remembered today as the discoverer of the Venus de Milo; for it was he who first recognized the statue when it was unearthed on Melos, and it is almost entirely due to his efforts that it stands today in the Louvre.

His expedition crossed the Antarctic Convergence in December 1837 and headed into the Weddell Sea, where a decade earlier British vessels had penetrated as far as 74° S. The ice, however, was more solid that summer and the weather a great deal worse; the *Astrolabe* and the *Zelée* were not strong enough to survive the buffeting of the Antarctic pack, and D'Urville found himself unable to penetrate to 64° S let alone to 74°. He spent a frustrating three months hovering between the South Orkneys and the South Shetlands, collecting data on ice formation and magnetism, and rediscovering, remapping and renaming a number of drab little islands; then, early in March, he headed north for the balmier sea lanes of the Pacific. His voyage so far had been pedestrian, the only flash of inspiration being provided by his artist, the young but dying Goupil, whose sketches of icebergs and floes (like those of Edward Wilson) combine authenticity with very real artistic merit.

The *Astrolabe* and the *Zelée* spent two years in the South Pacific, engaged in ethnological research; then in the summer of 1839/40 D'Urville again headed south.

According to his diary his purpose was 'to advance the science of terrestrial magnetism'; but his departure was undoubtedly hastened by his knowledge that both Wilkes and Ross were about to take expeditions to the 'unknown face' of Antarctica (i.e., the face which lay on the opposite side of the world to the Antarctic peninsula where the majority of sightings had been made to date); for here, according to persistent but unconfirmed reports by the sealers, a great south-reaching gulf lay astride the 180th meridian. D'Urville sailed from Tasmania on New Year's Day 1840, a few hours after the death of Goupil; and one can only wish that this gifted and dedicated artist had been with him to depict the remarkable discoveries to come. For unexpectedly, less than three weeks out from Hobart, D'Urville sighted land.

On the evening of 19 January 1841 his ships' companies were just preparing to welcome Father Antarctica aboard as they crossed the Circle, when they saw to the south 'a distinct appearance of mountains'. Next morning the weather was magnificent – no wind, no cloud and the sea a rich Mediterranean blue – and the land was clearly visible: a featureless unbroken coastline running from west-northwest to east-southeast as far as the eye could see. The shore appeared to consist of a sheer cliff of ice, some two hundred feet in height; and so clear was the atmosphere that the snow on the receding slopes was seen to be piled up into huge symmetrical drifts, like the dunes formed by wind in a desert. The *Astrolabe* and the *Zelée* picked their way through a network of icebergs towards the shore and at midday on 21 January D'Urville was able to fix his position – 66° 30′ S, 138° 21′ E – which places him only a couple of miles from the continent. His compasses were swinging wildly; no two were reading alike; and this convinced him that the South Magnetic Pole lay only a short distance inland. He was right. And indeed his estimate of the Pole's position – 72° 00′ S, 136° 45′ E – was remarkably accurate. For several days the *Astrolabe* and the *Zelée* followed the coast to the west, much hampered by icebergs. It was a voyage of awesome beauty; and D'Urville paints an evocative picture of his vessels sailing through the tortuous fairways as if they were threading their way through narrow streets between tall buildings, of the officers' orders echoing and re-echoing from the vertical walls of ice, of the sea rushing in and out of the ice caves and setting up dangerous whirlpools, and of the heat of the sun melting the snow on the flat-topped bergs so that water was continually streaming in great cataracts down their sides. On 22 January the *Astrolabe*'s longboat managed to land on a rocky island about a hundred yards offshore. The Tricolour was unfurled, rock samples were duly collected, a bottle of Bordeaux wine was ceremoniously drunk, and then, to quote D'Urville, following the ancient custom kept up by the English we took possession of the island in the name of France and also of the adjacent coast'.

It was one of the great moments in the history of exploration. For the first time a major expedition had sighted, surveyed and landed on what was undoubtedly part of the Great Southern Continent.

It could be argued too that D'Urville has another claim to fame: that of being the first man to recognize Antarctica for what it actually is. For his conception of the continent is both more accurate and more sophisticated than Bellingshausen's, witness the entry in his diary: 'the continent appears to consist of a formidable layer of ice, rather like an envelope, which forms the crust over a base of rock' – a description which, in basic essentials, it is hard to improve on.

All this was discovery on a major scale. But the weather now brought D'Urville's exploits to a premature end.

The coast of Adélie Land – D'Urville had named his discovery after his wife – is the most desolate and windswept on earth; the sun frequently is not seen for weeks at a stretch, and the wind day after day is a battering 60 knots. Ever since D'Urville's sighting the weather had been uncharacteristically benign; but now it showed its hand. On 24 January the *Astrolabe* and the *Zelée* were struck by a violent blizzard; they became separated; their canvas was ripped to shreds, and in six hours they suffered more damage than in the previous six months. Next day they managed to rejoin company; but in the weeks that followed, as snowstorm and hurricane-force winds alternated with dense banks of rolling fog, they were too preoccupied with survival to spare more than a passing thought for exploration. By the end of the month D'Urville had had enough. His ships were leaking, his crew were suffering

96  (above) Mt Erebus on the beautiful Ross Island with James Clark Ross's *Erebus* and *Terror* in
the foreground, 28 January 1841, by John Edward Davis, second master of the *Terror*
(below) *Erebus* passing through a chain of bergs, 13 March 1842, by John Edward Davis
(overleaf) Dumont D'Urville's corvettes *Astrolabe* and *Zelée*, 25 January 1840, drawn and
lithographed by Louis Le Breton and published by Auguste Bry, Paris

from frostbite and scurvy, and he was about to head for home when a strange vessel, flying the American flag, loomed unexpectedly out of the fog. D'Urville made more sail and attempted to close with her with a view to exchanging information; but she turned sharply away and vanished as suddenly as she had appeared into the spindrift and fog. Both commanders were subsequently to give a tart account of this encounter, and historians ever since have added fuel to the flames. But what happened was patently a misunderstanding; and the major cause of the ships failing to make contact was the appalling weather.

Nine months later the *Astrolabe* and *Zelée* were back in France, and D'Urville turned to the welcome task of preparing his report. As Hunter Christie puts it: '[he] was particularly suited to work of this nature and the ten volumes in which his report finally appeared are illuminated, not only by illustrations of outstanding merit (published separately in a two-volume *Atlas pittoresque*) but also by descriptive passages of the greatest beauty, well worthy of the pen that first described the classical outlines of the Venus de Milo.'

In spite of the importance of his discoveries and the magnificent manner in which he presented them, D'Urville's exploits, outside his native France, have seldom been accorded the recognition they deserve – his report for example, has never been translated into English. It can only be hoped that his reputation will in time become commensurate with his achievement.

The vessel which had appeared and disappeared so precipitously into the fog was, as D'Urville had guessed, one of the United States Exploring Expedition under the command of Charles Wilkes.

American expeditions today are characterized by the excellence of their equipment and the rapport among their personnel; it therefore comes as a distinct surprise to hear Wilkes's expedition condemned as 'the most ill-prepared, the most controversial and probably the most unhappy which ever sailed [into] the Antarctic'. Yet this is no overstatement. The truth is that the United States expedition had a traumatic birth from which it never recovered. It was conceived as early as 1821 when the House of Representatives resolved it 'expedient that one of our public vessels be sent South, to examine the coasts, islands, harbours, shoals and reefs, and to ascertain their true description'. America, however, had many other calls on her resources; she had not yet tapped the wealth of her own territory; and when she did feel the need for maritime expansion, the Pacific and the Caribbean held more obvious attractions than the Antarctic. It was therefore fifteen years before an Act of Congress to authorize the expedition was passed. There followed an incredible period of confusion: of personal feud, political intrigue, corruption, larceny and fraud. The ships selected were unsuitable, the budget was inadequate, the equipment was not up to standard, and the personnel did nothing but bicker, resign and desert. Indeed the whole project might well have come to nothing if, in March 1838, the command of it had not been offered to Charles Wilkes.

Wilkes's ancestry and portrait give the clue to his character. He was a descendant

(above) Celebrating New Year's Day 1842 on the ice floes in latitude 66° 32′ S, longitude 156° 28′ W, by John Edward Davis
(below) Watering *Terror* in the pack ice, 1842, by John Edward Davis

of John Wilkes, that champion of the peoples' rights who was such a thorn in the flesh of eighteenth-century Tories; his portrait depicts a firm though humorous mouth, a dominant nose, a stubborn jaw and sad disillusioned eyes; he was a born leader of lost causes. His appointment (he was only a junior lieutenant at the time) led to a further round of recrimination, but it was in fact a sound one; for although Wilkes was impetuous and domineering he was also a man of great driving power, tenacity and courage and it was largely due to his efforts that on 18 August 1838 the expedition at last got under way.

As Wilkes headed south that evening out of Hampton Roads he knew very well that his five ships were ill found and ill provisioned, and that his 345 men were ill tempered and ill equipped. Indeed he admitted in his diary that he felt 'like one doomed to destruction'. He was determined nonetheless to push farther to the south than man had ever pushed before.

His fleet arrived off Tierra del Fuego in March 1839, and he at once dispatched the *Porpoise* and *Sea Gull* to the South Shetland Islands and the *Peacock* and *Flying Fish* to the coast of Marie Byrd Land. The first two vessels had a most difficult time. The ice was especially thick and far to the north that season; the weather was even worse than usual, and conditions aboard the *Porpoise* and *Sea Gull* were miserable in the extreme. The former was a sloop of the line; her quarters were cramped, her timbers were rotten and her gunports open to the sea. The latter was an ancient New York pilot boat that leaked like a sieve. For six weeks this ill-assorted pair beat to and fro off the tip of the Antarctic peninsula, their crews becoming progressively weaker from exposure, malnutrition and exhaustion. Then came the last straw: an outbreak of scurvy; and in some difficulty and much distress the *Porpoise* and *Sea Gull* limped back to Tierra del Fuego. They had achieved nothing.

The *Peacock* and *Flying Fish* meanwhile had been exploring some thousand miles farther to the west. They were as ill suited to polar voyaging as their consorts; yet the cockleshell *Flying Fish* came close to achieving the impossible. Somehow and against all the odds, this tiny unstrengthened vessel of under 100 tons managed to force her way through near-solid ice as far as 70° S – almost to within sight of the inaccessible Marie Byrd Land. This was a truly heroic feat of endurance. It was, however, Wilkes's only achievement during his first Antarctic summer; and at the end of April his squadron stood north. All five vessels were in bad shape; their canvas was in shreds and their decks were stove in; the *Sea Gull* indeed was so battered that a couple of days out from Valparaiso she foundered with the loss of her entire company. As for the crews; half-frozen, half-starved and wholly exhausted, they were as sorely tried as their ships. Small wonder that on reaching Sydney a full quarter of them deserted.

Wilkes used the southern winter to patch up his battered fleet, though no amount of refurbishing could make good its basic deficiencies: poor ships and a lack of specialized equipment. Visitors to the vessels were quick to spot their lack of heating and watertight compartments, and several expressed the view that 'the crew seemed

(left) Charles Wilkes, by Alonzo Chappel after a photograph
(below) Wilkes's brig *Porpoise*, colour aquatint by W. J. Bennett

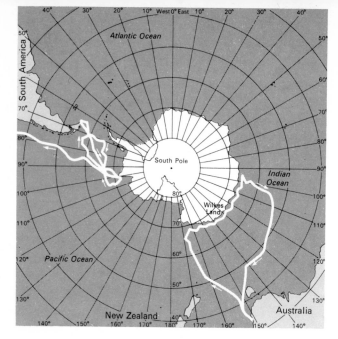

Map of Wilkes's route

certain to be froze to death'. Wilkes, however, was a determined man, and by the end of December he was again heading south, his destination the little-known sea lanes south of Australia, an area which D'Urville was also about to enter.

The events of the next few months are usually described as 'controversial'; and historians have pointed out that several of Wilkes's dates are questionable, and at least one of his sighting reports erroneous. This is so. Yet without doubt Wilkes made a major contribution to the unveiling of Antarctica. For between mid-January and mid-February 1840 he sighted and closely followed a large section of the continent which was previously unknown.

His first sighting took place on 16 January. It is typical of the controversy bedevilling Wilkes's career that his denigrators have accused him of deliberately predating this sighting from the 20th to the 16th so as to gain the kudos which would otherwise have belonged to D'Urville – the Frenchman, it will be remembered, had first reported land on 19 January. The evidence, however, points to Wilkes's earlier date being correct and to the land in question being the Balleny Islands. A couple of days later a more substantial landmass was reported: 'It had the appearance', Wilkes wrote, 'of being 300 feet in height, forming a sort of amphitheatre, grey and dark, and divided into two distinct ridges or elevations throughout its extent.' This, almost certainly, was the mainland of Antarctica some 400 miles to the east of Terre Adélie, where the coast has many bare strata of rocks which would tie in with Wilkes's description. This was a major discovery, and the prelude to a quite remarkable feat of exploration.

For more than a month Wilkes's cockleshell armada followed the coastline west, the vessels seldom out of sight of land. They skirted Terre Adélie, then made their way along the ice-encompassed shore of the territory which now bears Wilkes's name. It was a voyage of appalling hazard. One vessel, the *Peacock*, became ensnared in the ice. Her rudder was torn off, her anchors dragged, and for several hours she lay at the mercy of a rising sea, being smashed again and again against the jagged ice floes. Her longboat was crushed, her quarter was stove in, and her booms and davits were carried away. Mill gives a vivid description of the fight to save her.

> For several days the ship remained in the direst peril. . . . Her rudder was brought aboard. Mr Dibble, the carpenter, was on the sick list, but he rose from his bunk and toiled with the crew for four and twenty hours without intermission to accomplish the herculean task [of repairing the rudder]. Eventually, though in a very unsatisfactory state, it was hung, and the ship was able to struggle out of the bay in which she had so nearly perished.

She was still, however, in imminent danger of foundering, and it was obvious her only chance of survival lay in retreat. It says much for the fine seamanship of her captain, Lieutenant Hudson, that a month later the *Peacock* limped into Sydney harbour.

Wilkes meanwhile continued to follow the line of the continent. Snow, fog, high winds and heavy seas were his companions as he pushed steadily west, catching glimpses from time to time of snow-covered mountains. His crew suffered terribly from cold, exposure, malnutrition and exhaustion. Many were confined to their bunks; and early in February the surgeons took the almost unprecedented step of petitioning their commander that 'illness was so reducing [their] number as to hazard the safety of the ships and the lives of those aboard'. Wilkes, however, was adamant. 'I considered it was my duty', he wrote, 'to proceed and not to give up the cruise until the ship was totally disabled, or it should be evident to all that it was impossible to persist any longer.' He was particularly keen to set foot on the mainland, which was clearly visible day after day. The approaches, however, were everywhere blocked by ice too solid to penetrate; and Wilkes – like D'Urville before him and Ross after – had to be content with landing on an offshore island. This was accomplished on 14 February, not far from the 100th meridian; his ship's company going through the inevitable ritual of raising flags and collecting specimens. A few days later, much to the relief of his crew, Wilkes hauled away to the north, having followed the coast of Antarctica from close inshore for the better part of 2,000 miles – an achievement which, in his ill-found ships, can only be described as magnificent. A month later he dropped anchor beside the *Peacock*.

The aftermath of the United States Exploring Expedition was, unhappily, as tempestuous and fraught with drama as the voyage itself. In Europe Wilkes's achievements were recognized and applauded, and he was awarded the gold medal of the Royal Geographical Society – the *ne plus ultra* of exploration. In his own country, however, he was first hauled in front of a court-martial and charged with 'oppression, injustice, administering illegal punishments, falsehood and scandalous conduct', and then denied funds for the publication of his report – as late as 1861 a senator was recommending 'throw it into the Potomac; that is the best thing!' It could be argued that Wilkes brought many of his troubles on himself; for without

James Clark Ross, by J. R. Wildman

doubt he was impetuous, arrogant and quarrelsome; he seems also to have had a masochistic streak that made him positively revel in the suffering and injustice he was forced to endure. On the other hand it could be argued that he was more sinned against than sinning, and that the root cause of all his troubles was the failure of the United States administration to provide him with adequate tools for the job they expected him to do. Whichever view one holds, there can be no denying that he was a great explorer: a man of rare courage, tenacity and resource who discovered a large section of Antarctica.

Wilkes was a loner. The man who followed him into the Antarctic was the exact opposite: the chosen child of the Establishment, an explorer backed to the hilt by the resources of the greatest seafaring nation of the day.

James Clark Ross was born, with a silver spoon in his mouth, in April 1800. He had everything: wealth, influence, ability and good looks – he was said to be 'the handsomest man in the Navy', a compliment which his portrait appears to endorse. He went to sea at the age of twelve, and was to spend the rest of his active life in the service of three gods: his country, the Royal Navy and polar exploration. Between the age of eighteen and thirty-eight he spent seventeen years in the Arctic, in search of the elusive North West Passage; and at the end of this time what he did not know about handling ships in the ice was not worth knowing. His career seemed to reach its climax in 1831, when he became the first man to set foot on the North Magnetic Pole; a few years later, however, he was offered a change of locale: the command of an expedition bound not for the Arctic but for the little-known Antarctic.

Ross's preparations were as smooth and efficient as Wilkes's had been contentious and inadequate. He had the advantage of first-class ships: the *Erebus* and *Terror*. The former, like most British vessels used for polar exploration in the nineteenth century, was a bomb-boat: length 105 feet, beam 28 feet, draught 11 feet and displacement 370 tons; she rolled badly and was a clumsy sailer, but she had two great assets – her hold was enormous (having been designed for storing mortar shells and mines) and she was stoutly built and could stand a fantastic amount of punishment. The *Terror*, a veteran of many Arctic winters, was almost identical. Ross had both vessels strengthened still further. Their decks were taken up and replaced by two thicknesses of special planking with waterproof cloth in between; their bow and stern sections were scientifically shored up with interlacing beams of oak; all protuberances were smoothed from their hulls, which were then encased in a new outer skin, and their keels were not only sheathed in copper but double sheathed. At the end of this reconstruction neither ship had the grace and beauty of line usually associated with the swan-song days of sail, but for work in the polar pack ice they could not be bettered.

When it came to choosing provisions and stores, Ross was given a free hand. He took with him a great deal of specialized equipment (treble-strength canvas, ice saws, a portable forge, etc.), and sufficient food for three years (including a vast quantity of antiscorbutics – '2,618 pints of vegetable soup, 2,398 lbs of pickled cabbage and 10,782 lbs of carrots'); while to quote his own words, 'warm clothing of the best quality was furnished to both ship's companies, and every arrangement was made in the interior fittings that could contribute to health and comfort'. His crews were hand picked. His orders were flexible. It would, in short, be hard to imagine a better-found expedition than that which sailed from the Medway in the autumn of 1839. It was, however, an expedition with a limited objective; for its aim was not so much to explore as to establish weather stations and to study magnetic variation.

Throughout the winter of 1839/40 the *Erebus* and *Terror* pursued a leisurely course to the south, little dreaming that while they busied themselves with routine observations on temperature, humidity and magnetic dip, French and American expeditions were making their first groping contact with a new continent. They spent two months on Kerguélen Island where they built an observatory – 'on this most dreary and disagreeable place it snowed or sleeted on 61 days out of 63'; they ran into a hurricane – 'It was indeed an unusual sight', wrote the matter-of-fact Ross, 'to see the crests of the great waves driven completely over us in solid sheets'. Not till they arrived in Hobart was their expedition stimulated by the spur of urgency. For unwelcome news was waiting for them: not only had the French and Americans discovered land in the far south, they had discovered it in the very area where Ross had hoped to search for the magnetic pole. His reaction was typically forthright:

> Fortunately, [he wrote] in my instructions much had been left to my judgement in unforeseen circumstances; and impressed with the feeling that England had ever led the way of discovery in the southern as well as the northern regions. I considered it would have been inconsistent with the pre-eminence she had ever maintained, if we were to follow in the footsteps of any other nation. I therefore resolved to avoid all interference with their discoveries, and selected a much more easterly meridian on which to endeavour to penetrate south.

His choice of route is interesting. In the Arctic, Ross had often taken his lead from men who knew local conditions – the Eskimos and the whalers. Now, in the Antarctic, he did the same. He acted on the advice of the sealers, who told him how the pack ice fell away round the 180th meridian; he listened to their stories of how sealing vessels had sighted 'a lagoon-like expanse of open water' beyond the consolidated pack, and it occurred to him that with his specially strengthened vessels he might be able – for the first time in history – to penetrate the ice and force his way through to the virgin continent beyond. His expedition took on a new sense of purpose.

The *Erebus* and *Terror* sailed south from Hobart on 12 November 1840, and that night the flagship's doctor Robert McCormick made an entry in his diary which epitomizes their new-found sense of expectation: 'Our future promises to be full of interest, for we may soon make great discoveries in a region of our globe fresh

Adélie penguin (*Pygoscelis adeliae*)

and new as at creation's first dawn.' On 26 December they sighted their first iceberg. On New Year's Eve they crossed the Antarctic Circle. On 2 January they were brought up short by the consolidated pack.

It stretched away in front of them as far as the eye could see: a damask of white, solid at the edge but, much to Ross's satisfaction, with occasional leads of open water inside. The ships ran parallel to it for several miles, searching for a place to enter; but there seemed no flaw in its defences. Ross took a chance. He ran full-tilt at the edge of the pack.

Again and again his bow smashed into the ice. An ordinary vessel would have been stove in; but the *Erebus*, with her double skin and shored-up bow, was relatively unhurt. Strength alone, however, would never have forced the vessels through. It needs fine seamanship to run a sailing ship's bow again and again into the same place at the same velocity. This seamanship Ross took as a matter of course, and his account of breaking into the pack is prosaic and unemotional:

> After about an hour's hard thumping, we forced our way into some small holes of water, connected by narrow lanes. We found the ice lighter and more scattered than it appeared, and by no means as formidable as we had been led to expect. . . . At noon we were in latitude 65° 55′ S, and the sea was no longer discernible from the masthead as we pursued our way through the pack, choosing the clearest 'leads' and forcing the interposing barriers, at times sustaining violent shocks which nothing but ships so strengthened could have endured.

By nightfall they had penetrated 50 miles into the ice, and the omens were more auspicious than Ross could have dared to hope.

Antarctica, however, was not to yield her secrets without a fight.

During the night of 5/6 January the ice closed up and thickened, and dawn found the *Erebus* and *Terror* twisting anxiously this way and that to avoid being frozen in. But to no avail. At noon they were forced to heave to in a tiny circle of water out of which there was no escape. To start with Ross was not unduly worried; but the weather that evening took a turn for the worse. The barometer dropped. Storm clouds came rolling out of the west. By dawn on 7 January it was snowing hard, the wind had increased to a full hurricane and the swell had widened and steepened. It widened and steepened to such an extent that soon, to Ross's consternation, the pack began to split up, and great waves alive with solid blocks of ice came sweeping down on the imprisoned ships. Ross was to learn that day why no ship had ever ventured into the consolidated pack and lived.

Hour after hour the storm raged with such violence that there seemed no hope of survival. They tried to moor in the lee of a floe, but their hawsers parted. They tried to run with the wind, but their canvas was ripped to shreds. They rigged staysails, and alternatively backing and filling did their best to avoid the heavier conglomerations of ice. But they could not avoid them all. Again and again great blocks as hard as adamant and many tons in weight, crashed into the labouring vessels. They

Giant petrel chick (*Macronectes giganteus*)

Map of Ross's route

suffered terrible damage. The *Erebus*'s rudder was twisted and split, and the copper sheathing ripped from her hull; the *Terror*'s rudder was wrenched clean away, so that the luckless vessel broached to in the trough of the swell. And still the waves increased in fury, till they towered high over the yardarms. Even the phlegmatic Ross thought their last moment had come.

> Our ships, [he wrote] rolled and groaned amidst the fragments of bergs, over which the ocean rolled its mountainous waves, throwing huge masses one upon another then burying them deep beneath its foaming waters. . . . Each of us could only secure a hold, waiting the issue with resignation to the will of Him who alone could bring us through such extreme danger; watching with breathless anxiety the effect of each collision and the vibrations of the tottering masts, expecting every moment to see them give way.

But the storm was too violent to last for long. That night the wind dropped, the waves gradually lost their malevolence, and the vessels were able to limp for shelter behind a line of massive bergs. They had survived partly because of their special strengthening, and partly because of their fine seamanship. 'I must express my admiration', wrote Ross with typical understatement, 'of the conduct of the crew on this trying occasion: throughout a period of twenty-eight hours, during any one of which there appeared to be little hope that we should live to see another, the coolness, steady obedience and untiring exertions of each individual were in every way worthy of British seamen.' It was not within Ross's capacity to lavish higher praise.

For two days the *Erebus* and *Terror* lay in the lee of a chain of icebergs, effecting repairs. Then, once again, they got under way. They made good progress, for the storm had broken up the pack, and on the evening of 8 January open water was

112

'False sea leopard (*Leptonyx Weddelli*)' — now called Weddell seal (*Leptonychotes weddelli*), plate V in *The Zoology of the Voyage of H.M.S.* Erebus *and* Terror, by the zoologist who accompanied Ross to the Antarctic, Joseph Dalton Hooker

sighted to the south. Next morning the vessels broke free of the ice. The barrier that had remained inviolate since its creation had at last been breached, and the way to the continent lay open.

Ross's hopes were divided. The prospect of discovering new lands was alluring; but below in his cabin was the Union Jack that he had unfurled ten years previously, at the North Magnetic Pole, and to raise the same flag at the South Magnetic Pole was his most cherished dream. By the evening of 10 January the angle of magnetic dip had increased to 85°, and they realized the pole must be near. But even as they were calculating its position, an ice blink was sighted to the south, and it became a question of which they would discover first, new lands or the pole. The question was resolved that night:

Monday, January 11th, [McCormick wrote]. At 2.30 a.m. land was reported from the crow's nest. . . . It appeared at first indistinctly, through haze and a few light clouds, skirting the horizon on the port bow. I could just trace the outline of a mountain, with a steep escarpment streaked with snow. After about an hour this became so intermingled with the haze as to give rise to doubts about it being land at all. But by 9 a.m. the coast had become sufficiently well defined for me to get a sketch. It extended from S.E. to S.W.; very high, and was enveloped in snow. The whole of the upper part of this vast mountain range appeared to be a glaciation, relieved at intervals by the apex of some dark hummock or peak. . . . And [it soon became clear that] we had discovered a new land of so extensive a coastline and attaining such altitude as to justify the appellation of a Great New Southern Continent.

It was indeed a land of continental proportion which now unfolded peak by peak in front of Ross's eyes. All day he stood towards it, marvelling at the grandeur of the mountains, the dazzling white of the snow, the brilliance of the light and the silence that hung like a benediction over his advancing ships; and next morning he made a landing. It must have been an incongruous ceremony: the officers in their gold braid and wing collars, the seamen in their red frocks and Welsh wigs, the penguins which 'fought' the landing party, the ceremonial raising of the Union Jack and the three hearty cheers as Ross took possession of the newly discovered lands 'in the name of our Most Gracious Sovereign, Queen Victoria'. It was an occasion reminiscent of Wilkes's and D'Urville's landings, especially as it too took place on an offshore island. In one respect, however, Ross's landing was very different from his predecessors': it was not a finale but a prelude.

For several days the *Erebus* and *Terror* followed the land from a distance of no more than five or six hundred yards. It was this ability to stand close inshore which was the hallmark of Ross's expedition. Other explorers had seen Antarctica only from a distance, from beyond the consolidated pack. Ross had penetrated the pack; and in the lagoonlike belt of water between ice and land the wonders which his predecessors had seen only as through a glass darkly, he was now able to appreciate face to face.

On 15 January, rounding a cape, he was greeted by a scene of the utmost grandeur: a great chain of mountains, over 10,000 feet in height, stretching to the south in a single unbroken sweep from sea to sky. Ross named them after various sea lords about whom we know little and care less; not till he had been more than a week off the coast of Antarctica did he name a landfall after his fiancée – Cape Anne – his gallantry in this respect falling far short of D'Urville's.

For a week the *Erebus* and *Terror* followed the coastline, surveying the mountains, taking samples from the sea bed and marvelling at the great herds of whales, which, as Ross remarked with sad clairvoyance, 'had hitherto enjoyed a life of tranquillity beyond the reach of their persecutors, but would soon be made to contribute to the wealth of our country'. By 23 January they were in latitude 74° 23′, farther south than man had ever penetrated before. That night they drank to 'farther south still', and, since the coastline seemed to bear away to the southwest, to 'the discovery of the magnetic pole'. But it was something far more bizarre than the pole which they discovered.

> Thursday, January 28th, [wrote McCormick]. We were this morning startled by the most unexpected discovery in this region of glaciation: a stupendous volcanic mountain in a high state of activity. At 10 a.m., upon going on deck, my attention was arrested by what appeared to be a fine snowdrift, driving from the summit of a lofty crater-shaped peak. As we made a nearer approach, however, this apparent snowdrift resolved itself into a dense column of smoke, intermingled with flashes of red flame, emerging from a magnificent volcanic vent, in the very centre of a mountain range encased in eternal ice and snow. The peak itself, which rises to an altitude of 12,400 feet was named after our ship, Mount Erebus. Adjacent to it, and separated by only a saddle of ice, arose a sister mountain to the height of 10,900 feet, but now extinct. This received the name of Mount Terror.

It was a sensational discovery. But in the afternoon they were brought up short by something even more sensational. For to the east of Mount Erebus they found their way blocked not by a coastline, but by a vast barrier of solid ice, smooth as onyx and treble the height of their mast.

Ross's diary gives a vivid picture, both of the ice barrier and of his feelings at finding it blocked the way south.

> As we approached the land, we perceived a low white line extending east from the volcano as far as the eye could discern. It presented an extraordinary appearance,

gradually increasing in height as we got nearer to it, and proving at length to be a perpendicular cliff of ice, between one hundred and fifty and two hundred feet above the level of the sea, perfectly flat at the top and without any fissures or promontories on its seaward face. What was beyond it we could not imagine, but it was an obstruction of such a character as to leave no doubt upon my mind as to our future proceedings; for we might as well try to sail through the cliffs of Dover as penetrate such a mass. This was a great disappointment to us all. . . . At 4 p.m. (just as we were hauling round to follow the barrier east) Mount Erebus was observed to emit smoke and flame in unusual quantities, producing a most grand spectacle. A volume of dense smoke was projected at each successive jet with great force . . . and as the smoke cleared away the bright red flame that filled the vent was clearly perceptible. . . . That evening, favoured by a fresh north-westerly breeze, we made good progress along the lofty cliffs of the ice barrier. It would be impossible to conceive a more solid-looking structure; not the smallest appearance of a vent or fissure could we discover throughout its whole extent. But many small fragments lay at the foot of the cliffs, broken away by the force of the waves, which dashed their spray high up the face of them.

For two weeks and 250 miles the *Erebus* and *Terror* skirted the ice barrier, which, as they followed it east, grew steadily loftier and more intransigent. But the short Antarctic exploring season was now drawing to its close; young ice, the harbinger of winter, was already forming on the water between cliffs and pack; and in mid-February Ross was forced to haul away to the north to prevent his ships being frozen in. He spent several days searching in vain for an anchorage where it might be possible to winter. Then he stood north into the consolidated pack.

He devotes little space in his diary to this second crossing of the ice, and historians have tended simply to quote his comment that the passage was made 'without undue difficulty'. One entry, however, is significant:

March 7th. We found ourselves embayed in a deep bight of the pack, stretching across our bows. Much hampered by fields of pancake ice, we tried to haul to the wind. But at noon it fell quite calm, and the heavy easterly swell began to drive us onto a line of large bergs – from the mast-head we counted 84 large ones and some 100 of smaller dimension. . . . [After a while] we found we were fast closing this chain of bergs, so closely packed together that we could distinguish no opening through which the ships could pass; the waves breaking violently against them, dashed huge masses of pack ice against the precipitous faces of the bergs, now lifting them nearly to their summit, now forcing them again far beneath their waterline, and sometimes rending them into a multitude of brilliant fragments against their projecting points. . . . For eight hours we drifted slowly towards what to human eyes appeared inevitable destruction; the high waves and deep rolling of our ships rendered towing with the boats impossible, and our situation [was] the more painful and embarrassing from our inability to make any effort to avoid the dreadful calamity that seemed to await us. . . . Soon we were within half a mile of the range of bergs. The roar of the surf . . . and the crashing of ice, fell upon the ear with fearful distinctness, whilst the frequently averted eyes as immediately returned to contemplate the awful destruction that threatened in one short hour to close the world and all its hopes and joys and sorrows upon us for ever. In this our deep distress we called upon the Lord, and He heard our voices. A gentle wind filled our sails. Hope was revived: and the greatest activity prevailed to make the best use of the feeble breeze. As it gradually freshened, our heavy ships began to feel its influence, slowly at first, but then more rapidly; and before dark we found ourselves far removed from danger.

If this was voyaging 'without difficulty' the mind boggles at what perils must have beset Ross in the more eventful moments of his ice cruise!

By mid-March the *Erebus* and *Terror* had fought free of the pack, and under a full moon and brilliant coruscations from the aurora, were standing north for Hobart. They arrived on 6 April, after a voyage within the Antarctic Convergence of 145 days. Ross's ships were in excellent condition. Every one of the crew was in perfect health; and seldom on a major voyage of discovery can so many things have gone right and so few wrong.

Ross spent two more seasons in the Antarctic, his ships being frozen solid in the pack, coming into violent collision, and all but foundering in the lee of an iceberg whose walls literally scraped their rigging. His achievements on these voyages were far from negligible, but they did not break new ground; they simply extended his previous discoveries. Not till the autumn of 1843 did the *Erebus* and *Terror* return to England, after a commission of four years and five months, one of the longest in naval history.

Ross, on his homecoming, was showered with every kind of honour. He was knighted and awarded the gold medal of a host of societies, and a distinguished future seemed to be his for the taking. In fact, with the exception of one short voyage, he never went to sea again. He retired, married and settled quietly in Aylesbury – which in English terms is a long way from salt water. It would be no exaggeration to say that he had worn himself out, both physically and mentally, in the service of his three gods.

Within the space of eighteen months three great national expeditions had seen and landed on Antarctica. There had also been a number of important voyages made under the auspices of Enderby and Sons, oil merchants of London, the greatest being that of John Biscoe who in 1830–2 circumnavigated the continent from close in-shore, discovering Enderby Land, Adelaide Island and the southern reaches of the Antarctic peninsula. What these explorers found they did not like. It was clear from the reports they brought back that the new-found land was useless for colonization; scientists had for the time being more information than they could digest; and so we now enter what Mill has termed 'The Age of Averted Interest'. For half a century Antarctica was ignored. About the only people to go there were whalers, drawn to the Southern Ocean – like the sealers a century before them – by explorers' reports of the valuable harvest that could be wrung from the ice-cold waters of the south.

## CHAPTER 6

## THE RICH GREEN PASTURES OF THE SOUTH

WHALING IS A CONTROVERSIAL SUBJECT. It is hard to be dispassionate about a creature as sentient and in many ways as noble as a horse, plunging in agony at the end of a towline until it is stabbed to death. A fair summing up of the industry has, however, been made by F. D. Ommanney who for several years was whaling inspector aboard an Antarctic factory ship:

> The story of whaling, [he writes] is made up of a number of chapters each covering a few centuries and repeating the same pattern. Each begins with discovery and hopeful enterprise, passes through a phase of fierce competition and ruthless exploitation, and ends in diminishing resources, exhaustion and failure. In his pursuit of the whale man has been both blind and ignorant.

To understand the most recent, and in some ways the most tragic, of these chapters, whaling in the Antarctic, we need to know something of its antecedents.

An eighteenth-century engraving of a female whale showing the various implements employed to secure her capture and bring her ashore

Whales have been hunted for longer than history has been recorded, for their bones together with Stone Age harpoonheads have been found in middens dating back to 3000 B.C. Modern whaling, however, begins with the Basques.

Even today the carcasses of right whales are sometimes found stranded on the beaches of the Golfe de Gascogne; and if it seems curious that so powerful a swimmer should come to so ignominious an end, the fact is that whales are unable to 'go astern', so that once aground they are left high and dry by a receding tide. The Basques used to cut up the stranded carcasses, melt their blubber into oil and eat their flesh. The next step was predictable: fishermen took to going after the whales in boats, initially to try and drive them onto the beaches and subsequently to kill them and tow their bodies to the shore. By 1200 the Basques had perfected a technique of whaling which was to be followed for 700 years, and which indeed is still followed in many parts of the world today. A *chaloupe* (or shallow-draught whaling boat) would be rowed as stealthily as possible and as close as possible to its quarry; the harpooner would then fling his weapon into the 'shining cliff of the whale's body', his objective being not to kill the creature but to make it fast. The injured whale would then either run or dive, taking with it the harpoon line, which was often whipped out so fast over the *chaloupe*'s bow that it smoked and had to be dowsed with water. Once the first panic-stricken rush had slackened, the rope would be pulled taut and the whale 'played' like a gargantuan fish, until the time came – sometimes in minutes, usually in hours, but occasionally not for days – when the terrified and exhausted creature could be hauled alongside and stabbed to death.

> When the steersman was ready [writes Ommanney] he sent his lances home, three or four if possible, aimed at the heart. Now the boat had to back away quickly, for the whale, mortally wounded, would begin its terrible and pathetic death agony, thrashing the water with its tail in fear and pain, snapping its jaws and wallowing in a smother of foam, crimsoned with blood. If the boat did not pull away fast enough it was liable to be struck by the tail or snapped by the jaws. . . . Sometimes the whale had to be approached and attacked a second or even a third time. . . . Then began the long and arduous task of towing the carcass back.

One is torn between admiration of the whalers' courage, and pity for their huge but defenceless quarry.

Throughout the Middle Ages the Basques enjoyed a monopoly of Atlantic whaling. Early in the sixteenth century, however, there began a chain of events which was to be repeated many times in many oceans. The whales grew scarce, for the simple reason that they were being hunted to near extinction; by 1550 there was hardly a right whale left in the central reaches of the Atlantic; the industry collapsed, and with it the Basques' prosperity. Not until a new subspecies (the Greenland right) was discovered on the periphery of the Arctic did the industry revive. And this revival, when it eventually came about in the early seventeenth century, benefited not the Basques, but the rich seafaring nations who had sufficient

118       (above) Fin whale (*Balaenoptera physalus*), (centre) blue whale (*Balaenoptera musculus*),
(below) sperm whale (*Physeter catodon*).
The artwork shows the whales to scale with one another.
(overleaf) Flensing baleen (or whalebone) whales

ships and capital to support a distant, deep-sea fishery: the British and the Dutch.

The Dutch were the more successful. Their *Noordse Compagnie*, founded in 1614, was soon sending an annual fleet of big three-masted barques to the coasts of Greenland, Spitsbergen, Novaya Zemlya and Bear Island. They made handsome profits. For the Greenland right whales were slow swimmers, poor fighters, and when killed their bodies stayed obligingly afloat; they were also rich in oil. To start with the carcasses were simply towed to the nearest beach, dismembered and rendered down. In the 1620s, however, two events took place which set the pattern for the future. In 1623 a whaling station – Smeerenburg or 'Blubbertown' – was established on Spitsbergen; this, the prototype of a dozen subsequent stations in the sub-Antarctic, was equipped with slipways, winches, oil extractors and cookers, and was soon handling more than 600 whales in a season; while at much the same time the larger of the Dutch barques – the prototype of twentieth-century factory ships – took to rendering down their catches over an incinerator, built into their open deck. It is hardly surprising that under an assault of such sustained efficiency the Greenland rights soon disappeared from their traditional haunts. They retreated into the pack ice. Even here, however, they were tracked down by specially strengthened whalecatchers; and by 1850, like their Biscayan cousins, they had been hunted to the brink of extermination.

It was at this moment in history, when there were probably no more than a few hundred rights alive in the northern hemisphere, that D'Urville, Wilkes and Ross returned from their expeditions to the Antarctic. And each, in his official report, commented on the 'vast quantity of whales observed by the edge of the pack'. The stage was now set for the final scene of the tragedy.

Whaling in the Antarctic did not, however, follow the same pattern as in the Arctic. For there is a fundamental difference between the whales of the northern hemisphere and those of the southern. In the north the principal species – rights, greys, bottle-nosed and beluga – are harmless, slow-moving creatures which have neither the speed to escape their predators nor the inclination to fight them. In the south, on the other hand, the principal species – right, sperm, blue, fin, humpback and killer – include not only the largest creatures on earth but also some of the fiercest and most bizarre: protagonists who were to give a good account of themselves in the conflict to come.

This conflict, now to be fought out in the Southern Ocean, falls naturally into three sections, each concerned with the pursuit of a particular species: right or 'bay' whaling (1780–1840), sperming (1780–1880) and rorqual hunting (1890 to the present day).

The story of the southern rights is soon told. They were lumbering, inoffensive creatures, about 60 feet in length and 60 tons in weight, near relations of the Biscayan rights hunted half a millennium earlier by the Basques. In the early 1780s it was noticed by convict ships on the run to Botany Bay that the waters off Australia, Tasmania and New Zealand were alive with great herds of these playful,

(above) Southern right whale (*Eubalaena australis*), (centre) humpback whale (*Megaptera novaeangeliae*), (below) killer whale (*Orcinus orca*). The artwork shows the whales to scale with one another

123

A killer whale (*Orcinus orca*)

slow-moving creatures; and it became standard practice to equip the convict vessels with whaling gear, so that after they had landed their human cargo they could go whaling off the Australian coast. By the turn of the century some twenty-five vessels a year were making the outward voyage from England with a cargo of deportees and the homeward voyage with a cargo of whale oil and baleen. It was the start of a lucrative if short-lived boom. The whales were defenceless. Here is Hunter Christie's description of killing a southern right, *c.* 1800, off the coast of Australia – a description that might be transposed almost word for word with Ommanney's description of killing a Biscayan right, *c.* 1300, off the coast of France.

When a whale was sighted on the surface, the vessel would be hove-to within about half-a-mile and the boats launched. These boats, which still survive as the Royal Navy's whalers, were probably the most graceful ever designed to be propelled by oars, and, since beauty of line at sea as in the air usually goes hand in hand with efficiency, they were both fast and seaworthy. The harpooner, on whose strength and skill the success of the expedition depended, rowed in the bow and awaited the steersman's command to launch his harpoon – a wooden spear about five feet long, with a heavy barbed steel head to which was shackled a length of manilla line joined to a heavier cable carefully coiled down in the bottom of the boat. When, at a distance of 20 feet or less, the command was given, the harpooner rose to his feet, balanced himself in the heaving boat, and flung the harpoon with all his strength into the whale's flank in an attempt to force the steel head through the protective layer of blubber and into the lungs. If all went well the whale, which a moment before had been cruising quietly along on the surface at perhaps four or five miles an hour, would rush ahead, dragging the boat after it, while the harpoon line, which was looped round a post in the stern called the loggerhead and then through a ring in the bow, ran out at such a speed that it literally smoked, and water was thrown over it to reduce the friction. If the whale's first rush did not take out all the line, the crew would haul in and coil down the surplus until more harpoons or spears could be driven into the wretched animal's vital parts; then off he went again, spouting blood and viscera, and turning the surface of the ocean into a crimson foam before, often after many hours, dying from exhaustion and loss of blood.

A right would yield two tons of oil and a ton of baleen. It was the latter that made the whalemen their fortune. For the rise in nineteenth-century Europe of a prosperous, fashion-conscious middle class, all eager to elevate their bosoms and restrict their waists, created a demand for whalebone which far exceeded the supply. The price rocketed. By 1830 the baleen from a single right was fetching £2,500 – sufficient to finance a whaling voyage from Europe to Australia and back again. Small wonder the herds were hunted with such enthusiasm that their numbers dwindled. By 1840 the southern right, which for thousands of years had inconvenienced no one (except perhaps the Governor of Tasmania who complained that their 'snoring' kept him awake!) had suffered the fate of its cousins in the north. Man had not yet learned to temper his rapaciousness with either mercy or acumen.

The sperm whales, however, did not succumb so easily, and their story has a happier ending.

Sperm are the most numerous and ubiquitous of the whale family, being found in every ocean as far north as the Arctic Circle and as far south as the Antarctic. They have been dubbed 'the most unique form of animal life on earth', a description confirmed by their anatomy. Some 60 feet in length, a full third of their body is taken up by an enormous asymmetrical head which contains among other phenomena a buoyancy chamber filled with anything up to a ton of waxlike spermaceti, which acts as a stabilizer during deep-water dives; and their stomach not infrequently contains 50-pound lumps of ambergris, the world's only natural fixative for perfume. In character they are peaceful and playful, but if attacked will often show fight, and there are many well-documented cases of 'an ugly sperm' staving in and sinking vessels of up to 450 tons. They are also enormously strong and tenacious of life, all whalers agreeing that a sperm is the most difficult species to kill. Yet incredible as it sounds, the nineteenth-century whalers continued to use the old Basque technique of hunting them – transfixing the huge creatures with a hand harpoon, being towed after them (sometimes literally for days) in their flimsy boats, and finally stabbing them to death in a frenzy of churned-up water and blood, the boats frequently being swamped, capsized or bitten to matchwood in the process. This was the heroic age of whaling: the age of long voyages to far-flung corners of the earth, of desperate encounters, nauseating conditions, brutal punishments and fabulous rewards; the age of *Moby Dick*.

It was the New Englanders who were the most active sperm hunters. In the early nineteenth century some 600 whalers a year stood south from ports such as New Haven and Nantucket – indeed as Frank Bullen writes in *The Cruise of the*

*Cachalot*, 'one could [in 1800] hardly sail in the Main Ocean for twenty-four hours without coming upon a Yankee whaler chasing or stripping a Sperm'. When the industry was young the New Englanders concentrated on the easily worked breeding grounds off the coast of Brazil and in the Indian Ocean; but as the sperm inevitably grew scarce, they were obliged to extend their voyages north to Japan and south to the Southern Ocean. Eventually they were pursuing their quarry to the very periphery of the Antarctic. This must surely rank as the world's most hazardous calling.

Picture a close-reefed barque standing week after week into the lonely reaches of the sub-Antarctic, with an unremitting 30-knot wind in her rigging and greybacks sluicing in endless succession the length of her deck. Picture the tedium of the long search, broken at last by a cry from her masthead, 'Thar she blows!', as an oblique cloud of vapour rises for a moment above the waves. Picture launching the long-boats into a steep white-crested swell, and the long hard haul to close with the sperm – almost certainly a lone bull, swimming at anything up to 5 knots. Picture the hazards of coming alongside the labouring creature and thrusting a harpoon, by hand, into the glistening wall of its body. And this would be no more than a curtain raiser to the struggle to come. For once 'fix'd fast' the sperm might fight for its life for anything up to twenty-four hours, during which it could tow the longboats for anything up to 50 miles before being at last put out of its agony. The log of the *Royal Bounty* is eloquent testimony to at least one sperm's endurance. On the morning of 28 May 1817, we are told, one of the *Bounty*'s longboats succeeded in harpooning a 'great leviathan' – undoubtedly, from the description given, a bull sperm. This 'leviathan' immediately made off at 18 knots, towing the longboat behind it. During the course of the next few hours as many as five more longboats managed to harpoon the whale and attach themselves to it. Yet at sunset, eight hours later, it was still swimming strongly, dragging in its wake six boats, thirty-six men and some 5,000 fathoms of rope. During the night, a line was transferred to the *Bounty* herself. At dawn, however, the great creature was still struggling on, having towed a veritable armada, including a 350-ton brig, for a day and a night over a distance of more than 45 miles. One wishes the whale's strength and endurance had won him the freedom he deserved; but the *Bounty*'s log tells us simply that 'after twenty-five hours this most obstinate creature was despatch'd'.

It was not, however, always the whale that died; and the history of sperming is replete with hair-raising stories of boats overturned, stove in or towed to oblivion, and of men crushed to death by the whales' flukes or impaled on their jaws. Hardship, hazard and discomfort were the fabric of a sperm whaler's life and it is hardly surprising that on an average voyage 30 per cent of the crew deserted, 30 per cent were discharged and 5 per cent died. In compensation, the financial rewards – at least for those at the top – were considerable; and many of the crew undoubtedly enjoyed the *camaraderie* of those who together accomplish a dangerous and physically demanding task. It cannot be claimed that the New England sperm hunters made important discoveries in the Antarctic; but at a time when interest in the Southern Ocean was at its nadir, and explorers' interests were concentrated on Africa by land and the North West Passage by sea, they did preserve a link in the chain of man's contact with Antarctica.

The rorqual hunters, in contrast, played a major role in opening up the approaches to the continent.

The principal types of southern rorqual are the fin, the humpback and the blue. The fin is the most common. About 60 feet in length and 50 tons in weight, it is a magnificent swimmer and can, for short spells, keep pace with a naval frigate steaming at 25 knots. In character it is gregarious, usually being found about 50 miles from the edge of the ice in pods of 12 to 15, these pods occasionally coalescing to form a herd of anything up to 100. For a reason which is not altogether understood – though it almost certainly has something to do with the fact that fins swim on their side – there is always more white on the right of their body than on the left, which explains the harpooners' preference for shooting them from the starboard.

The humpback, some 50 feet in length and 40 tons in weight, is the ugliest of the rorquals in appearance and the most engaging in character. To quote Sanderson:

The form of the beast defies description . . . it appears to be permanently curved over, like a classical drawing of a dolphin; its body is short and extremely thick, the head is huge and the jaws unbelievably wide; the tail flukes are large and serrated. Most distinctive of all are the flippers, which are long, narrow, ragged and shaped like the wing of a jet-plane, thick at the leading edge and thin at the trailing. . . . Its skin is invariably scarred, abraded, covered with lumps, and infested with barnacles and molluscs – a humpback in fact has been described as 'a parasitologist's paradise'!

In character it is playful, rumbustious and unpredictable, blowing irregularly, sometimes staying submerged for as much as an hour and sometimes leaping clean out of the water. It seems to have a happy sex life – again to quote Sanderson: 'the mating of humpbacks can be best described as "quite something"! Apparently the fifty-foot creatures become highly skittish at this time, frolicking about and administering ten-ton love slaps to each other with their flippers by way of expressing affection. These caresses are audible for miles.' On a sadder note, it has been noticed by gunners that humpbacks are usually found in pairs, and that when one is harpooned its mate will frequently refuse to leave the body.

The blue or Sibbald's rorqual is the largest living creature on earth; it is also the most majestic, the most powerful and to some people's thinking the most beautiful; a full-grown cow may be over 100 feet in length and 100 tons in weight. Blues are usually found in family-sized pods of five or six, close to the edge of the ice. They are graceful, perfectly streamlined, beautifully coloured creatures that can swim for hour after hour at 20 knots and are unbelievably strong. Sanderson tells us that 'an eighty-foot female Blue, held fast by a harpoon-head

(left) Whalecatchers of former times in South Georgia (opposite) A now disused land-based whaling station at Leith Harbour, South Georgia. Antarctic whaling is now entirely carried out from floating factory ships as seen on pages 120 and 121.

attached to 3,000 fathoms of line, once towed a 90-foot twin-screwed whalecatcher, with its engines at full astern, for seven hours at a steady eight knots, without the slightest let-up or faltering, over a distance of more than fifty miles.' Imagine tackling such a creature with a hand harpoon and a rowing boat!

Bearing in mind the size and strength of these southern rorquals it is hardly surprising that they proved, initially, altogether too much of a handful for their pursuers, and that the early history of Antarctic whaling is a chronicle of failure. The experiences of the 1892 whaling fleet under Alexander Fairweather are typical. To quote Hunter Christie:

> From all points of view the expedition was a disappointment. They saw no Right Whales, but all around them spouted the fast-swimming Rorquals. It has been suggested that these carried insufficient whalebone to make it worth-while killing them; but this is not the whole story. The tough and experienced skippers were well aware that their tackle was inadequate for killing Fin Backs, and the experience of the *Active* confirmed this. One of her boats succeeded in getting three lines into a Fin, which at once made off, taking the boat with it. As it passed a second whaleboat, three more lines were secured, and away went the whale, trailing two boats and some 720 fathoms of two-inch cable behind it. In an attempt to save the harpoons, a third boat secured and managed to get the free end of the rope aboard the 340-ton *Active*, which also succeeded in picking up the lines from the other boats. Away went the whole procession, the boats trailing behind the ship on two ropes, and the whale pulling all four 'at a good rate'. [The experimental] rockets were fired whenever the whale surfaced, but their only effect was to make it go faster, and for fourteen hours the battle continued. At the end of that time, when all were exhausted except the whale, the engines were put into reverse, the lines broke, and the whale went off 'with half Jock Tod's smithy shop in its tail'. . . . It is scarcely surprising that, after this experience, the Rorquals were left severely alone.

Nor was it surprising that Fairweather's expedition, like many of its predecessors and many of its successors, turned in frustration to searching for seals off the little-known coast of Antarctica.

Inevitably, during some of these voyages, there were a number of random small-scale discoveries.

In 1874 the whaler *Grönland*, commanded by Eduard Dallmann, brought the German flag to Antarctica, discovering a series of straits and islands at the approaches to the Weddell Sea. In 1893 the whaler *Jason*, commanded by Carl Larsen, discovered an ice shelf and a great range of mountains off the east coast of the Antarctic peninsula. In 1895 Carsten Borchgrevink made a discovery of a different kind. While serving as an ordinary seaman aboard the *Antarctic* (a whaling vessel commanded by Henrik Bull) he landed on an offshore island in the Ross Sea and found the rocks coated with pale-green lichen – the first indication that the new continent could support any sort of life. And so, with the accumulation of small, almost incidental discoveries, the coastline of Antarctica took gradual shape on the cartographers' maps. But what was beyond this coastline man neither knew nor for the time being cared.

As for the rorquals, the staccato bark of the harpoon gun was soon to sound their requiem.

The idea of shooting whales with a gun was not new. In the 1820s two New Englanders patented a sort of bazooka; this was tried out in the Atlantic, but it made so much noise that it frightened away the whales and proved almost as dangerous to those who fired it as to their quarry! In the 1850s a bloodthirsty British clergyman, the Reverend Henry Cheever, who had gone whaling 'for the good of his health', suggested using both harpoon guns and inflationary bladders to keep the carcasses afloat; his inventions, however, were confined to theory. The first practical weapon came from Norway. This was the brainchild of Svend Foyn, who spent more than a decade experimenting with guns, harpoons, pulleys and compressed-air pumps from the deck of his schooner *Spes et Fides*. The device he finally patented in 1868 was lethal, and is still being used, with only minor modifications, today. In the bow of his schooner he built a raised platform; on this he mounted a swivel gun, and the swivel gun he loaded with a harpoon and line. The harpoon was designed with a twin-barb, so that the whale had no chance of shaking it free; the line was attached at one end to the shank of the harpoon, while the other end ran up one side of the foremast and down the other side to the waistdeck, where it passed over a slung pulley. Having used this equipment to kill and secure his whale, Svend Foyn kept it afloat by pumping compressed air into its stomach; he was then able to tow the carcass at his leisure, tail first, in the wake of the *Spes et Fides* – which is precisely the technique used by a whalecatcher in the 1970s.

With steam vessels able to match their 20 knots, and with harpoon guns able to pick them off at a range of several hundred yards, the rorquals were doomed. Ommanney summarizes their fate in a paragraph: 'Svend Foyn's deadly invention was taken up by the Norwegian whalers in 1880. It gave them a worldwide supremacy in whaling which lasted until 1950, when the Russians and Japanese arrived on the scene and the industry collapsed through over-fishing. It [the harpoon gun] took the glamour, but also the danger and hardship out of whaling, and led to the mass slaughter of the rorquals.'

The year 1904 saw the birth of modern whaling, when Carl Anton Larsen founded the first Antarctic shore-based whaling station at Grytviken, South Georgia. Within a decade more than two dozen stations and factory ships were operating in and around the sub-Antarctic islands. Initially both ships and shore stations had to be licensed; after 1925, however, factory ships took to operating in the open sea, unfettered by the necessity to license and free to hunt wherever their quarry were thickest. In a typical season (1930) the hunting group comprised 6 shore stations, 41 factory ships and 232 whalecatchers. Between them they killed over 40,000 whales; the herds dwindled and it seemed as though the tragedy of the Biscayan right, the Greenland right and the southern right was about to be repeated.

The more far-sighted whalers, however, both on commercial and humanitarian grounds, viewed the extinction of the southern rorquals with dismay. A small percentage of Grytviken's profits were offered to the British government for research, and it was these funds that financed the 'Discovery Investigations' of the 1920s and 1930s. The Discovery cruises carried out the first scientific studies of whale ecology, and their findings provided a platform for subsequent efforts at conservation.

In 1937 an International Agreement for the Regulation of Whaling was signed by nine nations. This, in theory, curtailed the length of the hunting season and restricted the weight and quantity of the catch, while species in danger of extinction were declared 'protected'. In practice, however, 1938 brought the greatest-ever number of kills – 46,039 whales, which yielded between them over half a million tons of oil. Bernard Stonehouse explains this apparent anomaly:

The Whaling Commission faced the impossible task of controlling a powerful, profitable, highly capitalized, fiercely competitive, multi-national industry, which had no intention of accepting controls other than on its own terms. Though the Commission

recognized that, under proper management, whales could be harvested rather than quarried, they had no powers to impose this view. Though they had powers to vary whaling procedure, amendments which were [genuinely] restrictive were seldom agreed to by all the delegates, and the demurral of one was usually sufficient for the proposal to be dropped by all. So conservation fell by the wayside. . . . Today the work of the Commission continues; but it is still without power, and no species of whale in Antarctic waters is safe from the threat of extermination.

How real is this threat in the 1970s?

The conservationists would have us believe that extinction is imminent. They point to the several species that man in his greed has exterminated in the past, and they quote statistics to prove that other species face the same danger in the immediate future. In particular they cite the case of the blue – a sentient, intelligent and peaceful creature which at the beginning of the century could be found in hundreds of thousands and is now reduced to a remnant of less than 600 survivors. They point out also the cruel manner in which the great creatures are slaughtered. Ommanney, himself a whaling inspector, admits that the modern harpoon gun and its explosive warhead is 'the most barbarous instrument used for slaughtering animals by any livestock industry in the world'; and in the name of both ecology and humanity the conservationists plead for whaling in the Antarctic to be brought under effective international control.

The protagonists of whaling – the Russians and the Japanese, who are the only nations nowadays to send pelagic expeditions to the Antarctic – point to the 'starving quarter of mankind' whom whalemeat helps to keep alive; they point also to the vast number of uses to which whale products are put – the manufacture of soap, candles, shaving cream and cosmetics, and the production of animal foods and fertilizers, to mention only a few. They also point out that thanks to the work of the Commission many species are now effectively protected.

There is truth in both arguments; and perhaps the final word in a controversial issue should be left with Ommanney who has a foot in both camps, being a conservationist at heart and a part-time whaler by profession.

> In the past man has exterminated his fellow creatures largely through thoughtlessness or ignorance. . . . The Greenland Right whale was brought to the verge of extinction because it never occurred to anyone that it did not exist in inexhaustible numbers. But if the great whales of the Antarctic disappear they will surely be the first victims of man's sheer greed and rapacity, wiped out by him in the full knowledge of what was happening, with the results of modern scientific research on the table and the remedies at hand.

If this in fact happens, there seems no reason why the big-game animals in Africa, the tiger in India, the fish from the continental shelves and the salmon from the Pacific rivers should not suffer the same fate, so that even as man struggles to lift himself to other planets his own becomes a desert in front of his eyes.

Sunset on Coronation Island as seen from Berntsen Point, South Orkney Islands

(right) Adrien de Gerlache de Gomery
(below) The *Belgica*

## CHAPTER 7

## THE FIRST FOOTHOLD

IN THE HALF CENTURY which followed Ross's expedition little interest was shown in the Antarctic. The seals had been exterminated, the whales were proving next to impossible to catch, and it was clear that the terrain itself was of no commercial value. British energies were therefore diverted to the North West Passage and the search for Franklin; American energies were dissipated in civil war; and it was left to the nations of continental Europe and Scandinavia – Germany, France, Belgium, Sweden and Norway – to send the occasional small-scale and privately sponsored expedition to the south. In 1895, however, the International Geographical Congress, meeting in London, provided a much-needed stimulus to the unveiling of Antarctica. 'The greatest piece of exploration still to be undertaken', this Congress declared, 'is that of the Antarctic'; and it went on to urge that scientific teams be sent there at once, 'in view of the vast addition to knowledge which would result'.

It was at this moment in history that the search for land was finally superseded by the more altruistic search for knowledge. First to respond to the beat of this *avant-garde* drum were the Belgians.

In 1894 Adrien de Gerlache de Gomery, a junior lieutenant in the Belgian Navy read a paper to the Royal Geographical Society of Brussels advocating an expedition to the Antarctic. Financial support, however, was slow to materialize; for the merchants and bankers who might have underwritten a traditional type of expedition in the hope of commercial gain were less enthusiastic at the prospect of subsidizing a search for something as unmarketable as knowledge. De Gerlache, however, was a determined man; he spent his winters in Norway experimenting with sledges, clothing and equipment, and his summers in the Low Countries campaigning for funds. And eventually, thanks largely to the patronage of a handful of scientific societies, his scheme got off the ground – albeit on a modest scale, since it was decided the expedition should consist of only one small vessel and nineteen men.

The vessel selected was a far-from-new Norwegian sealer, which de Gerlache re-christened the *Belgica*: a tough little battering ram of a ship, devoid of beauty or comfort but eminently suitable for work in the ice. She was sheathed in both greenheart and Swedish iron, her stern was 5 feet thick, her boiler gave her a speed of 7 knots, and her bow was angled up (like the runners of a sledge) so that she could ride over the ice. 'In a cosmopolitan harbour', wrote the expedition's doctor, Frederick Cook, 'she looked like a bull-dog amid a group of greyhounds – small, awkward and ungraceful. But she was to prove a craft of extraordinary endurance, withstanding the thumps of rocks and icebergs and the pressure of the pack-ice in a manner perfectly marvellous.'

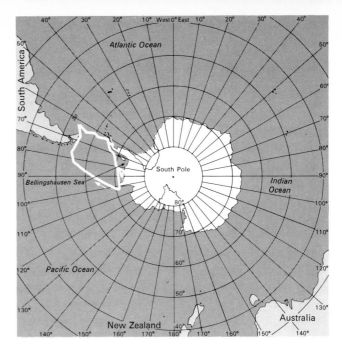

Map of de Gerlache's route

Her crew was cosmopolitan. Her captain, her first lieutenant, her engineer and five of her seamen were Belgian; the first mate and the other four seamen were Norwegian, the geologist and the meteorologist were Russian, the naturalist was Rumanian and the doctor American. Among them were men soon to become famous – Roald Amundsen (the mate) first to reach the South Pole, and Frederick Cook (the doctor) who claimed to be first to reach the North Pole; and several of the others were to achieve distinction in their particular fields – the meteorologist, Henryk Arctowski, for example, who was a pioneer in the study of Antarctica's climate.

The *Belgica* sailed from Ostend on 24 August 1897. It was five months before she entered the Antarctic, and de Gerlache has sometimes been criticized for spending an inordinate time in the region of Tierra del Fuego engaged in work 'of little importance'. This is unjustified. For de Gerlache's research among the Fuegian tribes, the Onas and Yaghans, sheds valuable light on the way of life of a race who were on the threshold of extinction even as he observed them. 'This noble band of human strugglers', he writes 'have endured for centuries the most testing climate in the world; but they now appear to be doomed, for the sheep farmers are taking over their land.' Prophetic words. For the Onas and Yaghans were indeed, in less than half a century, to succumb to the guns, greed and infectious diseases of the white man. De Gerlache's report and Cook's photographs provide a valuable commentary on this little-known tragedy.

It was January 1898 before de Gerlache stood south from Cape Horn, his objective being to survey the sea bed between Tierra del Fuego and the Antarctic peninsula. He was lucky. The weather that summer was uncharacteristically benign, and soundings and sea-bed samples were taken across the whole width of this previously unfathomed sea.

On 20 January the *Belgica* dropped anchor off the South Shetland Islands.

The night which followed [wrote Cook] was overcast. The sea rolled under our stern in huge inky mountains, while the wind scraped the deck with an icy edge. The sudden fall of the temperature and the stinging, penetrating character of the wind seemed to warn us that ice was near; but we encountered none. . . . It was a night of uncertainty, anticipation, and discomfort.

These three words epitomize the lot of Antarctic expeditions in general and that of the *Belgica* in particular.

Pushing south from the South Shetland Islands, de Gerlache entered Hughes Bay, where, nearly eighty years previously, Davis had made his historic landing. He discovered that the terrain which was known in those days as Palmer's Land consisted in fact of an archipelago divided from the mainland by a strait (Gerlache Strait), down which the *Belgica* now proceeded to sail. This was a geographical discovery of some importance; but more important still was the fact that no fewer than nineteen landings were made on the continent itself, and that these landings were carried out by scientists intent on collecting data and specimens. For the first time in history men were probing not only Antarctica's extent but also its content.

Cook gives a graphic, if unscientific, description of the first of these forays ashore.

January 23rd . . . a boat was lowered and we piled into it eagerly. It was a curious evening. Everything about us had an other-world appearance. The scenery, the light, the clouds, the atmosphere, the curious luminous grey of the water – everything wore an air of mystery. There was nothing in our surroundings which resembled any part of the antipodes or any part of the Arctic. . . . We landed in a small bight, on a ledge of rocks. I think Arctowski, with his hammer and geological bag, was the first to step ashore, followed by Racovitza. . . . The latter was soon turning up the stones along the shore where he found mysterious crawling things which he hailed with as much delight as if he had found nuggets of gold. [These were the wingless flies *Belgica antarctica*, about 2·5 mm in length and black in colour; and the oribatid mites *Podonominae* and *Paruchlus steineni*, about 5 mm in length and light brown in colour: to all intents and purposes Antarctica's only form of indigenous landlife.] The temperature [Cook-adds] was close to freezing, but the air was calm and dry. When engaged in rowing or climbing we took off our jackets; but even lightly dressed, we perspired.

Two or three such landings were made every day during the latter part of January; and towards the end of the month there took place a historic incident: for the first time in history men pitched a camp and spent the night on the mainland of Antarctica. In fact they spent six nights ashore, during which they endured all the hazards – wind and snow, crevasses and cold, humidity and fog – which even today make man's foothold on the continent no more than tenuous. Cook, once again, gives a good description of both locale and camp.

We disembarked at the foot of a prominent mountain [Cape Anna] whose face was perpendicular and free of snow to the shore. Here was life in profusion. The noise from the birds was so deafening that our attempts at conversation were inaudible. The lower rocks were lined with sea leopards. Columns of vapour rose from the water followed by a hiss like that of a steam-engine, and a second later the blue back of a whale, with long fin and ponderous tail, lashed the water into a foamy whirlpool. Above us rose a cliff to an altitude of about 2,000 feet, out of which projected shelf after shelf of rocks, which served as resting places for cormorants and sea-gulls. But our greatest surprise was the discovery of large quantities of moss and lichens, which made the spot a true oasis.

From this point we were able to see almost the entire length of the channel we had explored. We had not as yet, however, been able to make a running survey of the hinterland, and to get a better view of this, it was decided to ascend into the interior and scale one of the noonataks [icy hillocks]. In our preparations for this ascent we arranged to camp on the inland ice for a week. . . . Volunteers were called for, and those who responded were Arctowski, Danco, Amundsen and myself. Led by de Gerlache we landed on the afternoon of [January] 31st on a little point of land with a northern or sunny face. We climbed the steep slopes for about 500 feet, then camped for the night. But our first night was one of stormy discomfort. A wind came out of the bed of the glacier above us, against which we could hardly stand. It took two men to hold up the tent, and the combined efforts of all hands to keep our effects from being blown over the cliffs only a few yards away. On 1st of February we made another effort and struggled a few hundred yards into the interior, but fog and wind and crevasses made frequent halts necessary. The sledges were difficult to drag, and altogether the work of travelling and the discomfort of camping were such that life was miserable in the extreme. We succeeded, however, in climbing to the peak of a noonatak with an altitude of about 1,500 feet, and from here were able to make the necessary observations for a rough survey. . . . After a stay of seven days, the first camping experience in the history of south polar exploration, we gladly betook ourselves to our good old bark the *Belgica*.

It was clear that the new-found continent was going to prove by far the most difficult part of the world to explore. It had taken five men seven days to penetrate a bare mile into the interior. And at least one of these men, Roald Amundsen, must already have been doubting the good sense of trying to traverse such difficult country by man-hauled sledge.

On 12 February the *Belgica* emerged from the Gerlache Strait and nosed into the little-known approaches to Alexander Island. It was late in the year for exploration – most vessels by mid-February were heading hurriedly for home – but the weather was fine and de Gerlache continued to follow the coastline to the south, apparently unperturbed by the increasing number of icebergs. It must, to start with, have been an idyllic cruise, with an unknown and incredibly beautiful coastline unfolding peak by peak on their port bow. 'The scientists', wrote de Gerlache, 'are busily taking notes, and even the seamen are on deck with pencil and paper, drinking in the wonders of this new and mysterious land.' The Antarctic Circle was crossed on 15 February, and the next morning the *Belgica* met her first pack ice.

In the days that followed the ice thickened.

The events of the next fortnight are beyond dispute; it is how they are interpreted that varies. The fact is that de Gerlache held course to the south for so long that the *Belgica* became ensnared, gripped fast as a fly in amber by the consolidated pack. Was this through carelessness or by intent? The truth is, I think, that for reasons of national prestige de Gerlache was anxious to penetrate as far to the south as he could – certainly beyond Cook's 71° and if possible beyond Ross's 78°; the *Belgica* was proving unexpectedly ice-worthy, 'ploughing through the floes like something animate'; she was well stocked with fuel and food; and de Gerlache undoubtedly formed the opinion that if the worst came to the worst and the ice closed in behind her, she could survive. It was a calculated risk.

The *Belgica* therefore continued to fight her way through thickening ice floes deep into the Antarctic. Cook describes a typical day.

> February 22nd. . . . Navigation, to say the least, is difficult. We go ahead, squeezing through breaks in the ice until our path is barred by a floe; then we go astern to give the ship room for a new onslaught. In this way we batter and ram the ice until it seems as though every timber must break; but except for the bruising and scraping of her sides the *Belgica* receives no hurt. She . . . goes on cutting through great pans of ice five feet thick, and pushing aside floes 200 feet in diameter.

A couple of days later she ran into a storm.

> February 25th. . . . I cannot imagine a scene more despairing than the *Belgica* as she pushes into the pack this tempestuous night. The noise is maddening. Every swell that drives against the ship brings with it tons of ice, which is thrown against her ribs with a thunderous crash. . . . The ship keeps up a constant scream of complaint as she strikes piece after piece of ice. Occasionally we try to talk; but the noise of the storm, the straining of the ship, and the thumping of the ice makes speech inaudible.

The gale lasted twenty-four hours. It broke up the ice; and at dawn on 26 February long open leads stretched temptingly towards the southern horizon. Against the advice of his officers, de Gerlache stood into them.

During the course of the next few days the *Belgica* managed to penetrate a farther 90 miles to the south. Then the inevitable happened. The ice closed in behind her. And thickened. And she was trapped. The brief, matter-of-fact entry in Cook's diary gives no indication of how her crew must have felt.

> We now realize that farther progress is out of the question. The ice is too closely packed; the floes are heavier, and it is no longer possible to break them or push them aside. Indeed we are so closely hugged that movement in any direction is impossible. To the south several lakes are visible from the crow's nest, and to the northwest there are also spaces of open water; but after several efforts we found ourselves unable to reach them. . . . We are therefore forced to admit our inability to extricate ourselves. . . . Our position is latitude 71° 22′, longitude 84° 55′ – about 300 miles inside the Antarctic Circle and 1,100 miles from the geographical pole.

Here, on the rim of the world, the *Belgica* was to remain for 347 days!

There was nothing new in the concept of an expedition allowing itself to be frozen in for the polar winter, surviving as it were in limbo, and returning to the known world in the spring. This was a technique first used by Eric the Red in the tenth century during his discovery of Greenland, and subsequently perfected by Parry during his search for a North West Passage. Its practice, however, had been confined up to now to the Arctic. De Gerlache and his crew must therefore be. regarded as pioneers, the first men in history to face the physical and mental ordeal of the Antarctic winter – a far sterner test of endurance than previous explorers had undergone in the north.

They seem to have had surprisingly little idea of what they were in for. A couple of days after they had become frozen in, de Gerlache made a revealing entry in his diary: 'We had been led to believe', he wrote, 'that the temperature compared with the Arctic, would be moderate': an entry which demonstrates very clearly the total unpreparedness of his ship's company. They had no intimation of Antarctica's cold, of the strength of her wind or the humidity of her atmosphere; nor had they, it seems, the slightest premonition of the injurious effects, both mental and physical, of the long Antarctic night – seventy days of total darkness without a glimpse of the sun.

The first few months of their incarceration, however, proved more uncomfortable than hazardous. The crew had plenty to keep them occupied. They surrounded the *Belgica* with a wall of snowblocks; they built a covered passageway between her cabin and laboratory, they double-barred every window and door, they experimented with ventilation and heating, and they built a miniature observatory on the ice. This work was carried out in an atmosphere of depressing humidity – huge, moisture-laden snowflakes scything without respite out of a slate-grey sky. It was impossible to keep anything dry: clothes, equipment and bunks, all were beaded with moisture or veneered with ice. 'If only', de Gerlache lamented, 'we could be quit of this infernal humidity which plagues us like an agent of Satan!' But the snow fell month after month. The temperature continued to fall. And the nights lengthened.

To start with, it was the ship which gave them most cause for anxiety; for she had, to quote Cook, 'become like a football of fate: kicked, pushed, squeezed and ushered this way and that at the mercy of the pack'. The pack was never still: 5,000,000 square miles of restless ice, anything from an inch to twelve feet in thickness, drifting first one way then another under the influence of current and wind. If the *Belgica* had been carried onto a submerged reef, a line of bergs, or the shore of the continent, she would have been squeezed to matchwood. As it was, even in the open sea, she had difficulty in surviving the pressure of the ice. In Cook's diary for 16 March we read.

> The wind increased to a gale with snow, and continued fiercely all day. At 4 o'clock we noticed by the squeaking of the ice that a swell was rolling under us. We did not

feel its effects for several hours. Then, at about 7 o'clock, the ice suddenly cracked all about us, and was forced together with a pressure which aroused considerable fears for the safety of the *Belgica*. Huge hummocks rose up on every side, floes were forced over each other, and against the sides of the vessel. The paint was scraped off her, fragments of wood were gouged out of her, and she was thrown over on a floe where she lay enduring the thumps and the pressure with cracks and groans. But the good ship fought her battle bravely. At about 8 o'clock the pressure eased, the ice separated into small open leads and the *Belgica* settled back into the water on an even keel. . . .

As winter set in, the ice became more stable; and by mid-May de Gerlache must have felt reasonably sure that his ship would survive. He could not, however, have had the same confidence in his crew. For as the sun disappeared, and day and night coalesced into a single cold, humid and depressing twilight, his men began to suffer from anaemia, paranoia and a host of disorders and delusions which would have been the delight of a psychiatrist. De Gerlache was a sensible and reasonably efficient leader, but he lacked the inspiration needed to jerk his crew out of their depression. Cook was a sound doctor, but he lacked sufficient stability in his own character to be the ideal father-confessor to eighteen difficult patients who were suffering from a disease beyond the compass of textbook treatment. So the *Belgica* that winter had a supernumerary: the spectre of insanity and death.

The factors that contributed most to the mental and physical deterioration which towards the end of May began to affect de Gerlache's ship's company were cold, wind, humidity, isolation and darkness.

Cold was perhaps the least of their problems. It is true that during their year of incarceration the mean monthly temperature never rose above zero and was in some instances well below $-20°$; it is true too that this was colder than they had expected and colder by far than would have been experienced in a similar latitude in the Arctic. But the *Belgica* was well weatherproofed; she had plenty of fuel for her boiler and her crew had plenty of warm clothing. The cold, therefore, was more inconvenient than dangerous. Cook tells us that the scientists' fingers were frequently frostbitten, so that taking observations was difficult, and that a seaman who was hammering together a packing case and who carelessly put a nail in his mouth 'quickly snatched it out, bringing with it parts of his tongue and lower lip, and leaving ugly wounds such as might have been made by a red hot iron'. These mishaps, however, were hardly the fabric of madness. And as the meteorologist, Henryk Arctowski, says without ambiguity 'cold by itself was not a cause of serious suffering'.

Wind was a different matter. The winds of the Bellingshausen Sea are not nearly as strong as those in many other parts of the Antarctic – the coast of Terre Adélie for example. Nonetheless the *Belgica* had to endure blizzards of considerable ferocity, and the average wind strength throughout the year was well over 20 knots. It was Arctowski who first advanced the theory – now known to be true – that wind is as injurious to human health as cold, and that a combination of the two is liable to be lethal. 'We found', he wrote, 'that wind is an extremely important factor from the physiological point of view. In calm weather a temperature of −20°C is quite tolerable, even agreeable if the sun is shining; but with a light breeze one feels the cold at once, and in a strong wind it is impossible to remain in the open air at such a temperature.' The wind, that winter, was strong a great deal of the time.

Humidity is only a problem in the coastal regions of Antarctica, and even here, according to Arctowski, 'it plays a comparatively minor role in the physiology of the climate'. On the purely physical plane this may be so; but on the mental plane, prolonged and excessive dampness is a depressant. The meteorological records tell us that during the *Belgica*'s year in the ice, it was foggy on 255 days, that it snowed or sleeted on 271 days, and was overcast on 282 days. It is hardly surprising that several of de Gerlache's ship's company found this continual and excessive dampness the hardest of the crosses they had to bear: witness Cook's diary.

> April 11th. If I were to sum up in two words what causes us the greatest amount of suffering, I would say humidity and isolation. We try in every possible way, in the cut of our garments, in the construction of our winter quarters, in the arrangement of our bunks, to eliminate moisture, but our success is small. If we put our hands behind our beds we dislodge a great weight of frost; if a mattress is removed every nail is found to be covered with ice. . . . April 12th − Snow is falling in huge flakes. It is warm, dull and gloomy, making the air on board unendurable. Everything about the decks and the bulkheads is moist, and the hoar frost . . . is now melting making everything uncomfortably wet.

The effects of isolation are difficult to assess. The *Belgica* that winter was cut off from everyday life as effectively as if she had landed on another planet; there was not the remotest possibility of escape from the ice or of contact with the outside world; her crew were therefore thrown entirely on their own resources. In the wardroom one man was slowly dying, in the fo'c's'le two were being driven slowly mad; the prospect was hardly roseate. Cook canvassed each member of the crew personally to find out his complaints and longings. Among the officers the most ardent wishes, he discovered, were for news from home and for feminine company; among the men the most common wants were fresh food and sun, 'although two or three shyly admitted in tears that a few moments with the girl of their hearts would have been to their liking'. To start with, the improving of their quarters and the novelty of their scientific observations helped to occupy their minds; but as darkness closed in, no more improvements were possible, the collecting of data became routine drudgery, and time began to weigh on their hands. 'We long', Cook wrote, 'for some new fuel to prevent the fire of life from being snuffed out.' But there was no break in the monotony of the Antarctic night: only the everlasting wind, the unremitting snow, and the seemingly eternal darkness − 1,614 hours with never a glimpse of the sun.

It was the darkness which affected them most. During the first few days of May

Henryk Arctowski

the sun had appeared briefly above the horizon, like a faintly glowing lump of charcoal which can barely retain heat let alone give it out. On 17 May it disappeared altogether. It was not to be seen again for sixty-eight days. To quote the official summary of the *Belgica*:

> Gradually the members of the expedition became affected, body and soul, with languor. Each man continued to do his duty, but did it painfully. Polar anaemia preyed on them all. In some the pulse rate rose to 150 per minute, in others it sank to 47. The lack of fresh food began to make itself felt, and by mid-winter de Gerlache, Melaerts and Michotte were all showing symptoms of scurvy. One seaman had fits of hysteria which bereft him of reason. Another, witnessing the pressure of the ice, went mad with terror. On June 5th Lieutenant Danco died of heart disease. . . . The root cause of these disasters was the lack of sun.

This judgment is confirmed by Cook.

> During the months of winter darkness the life-giving rays of the sun are withdrawn, leaving the earth in despondent blackness. Bright artificial lights relieve this to some extent; but all animal organism is left in a condition similar to that of a planet deprived of direct sunlight. The skin grows pale, muscles grow weak, and the organs are unable to function with their usual vigour. This effect is most noticeable in the action of the heart, which, during the long night, is deprived of its regulating force, and becomes now quick, now slow, but never normal. The best substitute for the sun is direct rays of heat from an open fire. . . . I have stripped and placed men whose pulse was almost imperceptible in this sort of heat, and in less than an hour their heart action has returned to normal.

It was, in fact, largely due to Cook's heat treatment and to his insistence that the crew ate fresh seal and penguin meat, that they were still alive when, on 22 July, the sun once again appeared 'like a small withered orange' above the horizon.

The return of the sun marked the rebirth of vigour and hope. The *Belgica*, it is true, was still held fast by the ice; but as the days lengthened the crew's energy slowly returned, sledge parties set out to explore the surrounding terrain, and experiments were started with tonite to try to blast a path through the pack.

Neither sledging nor blasting met with success. The former was organized by Amundsen, who was forever experimenting with new types of clothing, transport and tent; it was as though, consciously or subconsciously, he was preparing himself for his epic journey thirteen years later to the Pole. Indeed it was probably during these abortive, man-hauled sledging journeys from the *Belgica* that Amundsen reached the decision that was to separate him so radically from Scott – that the best, indeed the only, form of Antarctic transport was the dog. As for the blasting, organized by Cook, this proved a disappointment. To quote the official report: 'In an effort to break the icefield in which the ship lay locked, heavy charges of tonite were exploded; but the ice was barely broached let alone breached. A hundred-weight of tonite made virtually no impression; it merely scooped out a shallow hollow, about 30 feet in radius.'

This was regarded at first as no more than a temporary check. But as spring gave way to summer and summer to autumn, and the *Belgica* still remained shackled to the ice her crew began to view with despair the prospect of a second incarceration throughout the Antarctic winter.

It was Cook and Racovitza who saved them.

> We have [wrote Cook], decided that if we do not help ourselves there is every possibility of our having to winter again in the pack. We therefore submitted a plan to the Commandant which involved cutting a canal through the ice, roughly a mile and a half in length. . . . This work was begun on January 11th and continued night and day until February 14th. . . . First we removed the upper sheets of ice and snow to the depth of about two feet. This left solid ice from 3 to 4 feet to be cut by saws. We kept at it day after day. No men ever worked harder or more faithfully.

They suffered many vicissitudes – the pack shifting and temporarily closing their canal, young ice forming as soon as they cut away the old, and the *Belgica* coming within an ace of being squeezed to destruction by a pressure ridge – but in mid-February they at last broke out of the floe that had so nearly become their tomb. They were not yet wholly free of the ice, and for nearly a fortnight were trapped off the edge of the pack; but eventually on 28 March 1899 the *Belgica*, battered but safe, steamed into Punta Arenas, having spent thirteen months inside the Antarctic Circle, during twelve of which she had been frozen solid in the pack.

De Gerlache and his crew were pathfinders: first of a long and distinguished line of explorers, men such as Nordenskjöld and Borchgrevink, Amundsen and Scott, Shackleton and Fuchs, who were to spend the long Antarctic night huddled in hut, igloo or tent, ready at the onset of spring to fight their way into the interior. This ability to survive the winter was a *sine qua non* of the continent's exploration by conventional methods; for the distances involved were so great and the exploring season so short that the hinterland could not be opened up unless this was done from a base that had already been established on the rim of the continent. That such a base could be established and lived in de Gerlache and his ship's company were the first to prove.

The *Belgica* was also the first ship to penetrate deep into the Antarctic with the express intention of making scientific observations. The data she brought back was valuable in itself; but perhaps even more valuable was the establishing of a tradition still in vogue today – the tradition of men going to the Antarctic to acquire knowledge and on their return making this knowledge available, freely and openly, to all. There is something heartening in this: that whereas the fruits of other continents were invariably fought over, the fruits of Antarctica should be shared.

Finally, we are left with a problem. The *Belgica* survived her winter in the ice far better than her crew, of whom one died and two were driven mad; and it must have seemed to contemporaries that the strain of the long Antarctic winter might be more than flesh and blood could endure. We know now that this is not so: that man *is* able to winter in even the most desolate corner of the earth and survive; but we can not even today be sure of the cost. . . . Much of this reconstruction of the *Belgica*'s voyage has been taken from Dr Cook's diary. His narrative strikes one as sensible and well balanced, and no one has ever cast doubts on its veracity. Cook was highly thought of by his companions – witness Amundsen: 'His behaviour won the respect, indeed the admiration, of all. He was the most popular man of the expedition. . . . Upright, honourable, capable and conscientious in the extreme – such is our recollection of Frederick Cook.' This was in 1898. Yet a decade later Cook was to be universally condemned as 'one of the greatest humbugs the world has ever known', a Munchausen among explorers, the man who claimed to have beaten Peary to the North Pole when in fact he never went near it. How did the honourable and conscientious doctor of 1898 become the charlatan of 1908? There would seem to be three possibilities: that Amundsen and the crew of the *Belgica* were wrong in their estimate of the doctor's character, that Cook did in fact reach the North Pole and is a much-maligned character, or that he suffered a personality change. The third is the only possibility that makes sense. The question is why? It is I think more than possible that the strain, hardship, isolation and lack of sun that winter aboard the *Belgica* had a malign affect on his personality: that he became, to use Amundsen's phrase, 'a psychological enigma'. If we accept this, it seems that returning explorers may sometimes have the same difficulty in adjusting to everyday life as returning prisoners of war. Little is known about the psychological effects of prolonged hardship and isolation. If ever a book is written on this subject one of its most interesting – and tragic – case histories will be that of Frederick Cook.

## CHAPTER 8

## PROBING THE HINTERLAND

DE GERLACHE AND HIS SHIP'S COMPANY were the last men to explore Antarctica by sea. The new century ushered in an era of exploration by land.

The most experienced seamen in the eighteenth and nineteenth centuries had undoubtedly been the British; and it is not by chance that the most successful voyages in this period – those of Cook and Ross – were made under the White Ensign. The British, however, had comparatively little experience of travelling in polar conditions by land; this was the forte of the Swedes, Norwegians and Finns; and it is not by chance that in the coming century the most successful land journeys – those of Nordenskjöld and Amundsen – were made under Scandinavian flags. Indeed the early twentieth century has been aptly described by L. P. Kirwan as the period of Scandinavian ascendancy.

Nordenskjöld's expedition, like de Gerlache's, had its roots in the International Geographical Congress of 1895. It had been decided at this Congress to launch a triple assault on Antarctica; and after several years of fund raising and preparing, three expeditions duly set sail: Scott in the *Discovery* to explore the region south of the Pacific, Drygalski in the *Gauss* to explore south of the Indian Ocean, and Nordenskjöld in the *Antarctic* to explore the area south of Tierra del Fuego. All were successful; but it was the Swedes under Nordenskjöld who spent the longest time in Antarctica, who suffered the greatest hardship and who brought back the greatest wealth of scientific material.

The *Antarctic* left Gothenburg on 16 October 1901. She was a stoutly built ex-sealer, veteran of several previous expeditions to both the Arctic and Antarctic. Her commander was Otto Nordenskjöld, an eminent 32-year-old geologist; her second-in-command was the experienced Carl Larsen, and her crew numbered twenty-nine, including a doctor, a botanist, a painter, a meteorologist, a hydro-grapher and a lieutenant from the Argentine Navy who was a specialist in both astronomy and magnetism.

The expedition arrived off the South Shetlands in January 1902 and spent several days exploring the west coast of the Antarctic peninsula in the hope of discovering a passage through to the Weddell Sea. When it was found that no such passage existed, Nordenskjöld retraced his steps, sailed between Joinville Island and the tip of the peninsula and began to explore its east coast. No great geographical discoveries were made, for on 19 January the ship was brought up short at the 66th parallel by solid ice. On the other hand a start was made on the sort of scientific observation that was, in its fashion, every bit as rewarding as the glimpse of an unknown shore. Off the coast of Paulet Island samples were taken from the sea bed at 75 and

(above) Members of the Swedish South Polar Expedition on their departure from Gothenburg: (standing left to right) Bodman, Skottsberg, K. A. Andersson; (sitting left to right) Ohlin, Nordenskjöld, Larsen, Ekelöf
(left) Bodman working at the dining table. On the wall the barograph, evaporimeter, the registering apparatus of the anemometer and the paper of the sunshine recorder
(below) 'We were, on the whole, well satisfied with our dwelling-house.'

150 metres, and each time the trawl came up it was found to be 'almost literally filled with a wonderfully rich mass of living organisms. . . . It was not only the number of specimens which amazed us', wrote Nordenskjöld, 'but their variety, size and peculiar appearance'. This was man's first intimation that the waters of Antarctica were to prove the richest on earth.

On 12 February, Nordenskjöld and five companions were put ashore on Snow Hill Island, off the east coast of the peninsula. Here they planned to spend the winter, while the *Antarctic* undertook research in the Drake Passage before returning to pick them up the following spring. Supplies and a prefabricated house were landed, and the six men were left, 'entirely to their own devices, the first settlers on a coastline as desolate as any on earth'.

Their first job was to erect the house and observatory which had been shipped in sections from Sweden. They found a good site, on level rock, about 100 yards from the water's edge, protected on one side by an ice wall and on the other side by an almost vertical cliff. They were lucky with the weather, and by 18 February the house was virtually complete. Here is Nordenskjöld's description of it:

> Its length was 21 feet, its width 13½ feet. It had double walls of ¾″ boards with an air-space in between, and a single roof. Both walls and roof were coated with tarred paste-board. The floor was double, and it too was lined with paste-board, and covered first with felt then with linoleum. The entrance was through a porch, which prevented snow and wind being driven in each time the door was opened. The loft, which occupied the whole of the upper part of the house was used as a storeroom; it was bitterly cold in the loft, but doubtless it helped to keep the lower floor insulated. On ground level were five so-called rooms, all diminutive; the largest of them was situated in the middle of the house and occupied its whole width, while on either side lay two smaller rooms, one of which served as the kitchen and the other three as bedrooms.

The house was well designed and strongly built; and this was as well, since the day after it was erected it was struck by the first of the storms which, during the next six months, were to rage with almost non-stop violence over the Antarctic peninsula.

'Ugh!' wrote Nordenskjöld, 'such *summer* weather! It blew a hurricane such as we had by the hundred afterwards, but were ill prepared for on this first occasion. The wind was a steady 55–60 m.p.h., the thermometer hovered round − 10° C, and the air was a thick swirling mass of driven snow against which we could scarcely stand.' The half-built observatory collapsed, a litter of puppies froze to death, a whaleboat was carried away.

Many times in the months to come Nordenskjöld's diary records a similar combination of wind, snow and cold:

> February 26th. For three days the wind has never dropped below 40 knots and has gusted to well over 70; the temperature has been a steady − 11° C, and the snow so heavy there is no chance of venturing outside. . . . May 28th. Another day of

cold, high wind and snow. At night the din is almost more than one can bear: the paste-board and ropes beating against the walls, and the whole house trembling and shaking. Nor is it better outside, where one can't see a dozen paces and all one is conscious of is the storm as it thrashes against ground and walls, clothes and face. And where on earth does all the powder snow come from? It sweeps over the ground in a never ending tide and is surely one of the most important phenomena of the Antarctic, although hardly anything, as yet, is known about it. . . . One of us compared our house in time of storm to the carriage of an express train, and the comparison is apt – the shaking which is so severe that the water in a basin trembles as though there were an earthquake . . . the wind howling and booming through every crevice, the door which each time it is opened lets in a cloud of condensed vapour – it all reminds one of a ramshackle carriage hurtling at top speed along an ill-constructed track.

At last, however, the winter storms subsided, the days lengthened and grew warmer, and it became possible to venture out of doors. In September Nordenskjöld began to prepare for a sledge journey to the south.

It would be idle to pretend that the trek which followed added a great deal to cartographical knowledge. It did, on the other hand, prove that men were able – albeit with the utmost difficulty – to journey considerable distances across the continent and survive; it also provided a valuable test for different techniques of polar travel. For at the same time as Nordenskjöld was striking inland from Snow Hill, Scott, on the opposite side of the continent, was striking inland from McMurdo Sound. It is interesting to compare their attitude to their dogs.

Our four-footed comrades [wrote Nordenskjöld] were lively and interested in everything that went on. It was as though they sensed the importance of the work they were about to embark on. Indeed they set off at such a pace that we had to run to keep up with them. . . . The dog-drawn sledge weighed 485 lbs, the man-drawn sledge 200 lbs, and I was amazed to find that the five dogs could pull their sledge quite easily, whereas the three men were hard put to get theirs on the move. The dogs in fact appeared to find it quite difficult to go as slowly as we did!

Scott's experiences were very different, as Kirwan points out:

Then began a period of intensive training. . . . Skiing, sledging, the handling . . . of dogs, all this had to be learnt from the beginning [for the] British sailors . . . were the rawest of recruits by comparison with the Scandinavians used from childhood to speeding swiftly over the snows. But control over the dogs was their greatest problem. At the merest touch of their inexperienced hands, it seemed, an apparently docile dog team would be transformed into a welter of snarling animals and tangled harness. . . . Man-hauling in the old traditional style soon appeared not only more reliable but infinitely preferable to these refractory beasts.

In this alienation of dog from man there were, for the British, the seeds of tragedy.

As for Nordenskjöld's journey, the facts speak for themselves. There were two sledges, three men, five dogs and 685 lb of equipment and food. In thirty-three days they covered 400 miles. In good weather and good snow they sometimes made 30 miles a day. In storm – and it was stormy on three days out of five – they lay huddled anxiously in their tent 'listening to the nerve-racking howl of the wind, knowing that our provisions are being used up, and realizing that our dogs and ourselves are growing weaker day by day'. By the time they got back, their feet, hands and lips were swollen and raw, their hair had turned white, they were suffering from frostbite, snow-blindness and insomnia, and each man had lost more than 14 lb in weight.

The unveiling of Antarctica, it was plain, was going to be no task for the faint-hearted.

By the time the sledge party was back on Snow Hill Island it was summer. Birds were nesting; penguins were crowding onto the shore, and the crew were running a sweepstake as to what day the *Antarctic* would reappear to take them home. The sea ice, it is true, had not yet disintegrated; but no one doubted that leads would eventually open up along which the vessel would force her way through to them. They spent the summer in scientific observation and research. It was Nordenskjöld himself who made what was perhaps their most interesting discovery. On the morning of 3 December he found the fossil of a land vertebrate of the Cretaceous period; and this made him think that some 100,000,000 years ago Antarctica must either have been joined to another continent or have enjoyed a more temperate climate. That very afternoon his speculation was confirmed. In a valley running up from the north coast he came across, to quote his own words, 'a number of brown, tuff-like rocks in which I found what I had for so long sought: several large, quite distinct, and well-preserved leaves belonging to exogenous trees'. These were subsequently identified as belonging to the *Sequoia*, *Araucaria* and *Fagus* genera: evidence which, again to quote Nordenskjöld, 'proved beyond doubt that during some period of the earth's development, Antarctica was not the icy wilderness it is today, but a land of luxuriant vegetation harbouring many forms of life'.

It was fortunate for the expedition that they were engrossed in work and buoyed up by discovery, for as December gave way to January and January to February the ice showed not the slightest indication of breaking up. Instead, on 18 February, it started to thicken, and it soon became all too obvious that the *Antarctic* would not be able to get through to them. Short of food and none too robust in health, they faced the prospect of spending a second winter on the peninsula.

This winter was to prove even more testing than the first, with winds of 75 to 80 knots, and the temperature, week after week, at under $-30°$ C. Their main problems were what to eat, how to keep warm and how to combat the depression which is almost an inevitable consequence of the long months of near perpetual darkness.

If it had not been for the seals and penguins they would have died of starvation. They killed thirty of the former and more than 400 of the latter. 'It would be difficult', wrote Nordenskjöld, 'to imagine a more unpleasant task. The killing of animals in large numbers is always a repulsive business, and especially so in Antarctica where the creatures have no fear of man and we had come to think of them as our friends. I often longed that autumn for the return of the *Antarctic*, but never more ardently than during this massacre of the innocents.' It was, however, a case of kill or be killed; for their weekly menu shows how dependent they were on this indigenous supply of meat.

Monday
*Breakfast:* porridge; herrings and potatoes; coffee
*Dinner:* breast of penguin and dried vegetables; pancakes and jam; coffee
*Supper:* pastry and cold penguin; tea

Tuesday
*Breakfast:* seal steak and dried greens; coffee
*Dinner:* tinned soup; *blodpudding* or sausage; coffee
*Supper:* reheated seal steak; cocoa

Wednesday
*Breakfast:* porridge; coffee
*Dinner:* fruit soup; salted penguin and beans; coffee
*Supper:* cold penguin; tea

Thursday
*Breakfast:* seal steak; coffee
*Dinner:* pea soup, salted penguin; pancakes and jam; coffee
*Supper:* reheated seal steak; cocoa

Friday
*Breakfast:* porridge; coffee
*Dinner:* salt soup; penguin and macaroni or rice; coffee
*Supper:* pastry and cold penguin; tea

Saturday
*Breakfast:* seal steak; coffee
*Dinner:* chocolate soup; dried fish and vegetables; coffee
*Supper:* pastry and cold penguin; cocoa

Sunday
*Breakfast:* lobscouse of kohl-rabi; coffee
*Dinner:* tinned soup; preserved meat and vegetables; fruit; coffee
*Supper:* sardines and cold penguin; tea

Keeping warm was less of a problem. To quote Nordenskjöld:

We had a fair amount of coal left, but in fact used little of it, since we found it preferable to burn the bodies of the seals. We threw both skins and blubber into the stove; surprisingly they gave off little smell and a great deal of heat, and indeed it was warmer indoors during the second winter than the first. . . . Our greatest bugbear was damp. Vapour became condensed on the walls, which each morning were covered in glittering arrases of snow and ice. These melted during the day, and soaked into the paste-board, so that everything became sticky and sodden. Papers turned to mould, and clothes and bedding became covered in mildew. A pea which had found its way into my blankets began to grow there. It had thrown out roots and a long stalk with embryo leaves – the latter a pale anaemic yellow since they had never known the sun.

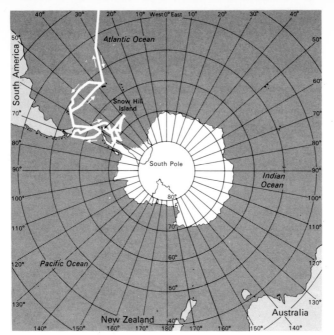

It says much for the common sense and strength of character of Nordenskjöld's ship's company that they survived these trying conditions with none of the mental aberrations that had afflicted the crew of the *Belgica*. This was due in part to the sensible frame of mind in which they approached their incarceration: 'When I told the men that we would have to spend a second winter in the Antarctic', writes Nordenskjöld, 'no one complained and no one showed any fear; but from that moment no one spoke again of the possibility of relief. When we talked of the future, it was always about how we should best employ ourselves during the long hours of darkness. . . .' They employed themselves principally in work. Nearly half the men marooned that winter on Snow Hill Island were scientists, and the observations they made were not only valuable in themselves, they were also valuable because the making of them took men's minds off their loneliness and discomfort. Spring found them in good heart and tolerable health; and since it would obviously be several months before relief got through to them, Nordenskjöld planned a second sledge journey, this time to the north.

He set out with a single companion – Ole Jonassen – and within a week there took place the first of the expedition's chance encounters which, had they featured in a work of fiction, would have been dismissed as too fantastic to be believed.

The morning of 12 October dawned much like any other morning: a high wind, a low temperature, and banks of mist dispersing gradually under the influence of the sun. Nordenskjöld and Jonassen were sledging quietly down the coast of Vega Island, when the latter stopped and pointed: 'What's that? Down by the shore?'

Nordenskjöld also stopped: 'It *looks* like a couple of men. But of course it can't be. They must be penguins.'

They sledged on. Then Jonassen came to a halt again: 'Have a look through your glasses.'

Nordenskjöld focused his binoculars. And as the figures came blurredly into focus, he found himself trembling. For without doubt they were men. The sledge was headed towards them. The figures waved in excitement.

> And what is this [Nordenskjöld wrote] that at last I saw before me? Two men, black as soot from head to toe: black clothes, black faces, black caps, their eyes hidden by black wooden frames. Never before have I seen such barbarous creatures. I am asking myself to what primitive sub-species they can belong, when one of them holds out his hand: 'You don't recognize us, do you! I'm Duse, and this is Gunnar Andersson. From the *Antarctic*.'

The story of Duse, Andersson and their companion Grunden – who was cooking a meal on the far side of an ice ridge and was picked up a few minutes later – is both an epic of survival and an affirmation of the indomitable spirit of man.

After the *Antarctic* had put Nordenskjöld and his five companions ashore on Snow Hill Island, she headed north. In Bransfield Strait she was hit by a blizzard, and came within a hairsbreadth first of foundering, then of being driven ashore; eventually, however, she managed to struggle into the Drake Passage, and after coaling at Ushuaia and calling at Port Stanley for supplies, she spent the winter in valuable but unspectacular research work off the coast of South Georgia. In November 1902 she again stood south for the Antarctic, intending first to survey the Orléans Channel; then, as soon as the ice receded, to pick up Nordenskjöld and his companions. She succeeded in surveying the Orléans Channel, the work being completed by 5 December, but when she tried to push round the tip of the peninsula towards Snow Hill Island, she was brought up short by a solid conglomeration of ice. Her captain, Carl Larsen, attempted to force the ice; and after a couple of days of ramming and battering, he succeeded in gaining an open lead which ran promisingly to the southeast. The lead, however, was to prove a chimera. It petered out. And the *Antarctic* found herself trapped. The diary of her doctor, Gunnar Andersson, describes her predicament:

> December 9th – Our prospects of reaching the winter station by sea don't appear very bright. We have therefore begun to consider the possibility of reaching Snow Hill Island by land.
> December 10th – In the morning we made a little ground to the east, but found we had drifted into a bay. We were therefore obliged to return to the northwest. Much thick pressure-ice.
> December 11th–18th – We are now held fast in the grip of the ice, being carried steadily northeast: farther and farther from our goal.
> December 19th – We are now off the coast of Joinville Island. And if any on board still doubted the necessity of a land journey, their doubts vanished at the sight of the great sea of impenetrable pack-ice which was seen to be covering Erebus and Terror Gulf.

They spent Christmas day in the pack: a Yuletide of dazzling sun, intense cold, and an atmosphere so clear that they could see Mount Haddington nearly 180 miles to the south – a peak which, they knew, was within easy sledging distance of Nordenskjöld's camp. A few days later they forced their way ashore onto Paulet Island; and the following morning three men set out by sledge: their objective, to trek the 200 odd miles across the ice to Snow Hill Island and to bring back Nordenskjöld and his party to where the *Antarctic* was waiting. The men were Andersson, Duse and Grunden: a doctor, a lieutenant in the Swedish army and a seaman; and their names deserve to be writ large in the roll of polar explorers. They left a small cache of food on Paulet Island, loaded the sledge with sleeping bags, a tent and food for twenty-five days, and set off into the unknown.

To start with all went well; but on the second day they made an unexpected and most unwelcome discovery. To quote Andersson:

On climbing to the top of an ice-shed we found our way barred by a broad sound: a mixture of sea-ice, islands and open water. The ice was in wretched condition, covered with slush and fresh-water ponds. . . . For five days we ploughed through the slush, our equipment, our clothes and our bodies getting wetter and wetter. At last, on reaching land, we discovered we were on an island, and still separated from our goal by Sidney Herbert Sound. This was in even worse condition than the sound we had just crossed. . . . And realizing we had not the slightest hope of crossing it, we reluctantly abandoned our attempt to reach Nordenskjöld and returned to Paulet Island. We arrived back on January 13th.

There was no sign of the *Antarctic*. This did not, at first, disconcert them, since it had been agreed that the vessel should continue to try and force her way through to Snow Hill Island, and that if she succeeded she would return with Nordenskjöld, and that if she failed she would return without him. The three men therefore settled down beside their somewhat meagre cache of food to wait. To start with they saw no reason for anxiety; but as January gave way to February and February to March and still the *Antarctic* failed to appear, they began to fear for her safety – and for their own. March 10 was the last date by which the vessel had undertaken to return; and when this passed without incident, Andersson and his companions realized they were faced with the prospect of having to winter, with no shelter and a quite inadequate supply of food, on the tip of the Antarctic peninsula. It was a prospect that would have daunted less resourceful and well-adjusted characters; but the three Swedes accepted their lot with a disarming nonchalance. 'When it became clear', Andersson wrote, 'that the ship would not return, we built ourselves a stone hut. Since our food was inadequate, we killed about 100 penguins to supply us with fresh meat. Since we had little fuel, we burned seal blubber. And the winter passed un-eventfully and without accident. . . .' There was, however, considerably more to their story than this masterpiece of understatement might lead one to suppose. For never before and seldom since have men so inadequately equipped lived through the long Antarctic night.

Their hut consisted of heavy blocks of stone, plastered together with gravel and snow, with the sledge built into the roof, a double floor, a dog-legged entrance, a snow cellar for the meat and a recess for the lavatory, all crowded into an area less than 7 feet square. Their food was inadequate and monotonous; about their greatest luxury was porridge, which they enjoyed twice a week, 'looking forward to it as though it were caviar'. And although they burned a great quantity of seal blubber, the average temperature that winter inside their hut was $-14°$ C at the roof and $-20°$ C on the floor. On the purely physical level their survival was little short of a miracle.

On the mental level, it would hardly have been surprising had they gone mad. In fact they not only kept their sanity, they remained on remarkably good terms both with themselves and with each other. This was partly because they were well-balanced characters, and partly because they made a conscious effort both to keep themselves mentally occupied and to observe little civilities – such as the punctilious use of the traditional Swedish formula in which those who have enjoyed a meal thank the person who prepared it. Andersson paints an evocative (if somewhat roseate) picture of life in the hut.

> Evening is the most pleasant time of the day. Before the cook creeps into his sleeping bag, he hangs up the lamp for the night. . . . This is the best time for chatting, and we take it in turn to entertain each other. One evening, for example, Duse would explain how a cannon works; another evening I would recount episodes from one of my favourite stories – *The Count of Monte Cristo* or *The Three Musketeers*. In this way the time slips by, surprisingly quickly. . . . It is true that on one or two occasions we had disagreements and harsh words were spoken. But reconciliation was always swift and sincere. And out of our ordeal that winter we managed to wring one of life's greatest treasures: the knowledge that with the gift of companionship man can triumph over the most extreme adversity.

As winter gave way to spring the danger from cold receded, but the discomfort from dampness increased. As Andersson puts it:

> During the winter storms, our hut was a secure refuge which we praised with grateful words. But when the thaw set in, we cursed it for an ill-made hell-hole; for both walls and roof had been plastered with snow, and the milder temperature caused this 'plaster' to melt, so that we became deluged with water. On several occasions we were drenched to the skin, the water lay inches deep on the floor, and it needed no little courage to crawl into our cold and sodden sleeping bags.

When we remember that the three men had no spare clothes into which they could change, were so short of food and fuel that they dare not heat so much as an extra mug of coffee to warm themselves, and that they spent more than three months snowed up in this cell-like hovel without once seeing the light of day, we begin to appreciate the scale of their suffering – and of their fortitude.

In September, however, they were able to dig themselves out, and to think of the future. Realizing they could not count on the *Antarctic* (or any other vessel) returning to pick them up, they decided that their only hope of survival lay in trying once again to trek south to Snow Hill Island. They therefore made what preparations they could, assembled their sledge and the last of their food, and at the end of September set off across the ice.

Behind them they left the traditional message in a bottle, and a plaque on which Duse with his penknife cut the inscription:

J. G. ANDERSSON, S. DUSE, T. GRUNDEN
from S.S. *Antarctic*
wintered here 11/3–28/9 1903.

Matter-of-fact words that describe a saga.

They had a difficult journey. On the second day they were hit by a violent storm, their tent collapsed and they were forced to lie in their sleeping bags literally frozen into the ice for thirty hours; they suffered from snow-blindness, frostbite and malnutrition; indeed if they had not succeeded in shooting a pair of seals they might never have survived. It says much for their dedication that throughout this taxing journey they continued their scientific work, Duse piecing together a map and Andersson and Grunden collecting geological specimens. After a fortnight of sledging they were barely halfway to Snow Hill Island and were a great deal weaker than when they set out. But the next day, off a headland they aptly named Cape Well Met, by a million-to-one coincidence, their path crossed that of Nordenskjöld and Jonassen. A week later they were back in the expedition's winter quarters which, after their hut on Paulet Island, must have seemed a veritable palace.

Dramatic events now followed one another in rapid succession. On the morning of 8 November the masts of a vessel appeared over the rim of the pack ice, and a couple of hours later men were seen approaching the house. No one doubted that the vessel would be the *Antarctic* and that the men would be led by Larsen. In fact, however, the ship turned out to be the *Uruguay*, commanded by Captain Irizar of the Argentine Navy; for realizing that Nordenskjöld and his men must be in difficulty, a relief expedition had been mounted from South America.

Nordenskjöld's thankfulness at being rescued was tempered by his anxiety for the *Antarctic*, which he had not seen for more than eighteen months and which appeared to have vanished off the face of the earth. It was agreed, however, that the men on Snow Hill Island should be lifted off in the *Uruguay*, and that evening they began to crate up their specimens and possessions. Within twenty-four hours the house would have been deserted. . . . It was quite late that evening, a little after 10 p.m., when the dogs began a discordant howling. Most people were either asleep or too busy to bother with them; one man, however, Gösta Bodman, went to the door and shouted at them to be quiet. As he looked out he saw, to his amazement, another group of men skiing towards the house. His first thought was that Captain Irizar must have ordered some of the *Uruguay*'s crew to join them. Not till the strangers had almost reached him did his excited shout bring his companions tumbling out of their bunks. 'Larsen! It's Larsen. And the crew of the *Antarctic.*'

After she had dropped Andersson, Duse and Grunden on the shore of Paulet Island, the *Antarctic* continued her efforts to push south. Her botanist, Carl Skottsberg, takes up the story:

> January 1st [1903]. Imprisoned again! We are being carried helplessly this way and that in the ice, now stern first, now broadside on; sometimes squeezing between the enormous flat-topped bergs, sometimes drifting over hidden reefs. It is miraculous that the ship has not been more seriously damaged. Larsen orders us all to sleep with our clothes on. . . . January 4th. A lead has opened up, so that once again we can use the engines. Our captain hopes that we shall now be able to make direct for Snow Hill Island; but, alas, by late evening we are again hemmed in by ice. . . . January 10th: a violent snow-storm, with wind screaming through the rigging, and the whole ship – decks, masts and funnels – coated with a veneer of ice. Late in the evening the pressure begins to build up, the vessel trembles like a leaf, and a violent crash has us all rushing on deck. The scene is terrifying. The *Antarctic* is being lifted bodily up, stern first. . . . Late that night comes another and still more violent crash, as though the hull is caving in. Again we rush on deck. The pumps are manned, and after an anxious hour comes the message 'the vessel is holed, but pumps are keeping the water down'.

It was, however, the beginning of the end. For almost a month the unfortunate vessel endured the squeezing and buffeting of the ice, unable to advance towards Snow Hill or to return to Paulet. Her pumps, both steam and hand, were in action round the clock; but a whole section of her hull had been ripped away, leaving a wound which no human ingenuity could heal; and inevitably there came a time when the water level began to rise. On 12 February Larsen gave the inevitable order: 'Stand by to abandon ship.'

Skottsberg describes her last moments:

> Huddled together on the edge of an ice floe, we couldn't take our eyes off her as she settled deeper and deeper in the water. Her engines were turning over, for although her fires had been dowsed there was still a sufficient head of steam in the pipes to revolve her screws. Her pumps were working too; but as the water rose the sound of them became more and more muffled. . . . She sank lower and lower, on a perfectly even keel. Now the name on her stern disappears from sight. Now the water is up to her rail, and the sea and the ice swirl in with a rattle across her decks – I shall remember that sound as long as I live. Now the blue and yellow of her flag is swallowed up by the sea. Her mizzen strikes the edge of a floe and is snapped off; her crow's nest disappears, now her pennant, now the very tip of her main-mast. And she is gone!

The *Antarctic* sank in Erebus and Terror Gulf, about 25 miles from land. For a fortnight her crew hauled their sledges and boats towards the distant coast, man-handling them from floe to floe, encompassed by blizzard and mist, compelled to drift sometimes towards their goal and sometimes away from it. At last, on 28

February, they struggled ashore. 'Who', wrote Skottsberg, 'can describe our feelings as the boats grounded? What joy in finding, once again, solid earth under our feet!' Their troubles, however, were far from over. For they were marooned on a shore of the utmost desolation. And it would soon be winter.

They built themselves a stone house, 34 by 22 feet with walls three and a half feet thick and six feet high. They killed some 1,100 penguins, and settled down to endure, as best they could, the onslaught of winter. 'The cold', wrote Skottsberg, 'becomes more and more terrible, paralysing the will to work or even to think. All our energies are concentrated on the one objective: survival.' And survive they did, all except the unfortunate Ole Wennersgård who, after an illness borne with great fortitude, died in midwinter of consumption. With the return of the sun, Larsen prepared to sledge south to Snow Hill Island.

The coming of spring marked the end of one crisis. But others remained; and without doubt throughout almost the whole of 1903 Nordenskjöld's expedition was in real jeopardy. It had become split into three widely separated fragments, none of which could contact the others or knew where they were, and none of which could have lived through another winter. One doubts if a bookmaker would have given odds on their survival. Yet within a month, thanks to a series of almost un-believable coincidences, the members of the expedition were reunited and on their way home.

They were lucky – if Nordenskjöld's track had not, by a million-to-one chance, coincided with Andersson's, the latter might never have reached Snow Hill; if the *Antarctic* had sunk a few miles further to seaward, her crew might never have reached the shore; if Larsen and the crew of the *Antarctic* had arrived twenty-four hours later on Snow Hill Island, they would have found Nordenskjöld and the relief ship gone. All this, it is true, adds up to a cornucopia of good fortune. But it is also true that the Swedes deserved their luck. There is a saying that God helps those who help themselves, and Nordenskjöld and his ship's company did exactly this; never once were they found lacking in fortitude or resource. Perhaps their most remarkable attribute, however, was their dedication to their work. On the trek to Snow Hill, for example, the partially snow-blinded Duse continued to work on his survey, and when the crew of the *Antarctic* abandoned ship they left behind them clothes, food and personal treasures, and loaded the whaleboat with scientific specimens and reports.

They arrived back in Sweden in January 1904, after an absence of nearly two and a half years. They had proved two things: that Antarctica was, to use Nordenskjöld's words, 'a vast refrigerated storehouse of knowledge', and that human beings *could*, albeit at appalling hazard, both survive in and traverse the continent.

Man's nature being what it is, his next move was predictable: that he should set his sights on the most desolate and inaccessible part of this continent, the Pole.

(left) Sastrugi on Barne Glacier,
by H. G. Ponting, 21 February
1911
(below) Young ice forming, by
H. G. Ponting, 7 March 1911

## CHAPTER 9

## THE RACE FOR THE POLE

ON 14 DECEMBER 1911 five men and seventeen dogs stood where no living creatures had stood before: at the South Pole. To preclude any chance of their navigation being at fault, their leader, Roald Amundsen, decided to make sure they had indeed reached their objective by circling the spot at a radius of some dozen miles. His men had already trekked 18 miles that day; but when one of them (Olav Bjaaland) said 'Let's do the encircling right away', the others agreed, and they set off at once, 'neither dogs nor men in the least exhausted, and the sledges fairly skimming over the snow'.

On the same day, about 400 miles to the north, another five men were having a very different sort of journey. 'A most damnably dismal day,' wrote their leader, Robert Falcon Scott. 'The pulling terribly bad, the sledges plunging into soft snow and stopping dead. We made desperate efforts to get under way, but became ever more and more bogged down. . . . We have advanced a bare four miles today. Outlook not hopeful.'

Why, one wonders, should Amundsen's journey to the Pole read like a summer idyll and Scott's like the road to Calvary? The answer lies in the fundamentally different method by which they travelled – the former with his sledges hauled by dogs, the latter by men. And if one asks why two seasoned campaigners should have put their trust in such diametrically opposed techniques, the answer lies in their different character, background and experience.

Roald Amundsen was born in 1872 in the district of Borge in southeastern Norway. When he was fifteen he was given the works of Sir John Franklin; and these, to quote his autobiography, 'thrilled me as nothing I had ever read before. What appealed to me most was the sufferings that Sir John and his men had to endure. A strange ambition burned within me, to endure the same privations. . . . I decided to be an explorer.' Having pinpointed his goal, the young Amundsen set about achieving it with a singlemindedness that was to be the hallmark of his career. He slept in midwinter with his bedroom window open, 'as part of a toughening process'; disliking football, he nonetheless played it 'in order to train my body to endure hardship'; he undertook military service 'gladly, because of the opportunity it provided to strengthen my physique'; he skied in a blizzard across a range of mountains which had never previously been crossed, nearly dying of exposure and exhaustion *en route*. By the time he was twenty-two, knowing himself to be well equipped for exploring by land, he decided to gain experience at sea and signed on as a deckhand aboard an Arctic

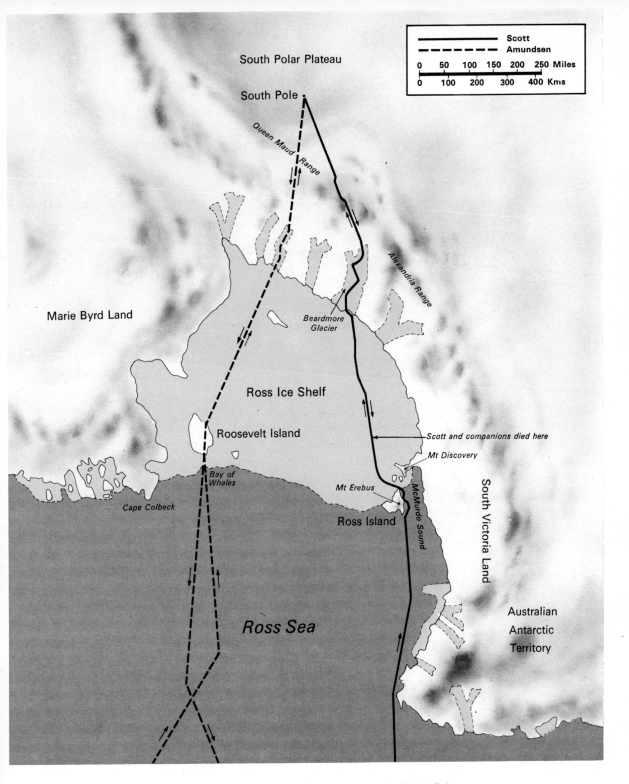

South Polar Plateau

South Pole

Queen Maud Range

Alexandria Range

Marie Byrd Land

Beardmore Glacier

Ross Ice Shelf

Roosevelt Island

Scott and companions died here

Mt Discovery

Bay of Whales

Mt Erebus

Ross Island

McMurdo Sound

South Victoria Land

Cape Colbeck

*Ross Sea*

Australian Antarctic Territory

Scott
Amundsen

| 0 | 50 | 100 | 150 | 200 | 250 Miles |
| 0 | 100 | 200 | 300 | 400 Kms |

Map showing Amundsen's and Scott's routes to the South Pole

whaler. In the words of his biographer, Bellamy Partridge, 'he proved so diligent and industrious that he quickly worked himself up to the position of mate; he also studied late into the night in order to sit for his master's certificate'. In 1897 he took the first step in his chosen career, serving as de Gerlache's mate aboard the *Belgica* – an initiation to polar conditions which would have daunted a less resolute character.

The voyage of the *Belgica* provided Amundsen with valuable experience; it also brought out one of the more attractive traits in his character. For it was during this expedition that he formed, with Dr Frederick Cook, a friendship which neither the years nor the latter's misfortunes was in any way to diminish. Amundsen was not a man who made friends easily; but the friendships he did make were both deep and lasting.

No sooner was he back from the Belgian expedition than he began to plan one of his own: his objective the navigation of the North West Passage, a quest which many had set out on but none had completed. He received little official support. To quote his own words, 'though I tapped every possible source of funds, both learned societies and private patrons, the money was not forthcoming, and there were times when despair almost overcame me.' Eventually, to escape his creditors, he clambered aboard his vessel, the *Gjøa*, by night and slipped away in the middle of a rainstorm! If he had failed in his quest for the Passage it would have been the end of his career. But he did not – the word failure had no place in his vocabulary – and thanks to his sensible preparations and efficient leadership, the *Gjøa* became the first vessel in history to follow the coast of North

(opposite left) Captain Robert Falcon Scott, leader of the 1901–4 expedition to Antarctica, aboard the frozen-in and snowed-up *Discovery* in McMurdo Sound. The ship broke free from the ice and sailed for home on 16 February 1904.
(opposite right) Scott just before leaving for the South Pole, by H. G. Ponting, 26 January 1911
(right) Roald Amundsen

America from ocean to ocean. Returning in triumph, Amundsen was able both to repay his creditors and to begin preparations for what was the great ambition of his life: to lead the first expedition to set foot on the North Pole. He bought a suitable vessel (Nansen's *Fram*), and refitted her. He then got together a first-class team of scientists, several first-class packs of dogs, and provisions and equipment for three years, every item in his manifest being meticulously selected and tested. He was about to sail on the first leg of his journey, to the Bering Strait, when his expedition received what was apparently a death blow – the news that Admiral Peary of the U.S. Navy had succeeded in struggling through to the Pole. Most explorers in Amundsen's position would have thrown in their hand. The Norwegian, however, was not the man to admit defeat. He sailed as though nothing had happened; then, while reprovisioning at Madeira, announced a dramatic change of plan. He had, he told his assembled ship's company, decided on a new objective: his expedition was now heading not for the North Pole but for the South!

The decision was typical of the man: forthright and unequivocal. It was typical too of his attitude towards exploration: an attitude epitomized in the quotation which he used to preface his book *The South Pole* – 'Success is a woman who has to be won, not courted. You've got to seize her and carry her off, not stand under her window with a mandolin.' Amundsen's liking for this quotation tells us a good deal about him. He was a man who knew exactly where he was going and who believed in getting there by the shortest possible route – and woe betide anyone who stood in his way! Baulked by Peary at the North Pole, he had no intention of being baulked by anyone at the South. A number of historians (most of them British) have seen fit to castigate him for what they describe as his unduly competitive attitude in switching his assault from the North Pole to the South. It is hard to see the logic of this. For the redoubts of the world are not the prerogative of any particular nation, but an open prize to be won by anyone with the requisite courage and expertise. Also it is worth remembering that Amundsen had the courtesy to inform Scott (whom he knew was also heading for Antarctica) of his change of plan.

Robert Falcon Scott, the other explorer who that year had his sights set on the Pole, was a very different character from Amundsen. Born near Devonport in 1868, he was a naval officer first and an explorer second. Indeed he only became associated with exploration through the whim of that formidable figure Sir Clements Markham, president of the Royal Geographical Society. The latter explains how this came about:

> When I was on board the *Active* in the West Indies . . . the lieutenants got up a service cutter race. The boats were to be at anchor with awnings spread. They were to get under way and make sail, beat up to windward for a mile, round a buoy, down mast and sail, pull down to the starting point, anchor and spread awning again. The race tried several qualities. For a long time it was a close thing between two midshipmen, Robert Falcon Scott and Hyde Parker. However, Scott won . . . and on the 5th he dined with us. He was then eighteen, and I was much struck with his intelligence, information, and the charm of his manner.

Scott indeed was Markham's beau ideal: a gifted and conscientious naval officer, whose character had been shaped by the disciplines and traditions of a Service to which he was dedicated with an almost religious fervour. Twelve years after the episode aboard the *Active*, the two men met again in London. Markham offered his protégé command of the *Discovery*, which was about to sail for Antarctica; and Scott accepted.

One is left with a slight feeling of bewilderment. Without wishing in any way to denigrate Markham or to belittle Scott, it may be wondered if prowess in a whaleboat race was the best possible qualification for leading a scientific team to the mainland of Antarctica.

Be that as it may, the *Discovery* expedition of 1901–4 was in fact outstandingly successful and Scott and his men were able to carry out the first extensive exploration by land of the Antarctic continent. A winter base was established in McMurdo Sound, sledging parties managed to penetrate a considerable distance both along the coast and into the interior, and a great deal of useful and very meticulous research was carried out. These achievements seem particularly commendable when one bears in mind that Scott and his ship's company were working in an alien element; that is to say they were seamen without a ship, and little they had learned in their professional training and nothing they had

In order to free the *Discovery* from her ice prison in 1904, successful blasting operations were carried out.

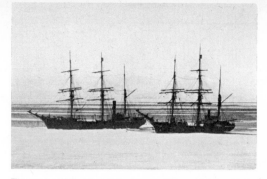

The two relief ships *Morning* and *Terra Nova* which were not needed when *Discovery* broke out of the ice

experienced in their private lives was a great deal of help to them when it came to exploring the mainland of Antarctica. In particular – and in contrast to the Norwegians – they were clumsy on skis and inept with sledge dogs. The latter failing was to have tragic repercussions. For it was the inability of the *Discovery* expedition to get the best out of its dogs which turned Scott against them as sledge haulers. Yet the dog-hauled sledge was the form of transport which offered by far the best chance of success in making a dash for the Pole.

On his return to England Scott resumed the more conventional duties of a commander at the Admiralty. There is, however, a saying that those who have been to Antarctica once always return, and his diary confirms that he had hopes one day of being offered another expedition. These aspirations were given a sense of urgency by Shackleton's *tour de force*, when the latter in 1909, in one of the greatest journeys ever made, ascended the Beardmore glacier and fought his way to within 97 miles of the Pole. Two paths now lay open to Scott: either he could command another *Discovery*-type scientific expedition, or he could lead an assault on the Pole. The tragedy was that in an effort to combine these two objectives he fell short of both. He was, it should be said in his defence, in a difficult position; for he had in effect three patrons – the Royal Navy, the Royal Geographical Society and the British public, all with a stake in his forthcoming expedition and all expecting different things of it. A more selfish character would have given his allegiance to one patron and lip service to the others. It is Scott's tragedy that in an effort to be sweetly reasonable and to please everyone he became burdened with a cumbersome, overweight expedition, part scientific and part exploratory, with diverse and indeed divergent aims.

By the summer of 1910 both Amundsen and Scott were on their way south. Their destination, however, was about the only thing they had in common.

Aboard the *Fram* were a compact close-knit team: nineteen men and ninety-seven dogs. They had one objective, to be first at the Pole. Their watchword was 'dogs first and last' (they even constructed a false deck so that the animals could, in the tropics, be kept cool and in first-class condition). And their leader had a simple, clear-cut and eminently practical plan.

Aboard the *Terra Nova* were sixty-five men, thirty-three dogs, nineteen ponies,

Emperor penguins (*Aptenodytes forsteri*), by Edward Wilson

(left) Evening in Amundsen's winter quarters: (left to right) Bjaaland, Hassel, Wisting, Helmer Hanssen, Amundsen, Johansen, Prestrud and Stubberud
(opposite left) Amundsen's ship the *Fram*
(opposite right) Members of Amundsen's team with dogs and sledges

three motor sledges and a plethora of scientific equipment. Their leader had 'no confidence in dogs', and his plans embraced not only a dash for the Pole but a full programme of scientific research together with a number of major journeys both along the coast and into the interior.

The end of each expedition was writ plain in its beginning.

Amundsen sighted the coast of Antarctica early in January 1911. For several days he ran parallel to Ross's Ice Barrier in search of somewhere to land, and on 13 January he found what he was looking for. In the centre of the Bay of Whales the Barrier was seen to consist of gentle slopes of snow no more than 20 feet high; landing would be easy, and the ice looked relatively stable. Here, Amundsen decided, would be the site for Framheim, his winter quarters.

Amundsen's winter quarters had several advantages over Scott's – which the latter was concurrently setting up some 450 miles to the west-northwest. It was nearer the Pole, it commanded a better route to the Pole, and it enjoyed better weather. It has sometimes been implied that Amundsen was lucky to find such a site; the truth is that he was skilful. Here is his account of how the position came to be chosen:

> The ice barrier is in fact the lip of a gigantic glacier which presses down from the heights of the Antarctic plateau to the sea. This glacier is hundreds of miles in width and between 100 and 200 feet in height. Like all glaciers, at its lower end it is constantly breaking away into icebergs; and the idea of setting up a camp on the edge of such a barrier had always been dismissed as too dangerous. I had, however, carefully pondered over the works of previous explorers, and been greatly struck by the fact that the shore of the Bay of Whales had not changed in outline since it was first discovered by Ross in 1842. 'Surely', I said to myself, 'if this part of the glacier has not moved for sixty-eight years, it can be for only one reason: that the ice must here be wedged firmly against the rock of an island'. The more I thought of this explanation, the more I became convinced of its truth; and I therefore had no fear as to the stability of our camp at Framheim. This faith was to prove entirely justified. We made use that winter of the most delicate instruments to make recordings, and there was never the slightest movement in the ice.

Amundsen's choice of a winter base has been looked at in some detail because it demonstrates very clearly his chief characteristics as an explorer. First, his common sense: he picked a site as close as possible to his goal – what a difference it would have made to Scott if he had, on his return journey, had 60 less miles to travel! Second, the painstaking research on which his decision was based – if he had not studied the problem of where to winter with care and in depth, he would never have realized the built-in safety potential of the Bay of Whales. Third, his willingness to take a calculated risk: Framheim was undoubtedly built on floating ice and *could*, with fatal consequences, have broken away and drifted into the Ross Sea. All of which adds up to the fact that Amundsen was preeminently shrewd: a man who was not afraid to gamble, but who invariably knew the odds.

The exact site of their hut was selected with care: a cwm, about two miles from the sea, between vast but stable pressure ridges, 'a spot which looked not only sheltered and cosy but above all safe'. The building itself measured 26 by 13 feet; it was high-gabled and had double 3-inch walls, insulated with cellulose pulp and coated with tar. It took a fortnight to erect. And a few days after it was completed Amundsen had visitors. Late on the night of 4 February, Scott's *Terra Nova* came nosing unexpectedly into the Bay of Whales.

The events of the next twenty-four hours do much to disprove the myth of a bitter personal antipathy between Amundsen and Scott. For visits were exchanged between ship and shore; the British offered to take home the Norwegians' mail, and the Norwegians invited the British to winter at Framheim and offered them half their dogs. 'One can not help liking them', writes an officer from the *Terra Nova*. 'And they are going out of their way not to get information from us which might be useful to them.' It is, however, Amundsen himself who deserves the last word on the subject of rivalry:

Scott was a splendid man, and nobody could hold a higher admiration than myself for his courage. . . . But just as in time of war while the soldiers of opposing armies often have a high regard for their foes in uniform and the non-combatants at home feel obliged to indulge in hymns of hate, so in exploration whereas the men in the field usually hold their competitors in high esteem the stay-at-homes frequently feel obliged to belittle the success of an explorer if he is not of their own nationality.

Amundsen, it is sad to relate, was writing from personal experience; for neither during his life nor since his death have English-speaking historians given him the credit he deserves, and even today a high percentage of British schoolchildren still believe that Scott was the first man to reach the Pole.

Before his winter hut was erected and long before the arrival of the *Terra Nova*, Amundsen had begun to lay food depots along the route he would take the following spring. During February and March he managed to lay three such depots. At 80° S (about 100 miles from Framheim) he left two tons of supplies; at 81° S (about 160 miles from Framheim) he left one and a half tons; and at 82° S (about 230 miles from Framheim) he left half a ton. This depot laying was one of the reasons for Amundsen's success. And it is indicative of what was to come the following spring that Scott, in the same period, managed to lay only one small depot and that pathetically close to his winter base.

It has been suggested that whereas the Norwegians concentrated all their energies that autumn on depot laying, the British dissipated theirs in scientific research, subsidiary journeys and experiments with different types of transport. There is some truth in this. There was, however, a more fundamental reason for the disparity in their achievement: their attitude to dogs.

Amundsen made use of his dogs for depot laying because he believed – quite rightly – that they were the best possible form of polar transport. In his book *The South Pole* he reiterates and enlarges on this:

> The great difference between Scott's expedition and mine lay in our choice of draught animals. Scott had come to the conclusion that Manchurian ponies and motor sledges would be superior to dogs as a means of transport. I don't suppose I was the only one to be amazed at this! For it seemed to me that conditions on the Antarctic ice-cap were precisely what one would desire for sledging with dogs. There must, I told myself, be a basic misunderstanding in the British attitude. Perhaps the dog didn't comprehend its master – or was it that the master didn't comprehend his dog?

Another reason for Amundsen's faith in dogs was that he saw them not only as draught animals, but also as a source of food. In his autobiography he wrote:

> Since there are 50 lbs of edible meat in the carcass of a husky, it was obvious that every dog we took south with us meant 50 lbs less food to be carried and cached. I worked out the precise day on which I intended to kill each dog as its usefulness for pulling supplies diminished and its usefulness as food increased. And this schedule was kept to, almost to the exact day.

Scott's views on dogs were altogether different. Firstly, he doubted their effectiveness: 'Bit by bit', he wrote on 12 March, 'I am losing all faith in them. I am afraid they will never go the pace we look for.' Secondly, he disliked using them on humanitarian grounds. His attitude is described by Markham: 'With regard to dogs, there were two ways of treating them: the idea of bringing them all back safe and well, and the idea of getting the greatest amount of work possible out of them and then using them as food. Scott had an unconquerable aversion to the employment of them in the second way.' As if to confirm this, Scott himself subsequently wrote, 'No journey made with dogs can approach the sublimity of a party of men who succeed by their own unaided efforts. Surely in this [latter] case the conquest is more nobly and splendidly won.' These sentiments do the greatest credit to Scott the man; to Scott the explorer they were a stumbling block which was to prove fatal.

Amundsen completed his depot laying early in April. He was only just in time, for the temperature was now dropping fast: $-33°$ F on 10 March, $-45°$ F on 17 March, and $-52°$ F on 3 April. A few weeks later the sun disappeared. 'For a couple of days it rested like a bright red ball on the horizon, surrounded by a sea of flame; then it vanished behind the pressure ridge to the north. We were not to see it again for four months.'

The Norwegians spent a spartan but trouble-free winter in their hut at Framheim. Their food was plain – 'I never thought it necessary', wrote Amundsen, 'to take a whole grocery shop with me' – but it was well balanced and contained plenty of fresh (seal) meat and antiscorbutic vegetables. Their environment was bleak; personal bric-à-brac was frowned on, and there was no more than a bunk and a stool for each man. As soon, however, as their hut was completely snowed under, they began to excavate an underground village in the snowdrift that piled up to leeward – a carpenter's shop, a smithy, a sewing room, a packing room and a steam bath, all connected by a series of passages under the snow. The winter was spent in rest and in preparation for their dash to the Pole. So anxious was Amundsen that everyone should be 100 per cent fit, both physically and mentally, for their coming journey, that he forbade the taking of meteorological readings by night, lest the men's sleep should be disturbed – a striking contrast to Scott's winter in McMurdo Sound, where an arduous programme of research, including sledge journeys along the coast, was sedulously adhered to. Another contrast between the two expeditions was that whereas Scott's winter hut was subdivided by packing crates into a wardroom (for the officers) and a mess deck (for the crew), life at Framheim was egalitarian. 'They seem', writes L. B. Quartermain, 'to have been a happy group. In the hut there was real camaraderie, no trace of class distinction, a wealth of invention, and much rough humour and hearty laughter, often led by Amundsen himself, who was a leader who could enjoy a joke, even if he were the butt of it.'

The return of the sun, on 24 August, found them in good health and high spirits, and, like their dogs, 'fairly bursting with energy and eager to be on their way'. They had a trial run between 8 and 15 September, during which they finalized their plans; then it was simply a question of waiting for suitable weather. By mid-October the temperature had steadied at about −15°, seals and sea birds were appearing in increasing numbers, and the sun had a touch of warmth. They set out on 19 October 1911, five men and fifty-two dogs. Their goal – one of the last great geographical sites on earth that man had not yet conquered – lay 870 miles to the south.

They travelled light. For they took with them only sufficient food to reach their first (80° S) depot. From there on they planned to live off the food they had cached the previous autumn. And their dogs.

The first half of their journey lay across the Ice Barrier. They made good progress; for the dogs were fresh and the sledges light. Most of the time the men allowed themselves to be towed on skis in the sledges' wake, and only when they came to difficult ground did one of them ski on ahead to blaze a trail. They averaged 25 miles a day – thereby utterly refuting Scott's contention that '[dogs] will never go the pace we look for'; and on the evening of 22 October they arrived at the first of their depots. Amundsen now made two decisions which indicate very clearly the effectiveness of his preparations. First, he decided to have a couple of days' rest 'because we are well ahead of schedule'; and second, he decided to leave three sledgeloads of food at the depot 'because we have no need of it and it might come in useful to someone'. The fact is that thanks to the excellence of his planning, Amundsen's journey from start to finish was to prove almost ridiculously easy.

They left their first depot on 25 October, and set themselves a target of 17 miles a day. This they kept to without difficulty – 'indeed we could', wrote Amundsen, 'have covered twice this distance had we been pushed'. They had in fact so much time on their hands that they stopped to build snow beacons every 5 or 6 miles along their route; these were 6 feet high and marked with flags, and embedded in each was a waterproof paper giving the course to steer in order to reach the beacon immediately to the north – a premium for their safe return.

On 6 November they left the last of the depots which had been established the year before. They were in virgin country now, and could see ahead of them the great semicircle of unknown mountains (Queen Maud Range) which mark the boundary between the Ross Ice Shelf and the central plateau. Here is Amundsen's account of the next few weeks:

> Our journey from 82° S to 83° S was a pure pleasure trip, with both weather and surface as favourable as one could wish. Everything went swimmingly. . . . On November 16th we approached a spot where the coastline intersected our route. To start with this presented little difficulty, the ice simply swelling up in a succession of ridges, some 300 feet in height, like waves approaching a shore. We established a depot here, then pressed on carrying food for sixty days. The terrain in front of us, which we had somehow to ascend, looked formidable in the extreme: a chain of steep glacier-clad mountains some 10,000 feet in height, with a further chain of almost 15,000 feet seen dimly to the southeast. . . . Next day we began the ascent.

The week that followed was the most arduous of their journey. For the climb turned out to be both steep and technically difficult: a succession of ice falls, glaciers and innocent-looking snow slopes which, on closer inspection, proved to be criss-crossed by a network of hidden and apparently bottomless crevasses. Amundsen makes light of their troubles. A careful reading of his diary, however, reveals some hair-raising facts. For most of the way the slope was so steep that the sledges had to be manhandled; three times men or dogs disappeared into gaping chasms and had to be hauled to safety; when they camped one night on a glacier there was so little level ground that their tents had to be pitched on one side of a crevasse and their tent pegs driven in on the other. No one has climbed in this area since Amundsen's day apart from Wally Herbert; and he, it is interesting to note, found the ice falls highly dangerous. 'Frankly', he writes, 'I didn't like them at all!' Yet the Norwegians took the ascent so much in their stride that halfway up they made a detour to climb Mount Betty (named after Amundsen's nurse), bringing back rocks of some interest and considerable beauty – granite rich in mica, schist crisscrossed with veins of quartz, and granite aplite dappled with small red garnets. Incredible as it sounds, it took them a bare five days to make the ascent from ice shelf to plateau: a climb of more than 60 miles and 8,500 feet. Then, in latitude 85° 36′ S, they came to more level ground. This was the site of their first depot on land: the site too of the most controversial episode of their expedition, the massacre of the dogs.

It had been agreed before they left Framheim that as soon as they reached the central plateau twenty-four of their forty-two dogs would have to be killed, in order to provide fresh meat for the remaining dogs and the men. There was sadness that night in the Norwegians' tent. It would be idle to pretend that Amundsen was as sensitive as Scott to the fate of his animals; on the other hand there is plenty of evidence that he viewed the killing of them with revulsion. He describes how, as the hour of the massacre approached, he pumped up the primus stove in his tent to high pressure hoping to generate sufficient noise to deaden the sound of the shots.

It was hard [he wrote], but it had to be. We had agreed to shrink from nothing in order to reach our goal. The pemmican was cooked remarkably quickly that evening and I was unusually industrious in stirring it. I am not a nervous man, but at the sound of the first shot I found myself trembling. Shot now followed shot in quick succession, echoing uncannily over the great white plain. Each time a trusty servant lost his life.

These are not the sentiments of a callous man, but of a man who had screwed himself up to make a cruel but necessary decision. For, as Amundsen knew very well, if he had not, that evening at 'The Butcher's Shop', killed half his dogs, neither he nor his companions nor for that matter the rest of his dogs would have survived.

The weather, as if in retribution, now took a turn for the worse. The wind freshened to a full gale, snow came scything out of the east, and great banks of fog-cum-cloud-cum-driven snow came swirling low over the glaciers. For a fortnight the Norwegians clawed their way forward, resting when the blizzards were at their worst, and pushing on in the clear spells in between. They were in difficult country – witness the names on their map: Hell's Gate, Satan's Glacier, The Devil's Ballroom – an area between mountains and plateau which Amundsen describes as 'a mosaic of sastrugi and crevasses'. The former (close-packed and sharp-edged snowdunes) made sledging arduous; the latter made it dangerous. Several times that fortnight both men and dogs disappeared through the upper snowcrust and found themselves dangling over narrow chasms the bottoms of which were out of sight. Once, when they had pitched their tent by a haycock and Hassel had knocked off its top to get ice for the cooker, 'a dark and bottomless well was uncovered. So that no more than a couple of feet from our front door, we had a handy way down to the cellar!' On another morning, men and dogs disappeared no fewer than seven times into crevasses: 'We could see no sign of them', writes Amundsen, 'but for several miles the ground we were traversing quaked like a jelly. It was obviously hollow; and we felt as if we were walking along the top of a row of empty barrels.' But at last, on the morning of 3 December, they emerged onto snow that was blessedly firm and level: the plateau itself.

From now on progress was rapid: a steady 20 to 25 miles a day, with the explorers so well up to schedule that they found time to stop every $2\frac{1}{2}$ miles to build a snow cairn. Here is Partridge's description:

> Travel became less and less difficult. It would indeed have been positively monotonous if they hadn't been drawing ever nearer to the Pole. . . . There was a quickening of pulses as, on December 8th, they passed Shackleton's Farthest South. . . . The vast plateau stretched in front of them in all its featureless whiteness, mile after mile. The whole world seemed to be nothing but length and breadth. No sound was heard but the scuffing of skis, the creaking of sledges and the scratching of the dogs' feet, with now and then the crack of a whip or a shout from one of the drivers.

They were now able to calculate the day, almost the hour, at which they would reach the Pole.

In the early afternoon of 14 December Hanssen, who was driving the lead sledge, shouted to Amundsen: 'Will you go on ahead?'

'What for?'

'The dogs run better with someone in front of them.'

In this way they ensured that their leader was first at the Pole.

They arrived a little after 3 p.m. There was no cheering and no speeches; but the Norwegian flag was unfurled with ceremony, each of the five explorers grasping the pole as it was thrust into the snow. It was a historic moment – the attainment by man of the *ne plus ultra* of exploration, as for the first time he stood on the loneliest and most inaccessible part of his planet – and it adds to rather than detracts from Amundsen's stature that seldom can so difficult an objective have been so easily achieved.

They spent three days at the Pole, sledging over a wide area to be certain they had

Auroral corona with two figures, by Edward Wilson
      (overleaf) Hut Point, McMurdo Sound, by Edward Wilson

Snowy Petrel.

*Pagodroma nivea.*

Ross Sea, South Victoria Land. 1910.

Amundsen at the South Pole

indeed set foot on it, erecting cairns and tents, and leaving messages for Scott –
'He will be here sooner or later', Amundsen said to Hanssen. 'I hope for his sake
it will be sooner!' Then, on the evening of 17 December, they started the journey
back to Framheim.

Bearing in mind the tragic events that overtook Scott on his return, we might
have expected the Norwegians to be in some difficulty if not danger. Far from it!
Their homeward trip was – if possible – even easier and speedier than their journey
out. Amundsen says simply: 'The return journey was made chiefly by night with
the sun behind us, in order to avoid the glare and the heat. The going was splendid.
We were in high spirits, and bowled along at a cracking pace.' They had no difficulty
finding the way, for their snow cairns and depot markers stood out clearly. Both wind
and sun were on their backs, and their daily target of $17\frac{1}{2}$ miles was usually covered
in less than five hours. Amundsen noted that the dogs, far from being overworked
and exhausted, looked sleek and well cared for: 'Indeed', he wrote, 'they are actually
putting on weight.' The same was true of the men, who had such prodigious appetites
that their rations were increased.

And so, one by one, the depots were reached and the supplies in them picked up
according to a schedule that Amundsen was meticulous in adhering to. There was
never the slightest danger of their falling behind this schedule; indeed on several
occasions they had deliberately to dawdle in order to keep to it. As for food, they had
so much that pemmican and biscuits were left behind, and chocolate was given to
the dogs. After a while, becoming bored with their $17\frac{1}{2}$ miles a day, they began to
sledge and sleep as the mood took them, sometimes traversing 20 miles at a stretch,
sometimes 25 and occasionally 30. They arrived back in Framheim, in perfect health,
on 25 January – the very day which Amundsen, two years earlier in Norway, had
earmarked as the ideal date for their return. A week later the expedition, in the
warmth and comfort of the *Fram*, was on its way home.

Amundsen had triumphed.

Snow petrel (*Pagodroma nivea*), by Edward Wilson

But Scott, some 500 miles to the south, was in trouble. On the very day the *Fram* stood northwards out of the Bay of Whales, the entry in the British explorer's diary holds a hint of the tragedy to come. 'Friday, February 2nd. Three out of five of us injured. We shall be lucky if we get through. . . . We are pretty hungry. . . . Our [sleeping] bags are wet, and we ought to have more sleep.'

How, one wonders, could things have gone so well for the one expedition and so badly for the other?

Scott sighted the coast of Antarctica on almost exactly the same day and at almost exactly the same spot as Amundsen; but whereas the latter had made for the Bay of Whales at the eastern extremity of the Ross Ice Barrier, Scott made for McMurdo Sound at the western extremity. This had been the site of his winter quarters, nine years earlier, in the *Discovery*. It was 60 miles farther from the Pole than Amundsen's, and being on land ice rather than sea ice it lay in the path of the cyclonic storms which follow the coast.

Scott's first concern was to land men, equipment and supplies: his second to erect his prefabricated hut. Unloading began on 4 January and was completed by the 13th – though not without incident, for their dogs were pursued by killer whales, and one of their motor sledges (of which Scott had great expectations) fell through the ice and was lost. The hut was assembled on a pleasant, well-sheltered site. They moved in on 17 January, and were 'quite overwhelmed with its comfort'.

> It was [Quartermain tells us] a large building, about fifty feet long and twenty-five feet wide, efficiently insulated with quilted seaweed, and well heated by two stoves. Scott was always the Naval Officer, and a bulkhead of food-cases stretching from wall to wall separated the officers' quarters from the men's. The latter occupied about one-third of the hut, and included the cook's galley. The interior was well lit by acetylene burners fed by a generator in the porch; and the building itself was protected from the expected blizzards by two annexes, the pony stables to the northwest and a provision store to the southeast. . . . There was a steward, and none of the officers or scientists had to bother with household chores or with washing up dishes.

This was luxury indeed compared with Amundsen's arrangements. One wonders, however, if the rigid segregation of the British into officers and other ranks might not have diminished the spirit of cameraderie which was so important an element in the success of the Norwegians. Scott maintained that his arrangements were to the satisfaction of both parties, and bearing in mind the conventions of his day and the Service background of most of his personnel, he was possibly right. One can, however, glean something of the atmosphere of these different expeditions by the nicknames the men gave their leaders: Scott was 'the Owner', Shackleton was 'the Boss', Amundsen was plain and simple Roald.

The events of the next month, like the prelude to a Greek tragedy, both presaged and predetermined what was to follow. For whereas Amundsen had had a single

(above left) Clissold the cook making bread, by H. G. Ponting, 26 March 1911
(above right) Captain Oates and some of his ponies, by H. G. Ponting
(centre left) Officers' living quarters: (left to right) Cherry-Garrard, Lieutenant Bowers, Captain Oates,
Meares and Dr Atkinson, by H. G. Ponting, 9 October 1911
(centre right) In the wardroom of the *Terra Nova*, by H. G. Ponting
(below left) H. G. Ponting lecturing on Japan, 16 October 1911
(below right) Dr Atkinson in his laboratory, by H. G. Ponting, 15 September 1911

(left) The *Terra Nova* trapped in the pack ice, by H. G. Ponting, 13 December 1910
(opposite left) Leopard seal (*Hydrurga leptonyx*), by Edward Wilson
(opposite right) Emperor penguins (*Aptenodytes forsteri*)

objective (depot laying) and had achieved it by a single method (sledging by dog), Scott found himself burdened with a variety of objectives which he sought to achieve in a multiplicity of ways. He divided his men into five groups: a depot-laying party that headed south, a geological-survey party that headed west, an exploratory party that headed for King Edward VII Land, a party aboard the *Terra Nova* that sailed for the Ice Barrier, and a party that stayed in McMurdo Sound to improve their winter quarters. This was a fatal dispersal of resources. And even more damaging was the fact that the different groups, uncertain as to the best form of transport, found themselves experimenting with motor-sledging, dog-hauling, pony-hauling and man-hauling. Almost inevitably, with such a diversity of tasks, Scott became bogged down with minutiae, unable to see the wood for the trees. Anxiety – and indecision – can be traced in his diary. 'The motor sledges are working well, but not very well.' (The fact was that they were a sad disappointment, but he did not like to admit it in case it should lower morale.) 'The dogs don't inspire confidence . . . I am losing all faith in them.' (The fact was that the British lacked the specialized knowledge to get the best out of their dogs; they had little idea of what to feed them on, or how to handle them.) 'The ponies are not turning out so well as I expected. I am not sure they are going to stand the cold.' (The fact was that the horses never came up to expectations, and bringing them to Antarctica was a serious error of judgment.)

As autumn gave way to winter it became increasingly obvious that the achievements of the British expedition were not commensurate with their efforts. No body of men ever worked harder, more selflessly or more harmoniously; but their motor sledges proved unworkable, their dogs proved intractable, and their ponies died; they succeeded in laying only a single small cache of food, and this was well short of the 80th parallel; and, what was worse, because of the failure of all other methods of transport, their leader became convinced in his mind that their only hope of reaching the Pole was by means of man-hauled sledge.

It is Scott's tragedy that his aims were unattainable by the methods he used.

The winter of 1911, however, passed pleasantly enough. Their hut was comfortable; the men were a contented team – 'there are no strained relations here,' writes Scott, 'and a universally amicable spirit is shown on all occasions'. Valuable research work was carried out. And it is worth noting that Scott took his scientific programme very seriously indeed: witness his dictum, 'science is the rock foundation of all effort'; witness too the twenty volumes of reports that his expedition brought back, reports that are all very much in demand by working scientists today. In contrast to the Norwegians, who spent much of their time resting, the British were unbelievably energetic – playing football, bicycling, go-cart racing and doing exercises out of doors; while three of them, in the depth of winter, made what has been aptly described as the worst journey in the world.

On 27 June, Bowers, Cherry-Garrard and Wilson set out for Cape Crozier, 65 miles to the east: their objective, to watch the winter hatching of the emperor penguins. Seldom can men have subjected themselves to such suffering and danger for the sake of adding so small a brick to the edifice of knowledge.

The three men took with them two sledges and 750 lb of equipment and food. For the first few days they made good progress; then they were hit by a blizzard. For day after day the wind was a bludgeoning 60 knots. The temperature fell to $-77°$ F. Their sledges became coated with ice and so heavy that they had to haul one for 100 yards, leave it, and go back for the other. They averaged 3 miles a day. For an hour either side of noon there was a faint glimmer of light on the northern horizon; for the rest of the time they were in darkness. Sweat dripping

(left) Captain Scott working on his diary
(opposite left) Pitching a tent in a high wind, by Edward Wilson
(opposite centre) Three men inside a pyramid tent, by Edward Wilson
(opposite right) A bad-weather sketching box from the manuscript of *The South Polar Times*, by Edward Wilson. *The South Polar Times* was a newspaper compiled by the men and published in book form on their return to England.

down inside their clothing turned to ice: 'Once', Cherry-Garrard wrote, 'I raised my head to look round and found I couldn't move it back. My clothing had frozen solid as I stood. For the next four hours I had to pull with my head screwed round at an angle!' They suffered from frostbite, snow-blindness, optical illusions, hunger and, above all, from cold – 'one talks of chattering teeth, but when one's whole body chatters then you really know you are cold!' They reached Cape Crozier on 19 July, built an igloo and set out to look for the penguins. Almost at once they were brought up short by a wall of ice, a jumble of huge blocks where a pressure ridge had been squeezed against the cliffs of the coast. Eventually Bowers found a hole just big enough to crawl through; this led to a snow pit with vertical walls up which they had to cut steps, and from the top of this snow pit they found themselves looking down on the rookery. 'There weren't a great number of penguins,' writes Cherry-Garrard, 'probably no more than a hundred, but they made a tremendous row, a sort of metallic trumpeting. And there was no doubt they had eggs, for we saw them trying to shuffle along without losing them off their toes.'

The three men spent as long as they dared in the rookery, observing the birds and collecting eggs; then they headed for home. Their journey back was to prove even more hair-raising than their journey out. As they were about to set off they lost their tent, ripped away in a great gust of wind, and their igloo became filled with driven snow. 'We dived for our bags', wrote Bowers, 'and lay there for the rest of the day, covered with snow blocks and debris. I pedalled my feet, and sang all the songs and hymns I knew. Every now and then I would thump Bill [Wilson], and as he moved I knew he was still alive.' For forty-eight hours they had nothing to eat and nothing but melted snow to drink. On the third day the blizzard eased off, and they emerged 'bitterly cold and utterly miserable'. Without shelter it seemed impossible for them to survive; but by a million-to-one chance they found their tent which, like a closed-up umbrella, had folded round its supports and fallen no more than half a mile away on the ice. 'We carried it back', writes Cherry-Garrard, 'solemnly and reverently, as though it were something not quite of this earth.'

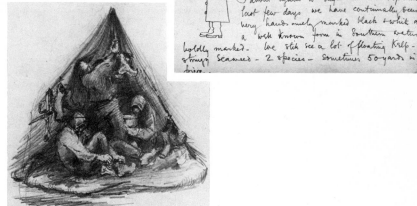

Ten days later they were back in McMurdo Sound. And if their saga – which has no direct bearing on the journey to the Pole – has been related at some length, this is because it epitomizes the spirit of Scott's expedition: indomitable (no men ever faced hardship so uncomplainingly or the prospect of death with such serenity) but amateur (professional explorers, men like Amundsen and Peary, would never have taken such risks). As the French might have said: *c'est magnifique, mais ce n'est pas l'exploration.*

The return of spring found the men in McMurdo Sound in good health, though their leader was not unnaturally worried by 'the ruin which has assailed our transport'. It was eventually decided to try to build up supplies by means of motor sledge and pony, to advance with ponies, dogs and more supplies as far as the Beardmore Glacier, then to make a dash by man-hauled sledge for the Pole.

They set out on 23 October – just four days later than Amundsen – and were in trouble before they were out of sight of their winter quarters. For their motor transport broke down. The two tractors may have been of value for experimental purposes, but from a practical point of view they had been more trouble than they were worth; they were finally abandoned on 29 October, less than halfway to the first depot, one with a split axle and the other with a cracked cylinder. 'So here', wrote Lashly, 'is an end of the wretched things. I can't say I am sorry.' The motor party now became a man-hauling party, toting 200 lb per man by sledge – 'and jolly tough work it was'. They did, however, manage to reach the depot more or less on schedule. The ponies, meanwhile, were also in difficulty. Only half of them managed, with the greatest difficulty, to struggle as far as One Ton Depot; and a few days later, on 18 November, Scott wrote:

'They are not pulling well. It's touch and go whether any of them scrape up to the [Beardmore] Glacier.' In fact none of them did. They grew progressively weaker, and as their strength gave out they were shot one by one – Chinaman on 28 November, Christopher on 1 December, Victor on 2 December, and the last survivor, Michael, on 4 December. It seems strange to modern eyes that Scott, who had such scruples over working and killing his dogs, should have been apparently little moved by the suffering and death of his ponies.

It was the despised and underrated huskies who now came to the expedition's rescue, hauling the sledges at an average of 15 miles per day to the foot of the glacier. Here they were struck by a summer blizzard which not only kept them tent-bound for four miserable days but transformed the glacier into a morass of slush. Wilson writes of 'snow like heavy wet sleet'; Evans says there was actual rain and that the surface was 18 inches deep in slush; Bowers paints an even gloomier picture: 'We are wet through, our tents are wet through, our bags are wet, our sledges are wet, our food is wet, everything on, round and about us is wet. . . . Scott is terribly depressed and thinks this will finish our chances.'

This blizzard – the one which hit the Norwegians just after they had climbed the plateau – may indeed have been the turning point in the British expedition's fortunes. For although Scott managed that December not only to climb the Beardmore Glacier but to catch up with Shackleton's timetable, the effort of man-hauling his sledges over soft, soggy and cloying snow was unbelievably exhausting: 'We are simply jerking our insides out', wrote Cherry-Garrard, 'with no result.' Bowers is even more descriptive: 'It was all we could do to keep the sledge moving for short spells of perhaps 100 yards. The starting was even worse than the pulling; it required from ten to fifteen desperate jerks on the harness to move it at all.' What a contrast to the Norwegians' easy 25 miles a day with their sledges hauled by dogs!

On 4 January 1912, not far from the 87th parallel and some 170 miles from the Pole, the last of the supporting parties turned back, and Scott and his four companions – Bowers, Evans, Oates and Wilson – set out on their journey of no return. They were in much the same latitude now as Amundsen. But the latter had already reached his objective and was on his way home.

> Such [to quote L. P. Kirwan] are the bare facts of Scott's approach to the Pole. The rest of the story, the exhausting march across the plateau, man-hauling all the way; the sight [when at last on 17 January he reached the Pole] of Amundsen's black flag tied to a sledge-bearer . . . the tell-tale marks of sledge tracks, skis, dogs' paws; the death of Evans, Oates, self-sacrifice, the utter dejection and tragic end of the homeward journey; these deeply moving events are part of our heritage.

There is only one word I would wish to alter in this concise summary: 'dejection'.

Dejection, depression and despair . . . there was, God knows, every justification for these feelings as, on the terrible journey back, the members of the British

(above) Opalescent alto stratus and a snowdrift 1–2 p.m., 17 August 1903, looking north towards McMurdo Sound, by Edward Wilson
(below) Sledge hauling on skis on a grey day on the Great Ice Barrier, by Edward Wilson

expedition succumbed one by one, in the most harrowing circumstances, to cold, exposure, exhaustion and lack of food.

Yet Scott's diary is utterly devoid of such sentiments. And it is this diary, I think, which raises the expedition from an unhappy chronicle of failure to an evocation of the unconquerable spirit of man.

Scott was not a great explorer. He saw too many sides to every question; and he made fundamental mistakes in strategy and day-to-day mistakes in tactics. He was, however, without doubt a noble and in many ways a great man.

We cannot fail to be conscious of this as we read the last pages of his diary, written only a few days – perhaps only a few hours – before his death.

> My dear Mrs Bowers,
>
> I am afraid this will reach you after one of the heaviest blows of your life.
>
> I write when we are very near the end of our journey, and I am finishing it in company with two gallant, noble gentlemen. One of these is your son. He had come to be one of my closest and soundest friends, and I appreciate his wonderful upright nature, his ability and energy. As the troubles have thickened, his dauntless spirit ever shone brighter, and he has remained cheerful, hopeful and indomitable to the end.
>
> The ways of Providence are inscrutable, but there must be some reason why such a young, vigorous and promising life is taken.
>
> My whole heart goes out in pity for you. . . .

To J. M. Barrie:

> We are pegging out in a very comfortless spot. . . . In a desperate state, feet frozen etc., no fuel and a long way from food, but it would do your heart good to be in our tent, and to hear our songs and the cheery conversation as to what we will do when we get to Hut Point. . . . Later – We are very near the end, but have not and will not lose our good cheer.

To his mother:

> Take comfort in that I die at peace with the world and myself – not afraid.

Scott, Bowers and Wilson died on about 31 March 1912. Bowers and Wilson in their sleeping bags – one likes to think in their sleep – Scott with his bag open and his arm resting on Wilson's shoulder. Their tent was a bare 11 miles from One Ton Depot, but even if they had reached this depot, they would have had little hope of covering the further 165 miles to McMurdo Sound.

The British expedition had been a failure. About the only thing that had not failed was the spirit of the men. It would be naïve to say that this spirit transformed disaster into triumph; but it did without doubt irradiate a tragedy which lingers in the mind more poignantly than Amundsen's well-merited success.

Wandering albatross and chick (*Diomedea exulans*)

## CHAPTER 10

## 'A NEW DIMENSION HAS BEEN ADDED TO EXPLORATION'

IT HAS BEEN SAID that the heroic age of exploration died with Amundsen and Scott: that once the Pole was achieved all else was anti-climax. This is not so. For the Pole was not a last step but a first. Its attainment may have been the ultimate in cartographical discovery, but a whole range of discoveries in other fields still remained to be made – the sort of discoveries that are now adding day by day to our knowledge of the world. Nor, for that matter, can Scott be termed the last of the heroic adventurers. For this niche in history belongs surely to Byrd.

Richard Evelyn Byrd was born in Winchester, Virginia, in 1888. From an early age he displayed a sturdy independence – he made an unaccompanied trip round the world before he was thirteen – and an almost obsessive love of flying: he recalls in his autobiography that when a serious ankle injury looked like preventing his learning to fly he worried himself to the verge of a nervous breakdown. It was World War I that brought him the chance he longed for. He was sent to the U.S. Navy base at Pensacola, went solo after less than six hours' tuition, and spent the rest of the war as an instructor – his ankle injury, much to his disappointment, precluding his being sent on active service. To quote from his autobiography:

> From the moment I became a full-fledged Navy pilot it was my ambition to make a career in aviation: not merely in the sense of routine flying, but rather in the pioneering sense. At the time I was learning to fly, the airplane was on the verge of becoming a tool which mankind could fit to its hand. My ambition was to test this tool to the utmost, through a series of long-range flights.

The end of the war saw him in command of an air station in Nova Scotia, trying to persuade the authorities to let him fly the Atlantic (a feat which had not yet been attempted) in the prototype of the Navy's latest long-range flying boat. Permission was not forthcoming, and Byrd resigned, 'believing that I could better advance my career in aviation outside the Service'. He teamed up with David MacMillan, who was making an aerial survey of north Greenland; and it was while crossing and recrossing the ice sheet that he conceived the idea of being the first man to fly over the North Pole.

This idea became reality in the spring of 1926 when Byrd and his co-pilot Floyd Bennett bought a three-engined Fokker monoplane which they shipped to Spitsbergen. The events of the next few weeks demonstrate very clearly the difficulties of early flying in general and polar flying in particular. The plane had to be ferried ashore on a makeshift raft, a path from ship to beach being

(above) Byrd wearing arctic kit with a
sundial compass, 1926
(left) Map of Byrd's flight

dynamited through the ice; once on land a runway had to be levelled out of the snow by men with shovels and picks working eighteen hours a day; on the Fokker's first two touch-downs her skis and landing gear were splintered to match-wood; on her first fully laden take-off she could not get off the ground and 'landed up on her nose, very nearly on her back, in a snowdrift'. Eventually, however, on 9 May 1926 the two men took off for the Pole. Their course lay over 1,600 miles of snow and ice, and their time in the air was expected to be more than fifteen hours, not far short of the limit of their endurance.

The flight itself proved unspectacular. 'I can only marvel', wrote Byrd as the Fokker levelled off at 2,000 feet, 'at the superiority of the airplane. To think that men toiled over this very ice at the rate of 3 to 4 miles a day, yet here we are travelling in luxury at 100 miles an hour . . . and opening up unexplored regions at the rate of 10,000 square miles for every hour we are in the air.' Returning in triumph to New York, Byrd was given a hero's welcome; and when Amundsen, at a civic reception, asked him what was going to be his next objective, he said half-jokingly: 'The South Pole.'

A year later he was more explicit: 'It is now my ambition', he wrote, 'not only to take an aircraft to the loneliest continent – Antarctica; but to take it to the loneliest part of that continent – the Pole.' Two factors helped him: Amundsen's advice, and the boom of the 1920s.

Amundsen was now nearer sixty than fifty, but he had young ideas and he had lost none of his clear-minded grasp of essentials. The three prerequisites of success, he suggested to Byrd, were a suitable plane, plenty of good dogs 'to act as the infantry of your assault', and good men. As regards the first, Byrd was probably the greatest authority of his day on the use of long-range aircraft. He bought a Ford trimotor monoplane with a 525 hp Cyclone in the nose and a 250 hp Whirlwind in either wing; this in theory enabled him to carry a payload of 15,000 lb at 110 mph for nearly 4,000 miles, though the plane's range and endurance would of course be drastically reduced in the Antarctic where much of the flight would be made over the polar plateau and hence close to her ceiling.

It would have been easy for Byrd to dismiss Amundsen's advice about dogs as an old-fashioned whim – indeed a great deal of pressure was brought on him to con-fine his transport to tractors and snowploughs. Fortunately, he decided in the end to take ninety-five dogs (seventy-nine Labrador huskies and sixteen Chinooks), and they proved invaluable. To quote his official report in *Little America*: 'The dogs have delighted me beyond words. I can see now that the wisest thing we ever did was to insist on bringing them.' And again: 'Rasmussen once said to me "I bless the fate which allowed me to be born in an age when the Arctic dog sledge was not yet out of date." And after seeing them race into Little America, team after team, I could only agree with him. . . . They were magnificent. . . . Had it not been for the dogs, our attempts to conquer the Antarctic by air must have ended in failure.'

Amundsen had warned Byrd that 'men are the doubtful quantities in the Antarctic. The most thorough preparation and the shrewdest plan can be destroyed by a worthless or incompetent man.' Byrd was therefore very conscious of his responsibility in choosing the best possible team. He was conscious too of the tenuous nature of the bond which would hold them together.

> Where is there another organization [he wrote] knit together like this one? It appears to lack all the factors that make for stability and co-operation. There can be no promotion for work well done, no increase in pay. Nor can there be punishment for misdeed or failure, no bread and water diet, no court-martial for disrespect. There is only one thing holding us together. Loyalty. Loyalty not only to a common purpose; but loyalty according to the ideals we live by: loyalty to family, to country, to one's fellow men, to oneself and to God. In this affinity I place my hope.

Byrd might have added another loyalty to his list: loyalty to one's leader. Such loyalty was a key factor in several Antarctic expeditions – Shackleton perhaps is the best example of a commander who enjoyed (and could not have succeeded without) the personal devotion of his men – and Byrd, albeit in a less flamboyant manner, possessed something of this magic quality of leadership. He was not particularly clever (academic work, he admits in his autobiography, never came easily to him), and he was not a particularly brilliant pilot (on many flights he left the take-off and landing to his crew); but he could be seen by all to be a good, dedicated and utterly selfless man; and these qualities earned him first the respect, then the cooperation and finally the devotion of his men.

The other key to Byrd's success was his timing. The late 1920s was a propitious moment for launching a privately sponsored expedition from the United States. Trade was booming, and philanthropic businessmen such as John D. Rockefeller and Edsel Ford were lavish in their patronage, and the U.S. Navy made a generous contribution towards supplying equipment and technicians. This was as well. For Byrd's expedition was, at the time of its sailing, the largest and most ambitious ever to set out for Antarctica. He himself has described the choosing, ordering, assembling and transporting of this mass of men and material as 'the hardest three years' work of my life. . . . Three years', he wrote, 'of being cartographer, dietitian, purchasing agent, fund-raiser, haberdasher and jack of all trades; and knowing all the while that our success or failure would be largely determined by the adequacy of our preparations.' He bought two ships, Amundsen's *Samson*, a wooden ex-sealer whose hull was 34 inches thick, which he rechristened the *City of New York*, and an 800-ton metal freighter, the *Chelsea*, which he rechristened the *Eleanor Bolling* after his mother. He chose three aircraft: a Ford trimotor monoplane, a Fairchild folding-wing monoplane and a Fokker Universal, all of which had to be stripped down, lightened and specially adapted for cold-weather, high-altitude flying. Clothing and food were assembled on a scale hitherto undreamed of: 1,200 boots, 2,000 socks, 500 crates of eggs, 1,200 lb

of cookies! And the ships' holds were filled to overflowing with vast quantities of coal and aviation fuel.

The expedition arrived in New Zealand in the early summer of 1928, and spent several weeks in Dunedin taking on last-minute stores. A few hours before they sailed, the story goes, an old man came up to Byrd: 'I've been there' – he pointed south to Antarctica – 'and I don't reckon I'll see you chaps again. Your ships won't make it. Too heavily laden.' And indeed as the vessels that December wallowed south it seemed as though the old man's prophecy might be fulfilled for, for several days, in a succession of violent blizzards, their decks were literally awash. At last, however, they gained the comparative safety of the pack ice, which, to quote Byrd, 'effectively dampened the sea'. It took them the better part of a fortnight to force their way through; then, on Christmas Day, 1928, they emerged into the lagoon of open water between ice and land. Late next evening they sighted their immediate objective, the Ross Ice Barrier.

Byrd was obliged to site his winter quarters even more carefully than Scott or Amundsen; for not only was his expedition larger than theirs, he also needed a level and stable area of ice as a landing strip. Eventually he found what he was looking for a little to the east of the Bay of Whales, and within a fortnight a veritable village – Little America he called it – had mushroomed on the lip of the Barrier. There were three main buildings: the Administration Centre, the Mess Hall and the Dormitory. These were placed some 100 yards apart, so that an accidental fire in one would not endanger the others, and also so that the men, having to move from building to building, would avoid the monotony of being cooped up in a single room for the winter. Surrounding the main blocks (which were built of prefabricated sections and painted orange so they could be seen easily from the air) were some dozen smaller huts, three aircraft hangars hollowed out of the snow, a storeroom for their 8,700 gallons of fuel, and a cluster of 70-foot radio masts. 'Little America', wrote Bryd, 'was a beautiful and eerie location. Out

(opposite) Dog teams of the geological party crossing the Great Ice Shelf on the way to the Queen Maud Range
(right) Admiral R. E. Byrd

beyond the shacks, the wireless masts and the spectral shapes of the anchored planes, were the vast stretches of the Barrier. The long, sweeping lines of the hills were tinted with constantly changing hues. It is as quiet here as in a tomb. Nothing stirs. The silence is so deep one feels one can reach out and take hold of it. . . .'

The Tuareg of the Sahara, it is said, believe that Allah fashioned their desert as a sanctuary, a haven of stillness and silence into which he could retreat from the pressures of the world. It is a belief one can understand and respect. But the peace of the Sahara, to judge from explorers' accounts, is neither so awesome nor so absolute as that of the Antarctic.

Byrd had been on the continent no more than a fortnight when he made his first flight. The date was 15 January 1929, his aircraft the Fairchild monoplane, and within a few minutes of take-off he and his crew were 'peering down on areas never before seen by man'. They were in the air for little more than an hour; but it was enough to give them a taste of both the difficulties and the rewards of Antarctic flying. Before take-off the engine and engine oil had to be heated by a torch held under fireproof covering, icicles froze onto the ailerons, and when the plane taxied cross-wind eight men had to hang onto its wing; in the air their compasses were useless because of their proximity to the Magnetic Pole, the glare from the ice was blinding, and distances were next to impossible to judge – a definite disadvantage when it came to landing! On the credit side, they had a magnificent, panoramic view of territory that was still largely unexplored, and even in the short time they were airborne they managed to photograph and survey more than 1,000 square miles of virgin ice.

It was nearly a fortnight before the weather was good enough for a second flight. Then, only some 100 miles from Little America, they discovered a great new range of mountains.

We were flying at about 4,000 feet [writes Byrd] when I saw far ahead a splendid peak, with the slate-grey of its rock clearly visible. As we drew near, a second peak, then a third, lifted its summit above the horizon. I counted 14 in all. They lay in the shape of a crescent, their spurs and crags rising austerely out of the snow. Here was something to put on the map: a fine new laboratory for geological research. As we flew parallel to the peaks I could not help thinking what an immense advantage the airplane gives an explorer. Prestrud's sledges [he was in charge of one of Amundsen's reconnaissance parties] had passed, day after day, within a few miles of these mountains but he had failed to see them because of bad visibility, yet we were now able to survey the whole range in a matter of minutes. I named them the Rockefeller Mountains. . . . [Returning to Little America] the setting, as we spiralled down, was one of wondrous beauty. An unbroken stillness: the cliffs and slopes of the Barrier rich with exquisite colors, which changed and shifted as we watched; and the lofty arch of the sky a clear blue, with a frieze of stationary clouds, some rose, some mauve. A few icebergs glittered on a sea washed with gold.

Early in March a team of geologists – Gould, June and Balchen – took off in the Fokker to collect rock samples from these newly discovered mountains. And the events that followed demonstrate very clearly the hazards of flying in the Antarctic.

On 10 March, Byrd, back in Little America, received a radio message from Gould. The geologists, the latter said, had finished their work; they had been about to take off when a storm had closed in; they would, the message concluded, fly back as soon as there was clear weather at both the Rockefellers and Little America.

There followed a long and vaguely disturbing silence.

Byrd now takes up the story:

As the days slipped by and the weather continued foul, our concern for Gould and his companions became very real. When we had good weather at Little America, they had storms; on the few occasions when it was clear in the mountains we had blizzards. It began to appear that good conditions might never be had in both places at the same time. And winter was approaching.

There was no word from Gould on the 15th. Nor the 16th. Nor the 17th. I became alarmed. The absence of radio communication was particularly puzzling; for June had two radio sets – one in the plane and one for emergency – and how both could be out of action unless the plane had crashed was difficult to understand. Yet how it could have crashed was even more puzzling; for it had been agreed that the Fokker would not take-off unless we radioed a favorable weather report, and this we had never been able to do. I began to prepare for a flight of investigation. The Fairchild was made ready. But the weather showed no sign of improving.

The long-awaited break didn't come until the evening of 19th March; then a small hole appeared in the cloud-bank to the east. It was late and the wind was still dangerously strong; but beggars couldn't be choosers, and we took-off a little after 5 p.m. The bumping was wicked; the shock of the skis' striking the sastrugi made the whole plane shiver and buck; but at last we were flung into the air in a whirlwind of snow. . . .

It was one of the worst skies for flying I have ever seen. The clouds were miles away, but they seemed very near, and merged into the ground without a shadow to show where the horizon met the snow. The instinctive reaction for a pilot was to fly lower and lower, to try to get under the clouds. But Smith kept his head, and managed to fly straight and level. . . . We soon lost the sun altogether, and the air became a confused whirl of dirty-grey through which we flew blind.

Shortly after 6 o'clock we managed to make out a mountain dead ahead. . . . It was getting dark now, but we could see below us sheets of drift [driven powder snow] streaming across the ice. 'Pretty tough to land in that!' Smith shouted. I thought so too, but said nothing.

They flew over the mountains, round the mountains and in between the mountains. They searched the slopes, the valleys and the peaks. But they saw nothing. They were thinking of giving up, when Smith spotted, away to the south, 'a column of smoke bending indistinctly on the wind, then the flashing of a light'. They spiralled down, and could just make out in the gathering twilight a landing 'T' marked out with flags. It looked rough, very rough indeed. They dropped towards it, 'with the sensation of falling powerless into a porcelain bowl'; and it needed all Smith's very considerable skill as a pilot to get them down safely, the plane bouncing, lurching and almost cartwheeling onto its back among the sastrugi. The moment they came to a halt Byrd jumped out and saw, to his relief, three figures running towards them over the snow. But of the Fokker there was no sign!

It was Gould who explained that night, as they rested in their tent, what had happened.

During their first two days in the Rockefellers the geologists had triangulated the major peaks and collected rock samples. Then, on the morning of 10 March, it had started to snow; the wind rose, and a particularly violent gust carried away the guy ropes securing the Fokker's skis. Tumbling out of their tent, the three men found the plane banging up and down, held only by its ice anchors. They tried to cut snow blocks out of a nearby drift and pile them onto the skis to hold the plane down, but the wind whipped the blocks off their shovels the moment they were cut. They did their best to anchor the wing tips; but the wind was too violent; it was numbingly cold, and the driving snow pitted into them like red-hot needles.

I never saw anything like it [June wrote later in his diary]. When I got in the plane to try and make radio contact, the needle on the airspeed indicator was registering 88 mph, and although she was only banging up and down on the snow, the aircraft was going through all the motions of flying. I looked out and saw Gould hanging onto a rope attached to one of the wing tips; he was blown straight out, horizontal, like a flag. The prop was turning over very fast, and the lines on the 'dead man' were so taut you could play a tune on them. It was blowing so hard, we could scarcely breathe. Gould believes that the wind reached a velocity of 150 mph. When it stopped it was so quiet that it hurt.

The end came suddenly. A tumult of wind, fiercer than any before, carried away both snow blocks and lines. The plane burst free. It rose into the air, flew backwards for more than half a mile, then crashed into the side of a mountain. When they managed, next day, to struggle across to it, they could tell at a glance that it would never fly again. 'The ski pedestals were split, the tail section broken, and the fuselage ripped open. It was as if a great bird had come to grief, and this was its carcass.'

A couple of days later both rescuers and rescued were back in Little America. 'The aviation season', Byrd wrote in his diary, 'is over.'

The winter passed comfortably, indeed almost pleasantly in their base at the edge of the Barrier, the men quitting the surface and settling down like moles in the catacombs they had hollowed out of the ice. Again to quote Byrd:

> As the sun went down for the last time, the darkness closed in and the aurora jerked into fantastic patterns across the sky, we burrowed deeper and deeper. The planes [there were only two of them now] were dragged into deep pits and covered with tarpaulins, the tunnels were roofed over, and the buildings became enveloped in snow. As blizzards pounded the surface, and the darkness above us was a never-ending cyclone of sound and drift, we were snug below. Time didn't drag; for we never lacked plenty to do.

Man was slowly coming to terms with the Antarctic winter.

Their main task during the hours of darkness was to prepare for their flight to the Pole. 'Victory awaits those who have everything in order,' Amundsen had written – 'people call this luck. Defeat awaits those who fail to take the necessary precautions – this is known as bad luck.' No expedition ever worked harder to ensure their 'luck' than Byrd's. Every detail of their forthcoming flight was discussed *ad nauseam* that winter; every possibility and combination of possibilities was meticulously catered for – they worked out their plane's payload, for example, down to the last roll of film and last half gallon of fuel – with the result that by the time it was spring everyone knew precisely what he had to do and how and when he was going to do it.

Towards the middle of August the northern horizon at noon became lit by flashes of red and gold, the skirmishers of the advancing sun. Some of the men climbed to the top of the radio masts for a preview. It was a magnificent spectacle they looked out on. In the north the flaming orb of the sun, magnified by refraction, was flinging up great shafts of light from below the horizon; while in the south a moon like green cheese hung without movement in a purple sky. But though the sun had returned, the cold remained. On 1 September the temperature in Little America was −63; that afternoon in New York, they learned by radio, it was +94, a difference of 157 degrees. It was mid-October before the dog teams could start for the interior.

Byrd's attempt to reach the Pole by air was planned to coincide with an attempt to reconnoitre the Queen Maud mountains by land. First a depot-laying party,

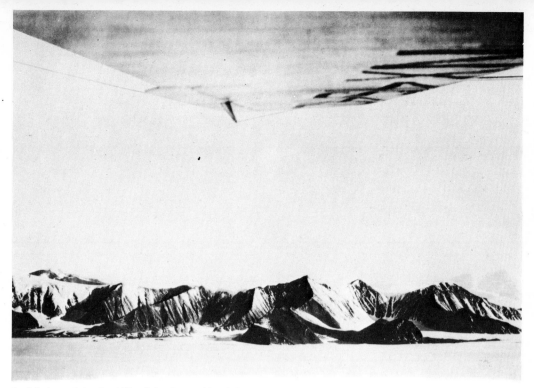

Aerial view of the foothills of the Queen Maud Range taken by Byrd

breaking the trail, would advance as far as the 83rd parallel. This would be followed by a geological sledging party, led by Gould, which would carry out research and exploration in the mountainous area that lay beneath Byrd's track – the idea being that if the plane was forced down, a rescue party might be reasonably close. As for the flight itself, this was planned in two stages: first a trip to the foot of the Queen Maud Range, where a cache would be made of provisions and fuel; then, a few days later, an attempt on the Pole itself, with the plane landing on its return journey to refuel. There was one big problem. Heavily laden with photographic equipment and fuel, the Ford was unable to climb above 11,000 feet. Yet most of the Queen Maud peaks were between 12,000 and 13,000 feet. The only way through would be via a glacial pass – no easy flight for an aircraft, in turbulent conditions, at its maximum ceiling.

The depot-laying party left on 15 October; and it was lucky they took dogs as well as motor sledges, for less than 80 miles from Little America the latter broke down in heavy snow. On 4 November, in easier conditions, the geological party set out in their wake. And next morning the Ford was manhandled out of its hangar and its engine tuned up. For a fortnight the plane was groomed for its big moment; its engine was serviced, its fuselage lightened, its tanks cleaned; a couple of test flights were made over the Bay of Whales; then it was a case of waiting for suitable weather.

November 19 dawned still and clear: one of those rare days when the Antarctic offers a pageant of almost unbelievable beauty. They took off at 9.40, circled once

An aerial photograph by Byrd captioned 'The land of eternal snow'

over the orange huts, and settled onto a course of due south. After less than two hours' flying they caught up with the geological party: a slow-moving column of ants who had been plodding south for a fortnight. They swept over them at 300 feet, dipping their wings. Byrd wrote:

> The poor devils were having a hard time. The men were in harness, pulling with the dogs; the dogs were up to their bellies in the snow. We caught sight of one or two white faces lifted up as we passed. . . . If ever a conclusive contrast was struck between the new and the old methods of polar travel it was at this moment. We dropped them some letters and equipment and continued on our way.

Soon, on their starboard bow, they could make out a magnificent range of mountains. These unfolded peak by peak: here a snow-clad shoulder and there an ebony expanse of cliff; here the shining blue-white of a glacier and there a truncated summit raised by refraction, 'a mirage suspended like Mahomet's tomb midway between heaven and earth'. As they neared the mountains Byrd did his best to identify them: 'I searched first for Mount Nansen – 15,000 feet, a blue-black look, a mighty hood of ice that raised its shining summit above all the rest; then for the Axel Heiberg glacier which rose in terraces up the mountainside, fearfully broken and disturbed, a great river of ice winding its way from Barrier to plateau.' But identifying mountains from the air is difficult, and it was some time before Byrd was able to pinpoint their position. They had made a near-perfect landfall, midway between the Axel Heiberg Glacier and the Liv.

But would they be able to land? They flew low over the Barrier. It looked unpromising: wave after wave of tall, knife-edged sastrugi which might have been designed to rip off their undercarriage and skis. Eventually, however, they spotted an area of more or less level snow at the foot of the Liv Glacier. They dropped smoke floats to gauge the strength and direction of the wind, picked the most promising-looking spot, and came in as slowly as they dared. A second before the plane touched down, Smith eased back on the control column so that the Ford stalled, hitting the snow firmly at no more than 50 mph. There was a great squeal of protest from the skis, a flurry of churned-up snow and ice from the Barrier, and they were down. Smith kept the engines ticking over, while the others unloaded cans of gasoline and oil and bags of food. 'It took us less than half an hour', wrote Byrd, 'to establish the most southerly base in the world.' Then they were airborne once again, heading south to reconnoitre the glaciers, one of which, they hoped, in a few days time would provide their pathway to the Pole.

The reconnaissance, however, was cut short by a most unwelcome discovery. They were short of fuel. On their flight out, the radio operator had discovered a leak at the base of their hand-operated fuel pump. This he had plugged with chewing gum. It had seemed at the time as though the leak had been staunched; but now that their tanks were sounded they were found to be three-quarters empty. They turned hurriedly for home.

About a hundred miles short of the coast all three engines cut simultaneously, and no amount of juggling with throttles and mixture controls would persuade them to restart. The Ford spiralled down, Smith searching desperately for a patch of level ice on which to land. They were lucky. If the engines had cut a few minutes earlier, they would have come down in the Devil's Graveyard, a network of sastrugi and crevasses. As it was, they cleared the danger area by a bare couple of miles, and Smith managed to make a perfect emergency landing. They drained their engines of oil (to prevent them freezing solid), set up their emergency radio and called for help. And a little before dark the Fairchild arrived from Little America with sufficient fuel to see them home.

In the week that followed, the fuel leak was repaired and the engine jets adjusted so as to give a thinner, and hence more economic, mixture. Then it was a case, once again, of waiting for good weather. November 28 dawned fine and clear at Little America, and the midday signal from the geological party reported light winds and perfect visibility over the Queen Maud Range.

'Go now,' the meteorologist said to Byrd. 'You'll never have a better chance.'

An hour later they were airborne for the Pole.

There were four men in the plane: Balchen the pilot, Byrd the navigator, June the radio operator and McKinley the photographer; and their load included not only fuel and food but aerial cameras, the latter far bulkier and heavier than those of today. The first part of their flight was uneventful, though they again passed low over Gould's geological party and dropped them photographs and a map. Then they were brought up short by the wall of the polar plateau, a continuous chain of peaks drawn up like a line of silver-armoured cavalry across their path. They could not climb over the mountains; they had to fly in between them; a prospect of no little hazard, since once they entered a valley there was every likelihood that they might find it too high to follow all the way through and too narrow to turn round in.

There seemed to be two possible routes: via the Axel Heiberg Glacier or the Liv. They had insufficient fuel for a reconnaissance. They had to make their decision, and stick to it. It was the layer of stratus at the top of the Axel Heiberg that decided them. Nothing would be worse than finding themselves among the peaks, unable to climb and enveloped in cloud. They headed into the Liv.

Flying was difficult.

> The stream of air pouring down the glacier [wrote Byrd] tossed the airplane about like a cork. The wings shuddered as they dipped this way and that in the changing pressures. . . . After a while the roughness of the air became so violent that we were forced to swing to the left-hand side of the valley. This brought us over a fearfully crevassed slope which ran up toward Mount Nansen, and here the down-surging currents damped our rate of climb.

They tried the right-hand side.

> Here the glacier floor rose sharply in a series of ice falls and terraces, some of which were well above the altitude of the plane. These glacial waterfalls, some 200 to 400 feet in height, were the most beautiful I had ever seen. Beautiful yes, but how rudely and with what finality they would deal with us if we crashed into them at 100 miles per hour!

Soon they were approaching their moment of truth: the 'hump' at the head of the valley.

They emptied the last of their fuel cans into the tank and jettisoned the empties – every pound of weight lost was a foot of height gained. Their altimeter was now reading 9,600 feet; but the controls were growing sluggish, and the Ford, wallowing this way and that, had become next to impossible to control. Nor, Byrd noticed, was she gaining height, for he saw to his dismay that strain as the engines might the top of the 'hump' remained obstinately above the rim of their cowling. He was in a dilemma. If he jettisoned fuel, they would have to forgo the Pole; if he jettisoned food, a forced landing would almost certainly lead to death from starvation. His crew helped him to reach a decision; they dragged a 200-lb food container to the trapdoor. Byrd nodded. The container spun down, to burst in a soundless explosion on the glacier below. And the plane, as if in gratitude, resumed her climb. But with painful slowness.

'Another bag!' the pilot shouted.

Again Byrd nodded. 'And the sacrifice swung the scale. The Ford literally rose with a jump; her engines dug in, and she gained steadily in altitude. It was the boost we needed. We crossed the dreaded "hump" with two or three hundred feet to spare, and saw ahead of us the level expanse of the plateau, an open pathway to the Pole.'

The rest of the flight was an anti-climax. They crossed the featureless expanse of the plateau without incident, taking sun shots to confirm their position; and at 1.14 a.m. Greenwich mean time all calculations agreed they were at the Pole. They did not land, but circled the spot a couple of times, taking photographs and dropping British, Norwegian and American flags – the last weighted with a stone from Floyd Bennett's grave. 'The Pole', wrote Byrd, 'lies in the centre of a limitless plain. And that is almost all there is to say about it. It is the effort of getting there that counts.'

They arrived back in Little America on the morning of 29 November. The journey, which had taken Amundsen three months and had cost Scott and his companions their lives, had been accomplished in less than sixteen hours. As the *New York Times* succinctly put it 'a new dimension has been added to the exploration of our planet'.

Byrd's account of his flight to the Pole is brief and unemotional, and it is clear that he did not regard it as his major achievement. His longest and most loving descriptions of the Antarctic are devoted to the surveys he made of virgin territory. History has endorsed his judgment. For we can see today that his most important contribution to the unveiling of Antarctica was indeed that he pioneered the use of aerial photography. His descriptions of this work have a freshness and enthusiasm that the years have done nothing to diminish.

> December 5th. . . . We continued to climb, and a little after noon were at 5,000 feet above Scott's Nunatak, with a splendid bird's eye panorama of the unknown area to the east. . . . At about 12.40 a mountainous mass appeared on the horizon. As we drew nearer, other peaks loomed up and there was the suggestion of a range: another first-class discovery. We were now advancing at the rate of 100 mph over an area unseen, unknown and unclaimed. Here was the romance of exploration, and seeing these mountains at last, after so much hoping and trying, brought us deep satisfaction; for aviation at last was doing what surface travel had for years failed to do; and best of all every foot of the area we discovered was being recorded precisely and in perspective by McKinley's camera. Our photographer's delight was beyond words. Everything of which an aerial surveyor dreams was before his camera in grand profusion – a new and undiscovered land, excellent visibility, a well marked coastline and scenery unlike any other known to man. . . . An air of drama foreshadowed every mile of progress; north, south, east and west – everything was untrodden and unknown. Here was the ice age in childhood. Here too was great beauty, in the way that things which are terrible can sometimes also be beautiful.

On this single flight Byrd saw a greater area of virgin territory than Scott and Amundsen set eyes on during all their years in the Antarctic. The old order was changing. From now on the continent would be mapped and opened up almost exclusively from the air.

## CHAPTER 11

# THE FIRST CROSSING

BY 1955 THE SURFACE OF ANTARCTICA had been roughly mapped. The coastline had been delineated, the interior had been photographed and its salient points such as the Geographic and Magnetic Poles had been attained. The continent had been crossed more than once by air – first by Ellsworth, who in 1935 flew a Northrop low-wing monoplane from the Antarctic peninsula to the Bay of Whales. It had, however, never been crossed by land.

The idea of such a crossing was first put forward as early as 1910 by the Scottish explorer William Bruce; and useful preparatory work was carried out the following year by the German explorer Filchner, who established a base at the foot of the ice shelf in the Weddell Sea which bears his name. These early schemes, however, were thwarted by lack of funds. For it was realized that the crossing of the continent would entail two major expeditions: one to land on the Ross Ice Shelf and to lay depots along either Scott's or Amundsen's route onto the central plateau, and one to land on the opposite side of the continent, to advance through the little-known Shackleton and Pensacola Mountains to the Pole, and to pick up supplies for the second half of their journey from the depots already laid. Because of the expense of mounting such a complex operation, only two attempts at a crossing have ever got under way: Shackleton's in 1914–17 and Fuchs's in 1955–8.

Ernest Henry Shackleton is a flamboyant, larger-than-life figure, whose character and achievements are steeped in controversy. His detractors regarded him as a vulgar seeker of notoriety; but to the men who served under him – and who should know better than they? – he was an inspired and well-loved leader whom they were happy to follow quite literally to the farthest ends of the earth.

He was born in Ireland in 1874, served for several years as an officer in the Merchant Navy, and had his first taste of polar exploration with Scott's *Discovery* expedition of 1902–4 – his first taste and very nearly his last; for he contracted scurvy, almost died and had to be invalided home. Five years later he was back again, leading a privately sponsored assault on the Pole. This assault culminated in what is sometimes regarded as the greatest sledging journey ever made, when Shackleton pushed to within 97 miles of his goal. Indeed he would almost certainly have been the first man to reach the Pole (predating Amundsen by a couple of years) if he had not, at a crucial moment, lost the last of his ponies down a crevasse. This left him short of food; and with his goal almost literally in sight, he was forced to retreat. To quote his friend and companion J. M. Wordie:

To have gone on a day longer would have meant the death of his whole party. Even as it was, they were left with the narrowest of margins, and on one occasion were 48

(left) Sir Ernest Shackleton
(below left) *Endurance*
(below) Map of Shackleton's journey

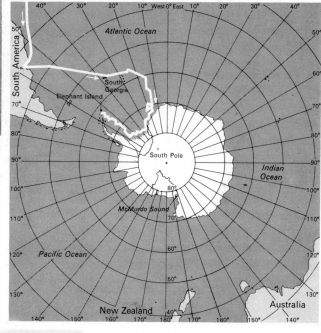

205

hours without food. The story of their return march is one of magnificent courage and endurance. Their daily average was 18 miles on three-quarters rations. And at the end of it all, Shackleton performed the astonishing feat of going back with the relief party for two members who had broken down. By doing this, he covered 100 miles without rest on top of a 1,700-mile journey. . . . His exploits fired public enthusiasm, and his reputation as an explorer was made. Honours were showered upon him, including knighthood, and the Gold Medal of the Royal Geographical Society.

His first thought on returning home was to raise funds for another attempt at the Pole. It was only when he was thwarted in this by Amundsen that he conceived, as an alternative, the idea of crossing the continent from coast to coast. He had become by this time what his biographers term 'an established public character'. His achievements, his books and above all his lecture tours kept him in the public eye; and he was able without too much difficulty to raise the £100,000 needed to get his expedition started, most of the money coming from private sponsors such as Sir James Caird, Miss Elizabeth Lambton and Dame Stancomb Wills.

He bought two vessels: the *Aurora* destined for the Ross Sea, and the *Endurance* destined for the Weddell Sea. He was about to sail when the storm which had been gathering all summer finally broke: on 4 August 1914 Britain was at war.

Shackleton at once offered his expedition – ships, equipment, men and dogs – to the government; but he was instructed to sail, as planned, for the Antarctic. This placed him in a dilemma – 'in a state of great mental strain', to quote his auto-biography, 'and on the point of chucking the whole expedition and applying to Kitchener for a job'. His friends, however, managed to persuade him that the war would be over in a matter of weeks and that it was his duty to go. So on 8 August 1914 the *Endurance* stood south out of Plymouth, her destination the Weddell Sea.

Meanwhile on the opposite side of the world the *Aurora* was fitting out in Sydney, and toward the end of the year she also headed south. Shackleton describes her objective:

> The *Aurora*, under the command of Captain Mackintosh, sailed for the Ross Sea on December 24th, 1914. My instructions to Captain Mackintosh were, in brief, to make a base at some convenient place in or near McMurdo Sound, land stores and equipment, and lay depots across the Great Ice Barrier in the direction of the Beardmore Glacier for use of the party that I expected to bring overland from the Weddell Sea. The programme would involve heavy sledging, but the ground to be covered was familiar.

These instructions proved none too easy to carry out; for the weather that summer was appalling – the snow 'too dreadful for words' – and the depot-laying parties soon found themselves crippled by hunger, scurvy, frostbite and exhaustion. They were fiercely determined, however, not to let Shackleton down, and eventually managed with great difficulty to lay four caches of food between 79° and 82° S and

Frank Hurley and Shackleton at Patience Camp, by Frank Hurley

Ice flowers in early spring, by Frank Hurley

two caches on the Beardmore Glacier, the latter involving the longest period of continuous sledge travelling in polar history. Their ship meanwhile was also having a difficult time. Early in May, she was caught in a blizzard that broke up the ice, carried away her anchors and moorings, and swirled her out of McMurdo Sound. 'At about 9.35 p.m.,' writes her Second Officer, Leslie Thomson, 'the moorings began to strain and the decks to groan, and we realized the ice was on the move. The wind was blowing fiercely, and it was so thick that we could see only a few yards. When the floe we were stuck fast in began to break up and we got amongst the loose pack, the pounding we received would have sent any steel ship to the bottom.' For nine months the *Aurora* drifted this way and that in the ice, battered, rudderless and desperately short of coal, trying first to get back to the men left stranded in McMurdo Sound, then, when this proved impossible, to force her way north into open sea. Not until February 1916 did she break free from the pack, and not until April of the same year did she manage to struggle half-foundering into Port Chalmers, New Zealand.

The party in McMurdo Sound, meanwhile, under Captain Mackintosh, were in real trouble. One man died; two were lost in a blizzard, and the remainder had no option but to eke out their provisions as best they could and wait for Shackleton. 'We didn't know whether the Boss would come overland from the south', one of them wrote, 'or by sea from the north. We only knew that he would come.'

The *Endurance* arrived in South Georgia about the middle of November 1914. It was a bad year for ice; and to add to Shackleton's problems Admiral von Spee and a squadron of German cruisers were known to be in the vicinity. He decided nevertheless to make for the Weddell Sea; and on 11 December managed to force his way into a likely looking lead in the pack. Progress was slow. The ice was unusually heavy and thick, and for three weeks the *Endurance* averaged no more than a mile to southward per day. At last, however, she broke through to the belt of open water between pack and shore. The first hurdle had been cleared and the vessel was now able to follow the coast towards Vahsel Bay, where Filchner, a few years earlier, had established his winter quarters. On 18 January, however, when he was still some 100 miles from his goal, Shackleton was brought up short by solid ice. And next afternoon the *Endurance* became ensnared: gripped fast as a fly in amber in a vast conglomeration of floes.

The situation at first was not regarded as serious. It was still summer, a gale would almost certainly have broken up the pack, and the *Endurance* seemed to be drifting southwest in the direction she wanted to go. But as week followed week, and the temperature dropped and the ice thickened and the ship began to drift north, Shackleton became anxious:

> The weather is foggy and unseasonably cold. Mirages are continually giving us false alarms. Icebergs hang upsidedown in the sky; the land appears as layers of silvery or golden cloud; cloud-banks look like land; icebergs masquerade as islands, and the distant barrier to the south is thrown into view, although it is really outside our range of vision. Worst of all is the deceptive appearance of open water, caused by refraction or by the sun shining at an angle on fields of snow.
>
> On the morning of the 14th [February] I ordered a good head of steam on the engines and sent all hands onto the floe with ice-chisels, saws and picks. We worked all that day and most of the next in a strenuous effort to get the ship into a lead. The men cut away the young ice and pulled it aside with much energy; and after 24 hours' labour we got the ship a third of the way to the lead. But about 400 yds of heavy ice, including old rafted pack, still separated the *Endurance* from open water, and reluctantly we had to admit that further effort was useless. Every opening we made froze up again owing to the unseasonably low temperature; and the young ice was elastic, and prevented the ship delivering a splitting blow to the floe. The abandonment of the attack was a great disappointment to all hands. . . . But the task was beyond our powers. I realized I had now to count on the possibility of having to spend a winter in the inhospitable arms of the pack.

A passage that epitomizes Shackleton's cheerfulness in adversity – in all his writings about the Antarctic there is never a word of self-pity or complaint.

For month after month the *Endurance*, embedded in the floe like a castle upon an island, drifted this way and that at the mercy of current and wind. Her boilers were emptied, a ring of 'dogloos' was built on the ice round her hull, seals were hunted, and the vessel was made as warm and as comfortable as possible for the winter. Her ship's company were a close-knit team, and their morale was high. Shackleton himself was both respected and loved: respected because although he

Frank Wild examining the wreckage of the *Endurance*, by Frank Hurley

was 'the Boss' he gave his crew the opportunity to discuss and participate in every activity; and loved partly because he refused any of the privileges a leader might have reserved for himself – 'if he had half a pipe of tobacco', wrote How, 'he'd share it' – and partly because he took the trouble to establish a warm and personal relationship with each individual man.

The winter passed uneventfully, the ship being drifted now to within 60 miles of Vahsel Bay, now as far north as the 70th parallel. With the approach of spring, however, the ice began to cause them anxiety. Like a monstrous flower whose sap was rising, it began to move, the floes sometimes splitting apart with a crack like a bull whip, sometimes thrusting on top of one another in a volcano-like eruption. Worst of all were the pressure ridges: great waves of ice built up by the force of wind and current, advancing like giant combers over the surface of the pack. On 18 October the *Endurance* was first lifted up on such a ridge, then dropped into a pool of open water. Before she could escape, she was squeezed between two converging floes and flung almost onto her beam end. Here, for 48 hours, leaking badly, she hung with a thirty-degree list. Then the ice moved again.

The massive and threatening pressure ridges [wrote Shackleton] testified to the overwhelming nature of the forces at work. Huge blocks of ice, weighing many tons, were lifted into the air and tossed aside as other masses rose beneath them. We were helpless intruders in a terrifying world, our lives dependent on the play of elementary forces that made a mock of our efforts. I scarcely dared hope now that the *Endurance* would live, and reviewed my plan for the sledge journey we would have to make in the event of our taking to the ice. We were ready, as far as forethought could make us, for every contingency. Stores, dogs, sledges and equipment were ready to be moved from the ship at a moment's notice.

The moment came on 27 October.

We have just finished lunch [writes the expedition's photographer Frank Hurley] and the ice mill is in motion again. Closer and closer the pressure-wave approaches. . . . Now it is within a few yards of the vessel. We are the embodiment of helplessness, and can only look impotently on. . . . The line of pressure now assaults the ship, and she is heaved to the crest of the ridge like a toy. Immense fragments are forced under the counter and wrench away the stern-post. Sir Ernest and Captain Worsley are surveying the ship's position from the floe, when the carpenter announces that the water is gaining rapidly on the pumps. All hands are ordered to stand by to discharge equipment and stores onto the ice. The pumps work faster and faster; someone is singing a shanty to their beat, as the dogs are rapidly passed down a canvas chute, followed by rations, sledges and equipment. The ship is doomed.

By 8 p.m. all essential equipment and food had been unloaded, but the men returned aboard for a last meal. This was eaten to the accompaniment of groaning timbers and crunching ice. As Shackleton left the wardroom for the last time the clock was still ticking on the wall; but water was swirling fast into the hold, and tongues of ice were being forced up through the riven deck. He wrote:

It was a sickening sensation to feel the deck breaking up under one's feet, the great beams bending then snapping with a noise like gunfire. I looked down the skylight and saw the engines dropping sideways as the stays and bed-plates gave way. I cannot describe the impression of relentless destruction as I looked about me. The floes, with the force of millions of tons of moving ice behind them, were simply annihilating the ship.

It was in the late evening that the *Endurance* gave what was literally her last flicker of life. 'You could hear the ship being crushed', one of her crew wrote, 'as the ice ground into her, and you felt as if your own ribs were cracking. Suddenly, inside her, a light went on for a moment and then went out. It seemed the end of everything.'

For nine months Shackleton had been incarcerated aboard the *Endurance*. Now she had gone, and with her his dream of an Antarctic crossing. With his twenty-seven men he stood huddled on an ice floe, hundreds of miles from land, without the slightest possibility of outside help. He had only one ambition now. Never on any of his previous expeditions had he lost a member of his ship's company: this record he was fiercely determined to preserve.

For nearly a month he kept his men by the wreck of the *Endurance*, salvaging equipment, food and timber out of a ship that was crushed beyond recognition but still held fast in the ice; not till the evening of 21 November did his shout 'She is going, boys' bring the men tumbling out of their tents.

She went down quietly, bow first, a little after 5 p.m. For perhaps a couple of minutes there was a small, dark hole in the pack, then the floes drifted together, and there was nothing to show that a ship had once floated there. Shackleton made only a brief entry in his diary – 'I can not write about it'. Yet in a way the disappearance of his vessel must have come as a relief; the dead past had buried its dead; he had nothing to think of now but the future, and a few weeks later he struck camp and set off for Paulet Island, some 400 miles to the north.

The going was not simply difficult, it was impossible. The floes were irregular: in some places rafted together to form ridges 12 to 15 feet in height, in other places so thin that the sledges fell through into the ice-cold water beneath. Sometimes the ice was so hard they had difficulty in chipping it away with their picks; other times it was so soft that dogs and men found themselves floundering deep in slush. Progress was tortuous and pitifully slow. At the end of an exhausting week they had travelled a bare 10 miles to the north, and the current had drifted them nearly 4 miles to the east. At this rate, Shackleton calculated, it would take them 400 days to reach Paulet Island! He decided to camp on the most solid floe he could find, wait for the ice to melt and then take to whaleboats which had been salvaged from the wreck.

On 29 December, he established a camp called 'Patience'. Here, cold, wet, short of food and in conditions as wretched as any on earth, his ship's company settled down to wait.

Patience did come easily to Shackleton. He was a doer – even when contemplating he liked to pace up and down – and it is perhaps the greatest of all his achievements that he managed that summer to curb his impetuosity and to present to his men a façade of placid unconcern. But his biographers, Margery and James Fisher, describe very well what were his real feelings.

> Deprived of exercise, Shackleton suffered more at Patience Camp than during any other period of the expedition. Hurley [with whom he shared a tent] remembers how sometimes at night their leader would call out in the grip of nightmare, and when he was woken, would describe some accident which his tired mind had too vividly foreseen. But once awake (and this was entirely characteristic of him) he would set himself there and then to think of a plan to circumvent the imagined danger; only then would he sleep again. He was always a planner; his diary had lists on every spare page – lists of boat parties or emergency orders – yet to few others was his anxiety apparent.

Indeed to his crew he was the epitome of self-confidence – 'He was always cheerful, and gave everyone confidence that we would get out. . . . The Boss was a tower of strength and endurance, and never panicked in any emergency.' But perhaps the most discerning tribute comes from R. W. James (who, like Hurley, was one of the men in his tent):

He had a wonderful power of inspiring confidence and an uncanny flair for the right thing to do. He kept his plans elastic, and did not hesitate to change them with changing circumstances. We did not always think his judgment right at the time, but it always turned out to be so. I do not think there is any doubt that we all owe our lives to his leadership and to his power of making a loyal and coherent party out of our diverse elements.

Patience Camp, to start with, was a tolerable enough base from which they were able to exercise the dogs, take observations and hunt for seals. As the summer progressed, however, the weather deteriorated, and their position on the disintegrating ice became more and more untenable. During February and March they were confined on nineteen days out of twenty to their tents, and 'walking became a virtually forgotten sensation'. 'We all grew very weak', wrote Shackleton. 'Because fuel was scarce, we had to resort to melting ice for drinking water by holding it in tins against our bodies . . . our meals were practically all seal meat with a single biscuit at midday. . . . On April 2nd we shot the last of the dogs.' To have survived at all in such conditions was no mean achievement. To have survived with sanity and cheerfulness was little short of a miracle.

By early April the floe on which they were camped had drifted as far north as the tip of the Antarctic peninsula, and the ice was breaking up fast. To quote Mill:

> The massive field, extending for hundreds of miles, in which the Endurance had been crushed had now thinned down. It had broken into a number of floebergs, an acre or so in extent, on one of which stood Patience Camp, with its tents, its blubber stove, its outlook post and its three boats. A great swell made the icefloes heave and tremble, and jostled them one against another so that they split farther apart. In the lanes of water in between, the men could see killer whales, greedy as sharks and no less dangerous.

Cracks began to open without warning in even the most solid-looking surface, so that men who were one moment asleep in their tents would the next be tumbled into ice-cold water. Three times Shackleton saved a member of his crew from drowning by hauling him to safety.

By the morning of 9 April Patience Camp was untenable: a morass of slush that would neither float a boat nor support a man. A little after midday their floeberg drifted into a patch of relatively open water, and this was the moment for which Shackleton had been waiting. Everyone knew exactly what had to be done; and tents, provisions, stores and men were piled quickly into the boats.

They had, by this time, drifted almost as far as the South Shetlands and could see, away in the distance, the conical peaks of Clarence Island. Between this island and their boats, however, lay 50 miles of ice-strewn sea: a mosaic of disintegrating floes, bergs of all shapes and sizes, and narrow waterways down which the tide-rips swept like a river in spate. So heavy was the swell that sheets of spray were flung 60 feet high over the tops of the bergs.

Our deeply-laden boats [wrote Shackleton] made heavy weather. They shipped spray which, freezing as it fell, coated men and gear with ice. Seeing we could not safely proceed, we ran for shelter and hauled up for the night on a big floeberg. . . . We were now on a piece of flat ice about 200 feet long and 100 feet wide. There was no sleep for any of us. The killer whales were blowing in the sea lanes all around as we waited for daylight and watched for signs of cracks in the ice. The hours passed with laggard feet as we stood huddled together or walked to and fro in an effort to keep some warmth in our bodies. We lit the blubber stove at 3 a.m., and with pipes going and a cup of hot milk for each man, we were able to discover some bright spots in our outlook. At least we were on the move!

This night on the floe was the prelude to sixty hours in the open sea: sixty hours of appalling hazard in which Shackleton's ship's company came very close to death from exposure, as their boats, now rowing and now sailing, now tied together and now separated, fought their way towards the comparative safety of the South Shetlands. Each member of the crew has his own particular memory of this gruelling journey.

To Green and How it was the nights spent in the boats, lashed together with a painter, hearing the whales moving about them. To Dr Machlin it was the combination of freezing seas, sea-sickness and diarrhoea from the uncooked dog pemmican they had been forced to eat. To Greenstreet it was the moment as they drew into the open sea. 'The pack was closed round us' [he wrote], 'a howling gale was blowing, and a terrific sea running. One moment we were up on the tremendous crest of a swell – you could see right away to the horizon, nothing but sea and ice and sky – then you'd drop into the hollow and see a great roller coming toward you filled with blocks of ice.'

Worsley remembers the cold:

The temperature fell to 36° of frost. It was so cold that our Burberry overalls crackled, and ice and frost fell off us as we rowed. When the moon came out, we saw that our beards were white with frost, moustaches were knobbed with ice, and each man's breath formed clouds of vapour, showing white against the darkness of his face.

It was Shackleton's leadership that saw them through. 'You felt', wrote Greenstreet, 'that so long as the Boss was in charge, everything was going to be alright . . . he was undefeatable.'

In the early morning of 15 April the three boats struggled into a bleak but mercifully sheltered cove on the east coast of Elephant Island. 'The men', wrote Worsley, 'were light-headed by now. Some, when they had landed, reeled about, laughing uproariously. Others sat on the shingle, and, like harmless lunatics, let it run through their fingers. It was the first land we had set foot on for 485 days.'

Their most pressing needs were for food and warmth. They were lucky. Within a couple of hours of landing they found and killed an elephant seal; and the great creature's flesh provided them with meal after meal of nourishing stew, and its blubber acted as fuel to a fire on the beach which was soon giving

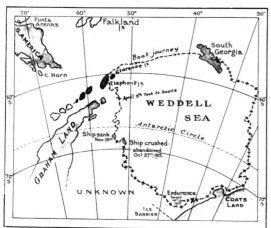

(top left) Tracks of the *Endurance* and
her boats
(top right) Drying clothes on Elephant
Island, by Frank Hurley
(above left) The arrival at Elephant
Island, by Frank Hurley
(above right) The living quarters on
Elephant Island, by Frank Hurley and
George Marston
(below right) Shackleton and his
companions setting off for help.
Possibly executed by George
Marston from memory

off more heat than the men had known for the past fifteen months. They slept well that night. 'There were sharp stones beneath our shoulders', wrote Worsley, 'but they didn't worry us. We were only too glad to feel solid land beneath us after living for six months on the heaving ice. And I think that most of us, before falling asleep, uttered a prayer of thankfulness for our escape.'

Their troubles, however, were far from over. It was clear from highwater marks on the encircling cliffs that the beach on which they had camped would be submerged during spring tides; they therefore moved next day to another. Here Shackleton paused to take stock of their predicament. Elephant Island was bleak, uninhabited and far from the usual track of whalers and sealers; nobody was likely to think of looking for them here. They could, he calculated, survive well enough on the island for a short spell, but not indefinitely. So the question had to be faced of where to go next. Many of his men were too weak for him to contemplate another voyage in open boats by the whole ship's company; he therefore had no option but to try to get help; and the only place he could possibly get help from was South Georgia, 800 miles to the northeast. It must have seemed extremely unlikely that a battered 22-foot whaleboat could survive so long a passage through one of the stormiest seaways on earth; but Shackleton knew it was their only hope. He decided to lead the rescue party himself, leaving the bulk of his men under the reliable Frank Wild to establish a camp in the comparative safety of Elephant Island.

One of their longboats, the *James Caird*, was strengthened and partially decked in; and on 23 April Shackleton and five volunteers embarked on a voyage as hazardous as any that had ever been attempted in the annals of the sea. Their departure was hardly auspicious. For while they were still within the shelter of land their boat almost capsized, two of her crew were flung overboard and a water barrel was stove in. Yet such, we are told, was the men's faith in the Boss, that beyond all the dictates of reason, those who were left never doubted that somehow, some day, he would be back to rescue them.

The *James Caird* headed north, picking her way through the remnants of last year's pack:

> The bergs and floes had broken down and melted into all sorts of grotesque and wondrous shapes [writes Worsley], and were heaving, bowing, curtseying and jostling together in the swell. They would draw apart, then close with a thud that would have smashed our boat like a gasmantle. Their colours were beyond belief: clear green at the waterline, shading first to a deep blue, and then at their summits to a snow-white purity. To our great relief we cleared this ice a little before dark and set more sail – Elephant Island a pale shadow astern.

Shackleton divided his men into two watches, four hours on and four off. During his duty watch one man took the tiller, one was in charge of the sail and one baled; those off duty could in theory sleep, though in practice they were usually too cold, wet and cramped to do more than doze for a few moments.

The sub-Antarctic Ocean [wrote Shackleton] lived up to its evil reputation. . . . Deep were the valleys and high the hills. So small was our boat that its sail would flap idly in the calm between the crests of the waves. Then we would climb the next slope and catch the full fury of the gale, while the wool-like whiteness of breaking water surged all about us. Always there were gales. At times we were in dire peril. . . . On the fourth day a severe southwesterly gale forced us to heave to. I would have liked to run before the wind, but the sea was too high and the *James Caird* was in danger of broaching to and swamping. We put out a sea anchor to keep our head up; but even then the crests of the waves would curl right over us and we shipped a great deal of water. A thousand times it seemed as though the boat must be engulfed; but she lived. . . . By daylight on the sixth day the *James Caird* had lost her resiliency. The weight of ice in her and upon her was having its effect, and she was becoming more like a log than a boat. It was a situation that called for desperate action. We broke away the spare oars, which were encased in ice and frozen to the side of the boat, and threw them overboard; two of the four sleeping bags (which were frozen solid and probably weighed 40 lbs apiece) went over the side. This reduction of weight relieved the boat to some extent, and vigorous chipping did more. We had to be careful not to put axe or knife through the frozen canvas, but gradually we got rid of a great deal of ice, and the *James Caird* lifted to the waves as though she lived again. . . . On the tenth night Worsley could not straighten his body after his spell at the tiller. He was thoroughly cramped, and we had to drag him beneath the decking and massage him before he could unbend enough to get into a sleeping bag. A hard northwesterly gale came up in the late afternoon. . . . At midnight I was at the tiller and suddenly noticed a line of what looked like clear sky to the southwest. I called to the others that the weather was clearing, then a moment later realized that what I had seen was not a rift in the clouds but the white crest of an enormous wave. During 26 years' experience of the ocean in all its moods I had not encountered a wave so gigantic. It was a mighty upheaval of the ocean, a thing quite apart from the big white-capped seas that had been our enemies for days. I shouted 'For God's sake, hold on!' Then came a moment of suspense that seemed drawn out into hours. The foam of the breaking sea surged white around us. We felt our boat lifted and flung forward like a cork in breaking surf. We were in a seething chaos of tortured waters; but somehow the boat lived through it, half full of water, sagging to the dead weight and shuddering under the blow. We baled with the energy of men fighting for life. . . . She floated again, and ceased to lurch drunkenly as though dazed by the attack of the sea. . . . On the thirteenth day thirst took possession of us. Lack of water is the most severe privation that men can be condemned to endure, and we found that the salt water in our clothing and the salt spray that lashed our faces made our thirst grow into a burning pain. . . . Things were bad for us those last few days, but the end was coming. At about 12.30 p.m. on May 8th we caught sight, through a rift in the clouds, of the black cliffs of South Georgia.

One does not know which to admire most: the men's endurance, Shackleton's leadership or Worsley's navigation.

Their troubles, however, were far from over. For that evening the gale increased to 'one of the worst hurricanes any of us had ever known'. The wind with insane malevolence tore off the tops of the waves and converted the whole seascape into a kaleidoscope of driving spray. For a day and a night they clawed desperately away from the island, glimpsing every now and then through rifts in the spume huge 3,000-foot crags disappearing into the sky. They were off a lee shore, in near darkness, and could only gauge their approach to the rocks by the roar of breakers. In the small hours of 10 May they came almost literally to within inches of death, when their boat was driven inside the yeasty backwash of seas flung back from the cliffs. Then, quite suddenly, the wind died away, and they drifted battered and exhausted onto a shelving beach where, as if in answer to their prayers, a stream of ice-cold water cascaded from glacier to sea.

As they were pulling the last few yards to the shore the locking pin (which secured their mast to the thwart) split and fell out of its socket. If it had come away a couple of hours earlier, during the hurricane, nothing could have saved them; their mast would have snapped like a twig.

They enjoyed that evening their first wholly satisfying drink and their first properly cooked meal for a fortnight: then, dead to the world, they crawled into a cave for the night. Shackleton, typically, took the first watch (from 8 p.m. to 1 a.m.), hauling the *James Caird* up the beach as the tide advanced and the others slept.

Two of the men, McNeish and Vincent, were at the end of their tether – the latter indeed had been bludgeoned to near insanity by suffering and hardship – and Shackleton realized they would never survive another voyage in the *James Caird*. He therefore ruled out the possibility of reaching the whaling station (which lay on the opposite coast of South Georgia) by sea – a voyage which would, in any case, have been long and hazardous – and decided that the men who were fit must try to cross the island on foot. This would involve climbing a precipitous, 6,000-foot range which had never before been crossed.

Four days were spent in setting up camp, in building up a reserve of food, and in rest and recuperation. Then Shackleton, Worsley and Crean set out on their climb – about as forlorn a hope as the voyage they had just, against all odds, completed.

They started at 7 a.m. on 19 May, their equipment a makeshift sledge, knocked up from the timbers of the *James Caird*, a Primus filled with oil, Bovril extract and biscuits packed into a spare pair of socks, forty-eight matches, the carpenter's adze (to use as an ice-axe) and fifty feet of rope. With no sleeping bags and inadequate clothing they realized the crossing would have to be made swiftly. By mid-afternoon they were lost in a switchback of valley and precipice-cum-scree in the centre of the island. Worsley describes how, at the top of a particularly high and difficult ridge, they paused exhausted, peering down into the misty darkness below.

It was impossible to see if there was a way down. After cutting steps for about 200 yards Shackleton halted the party on a little ledge. It was difficult to tell if the slope steepened to a precipice or eased off into the valley seen dimly below. Shackleton said: 'We'll try it.' I coiled my share of the rope beneath me as chafing gear, and straddled behind Sir Ernest: Crean did the same for me, and so, locked together, we let go. I was never more scared in my life than for the first 30 seconds. Our speed was terrific. Crean had hard work to prevent the adze coming round and cutting into us. Then, to our relief and joy, the slope curved out, and we shot into a bank of soft snow. I estimate we had covered a mile in three minutes, and lowered our altitude by 2,500 feet. We stood up and shook hands – very pleased with ourselves – until we inspected our trousers!

The moon was their ally; it shone brightly, showing up the crevasses as they picked their way over snowfield and glacier. In the small hours of the morning they crept exhausted into the shelter of an overhanging rock. Shackleton let his companions doze for a couple of minutes, altered their watches, then woke them and told them they had been asleep for an hour. They struggled on, and at dawn saw far beneath them the whaling station at Husvik. Their dramatic entry, with small boys fleeing in terror at their approach, is described by one of the whalers:

Everybody knew Shackleton well, and we very sorry he is lost in ice with all hands. We not know three terrible-looking bearded men who walk into office off the mountainside. Manager say 'Who the hell are you?', and terrible bearded man in the centre of the three say very quietly, 'my name is Shackleton'. Me – I turn away and weep. I think Manager weep too.

Later, when the three had fed, washed and rested, there took place an incident which shows very clearly the high regard in which Shackleton will always be held by those who know the Antarctic.

In the evening, [Worsley tells us] the Manager informed Sir Ernest that a number of seamen wished to speak to us. . . . Four white-haired veterans of the sea came forward; one spoke in Norse and the Manager translated. He said that he had been at sea over 40 years, that he knew the Southern Ocean intimately, from South Georgia to Cape Horn and from Elephant Island to the South Orkneys, and that never had he heard of such a wonderful feat of seamanship as bringing a 22-ft open boat from Elephant Island to South Georgia, and then, to crown it, tramping across the ice, snow and rocky heights of the interior, and that he felt it an honour to meet and shake hands with Sir Ernest and his comrades. He finished with a dramatic gesture:
    'These are men!'
All the seamen present then came forward and solemnly shook hands with us in turn. Coming from a great seafaring race like the Norwegians, this was a wonderful tribute.

The finale of Shackleton's expedition reads like a fairy tale come true. Within forty-eight hours of his arrival in Husvik a whalecatcher had rescued his three men from the opposite side of the island, and attempts to get through to the men on Elephant Island were under way. These attempts, it is true, did not bear fruit for several months; but eventually, aboard the Chilean vessel *Yelcho*, Shackleton fought his way through the winter ice to his marooned men. He was only just in time.

We are told that during the intervening months on Elephant Island Frank Wild had woken his ship's company every morning with the cry: 'Lash up and stow, boys. The Boss may come today.' And at last, on the morning of 30 August 1916, his optimism was rewarded.

'Are you all well?' Shackleton shouted anxiously from the deck of the *Yelcho*.

'All safe!' Wild shouted back. 'All well!'

Shackleton's face lit up, and the years seemed to fall from his shoulders. A few months later, aboard the repaired *Aurora*, he was standing into McMurdo Sound to pick up the men who for more than fifteen months had been marooned on the opposite side of the continent.

Many times during the last two years it must have seemed to Shackleton that not one of the *Endurance*'s ship's company would survive; instead, thanks largely to his leadership and to the fact that he never hesitated to place his own life in hazard, not one had been lost. His expedition, it is true, had failed. But history has endorsed Frank Worsley's comment that 'among all his achievements, great as they were, his one failure was the most glorious'.

It was more than forty years before Shackleton's dream was resuscitated, and then by a man of equal courage but very different character.

Vivian Fuchs was born in February 1908. He is a scholar first and an explorer second: a quietly spoken man whose unassuming manner hides a resolution every bit as inflexible as Shackleton's. In 1948 he took a survey team to the Falkland Island Dependencies; and it was, he tells us, while blizzard-bound in a tent at the approaches to Alexander Island that he first thought seriously of crossing the Antarctic. Five years later he was explaining his scheme to Edmund Hillary, the conqueror of Everest. In their book *The Crossing of Antarctica* the two men outline both the plan and the purpose of what was later to become the British Commonwealth Trans-Antarctic Expedition.

> One party [wrote Fuchs] was to travel from the head of the Weddell Sea [via the Pole] to McMurdo Sound in the Ross Sea, a distance of nearly 2,000 miles. They would use tracked vehicles, with dogs and aircraft in support. From the Ross Sea another party was to reconnoitre a route onto the polar plateau . . . from a base in McMurdo Sound; they would lay food and fuel depots along the expedition's route, thereby reducing the load which would otherwise have to be carried across the continent. . . . During the course of the crossing seismic soundings and a gravity traverse would be made to discover the depth of the polar ice sheet and the form of the rock surface beneath. . . .

> I felt that Fuchs's underlying urge [adds Hillary] came from an honest love of adventure and the prestige that he felt would accrue to his country if he were the first man to succeed in such a long and hazardous undertaking. And with this approach I heartily agreed – I have never needed a spate of excuses, scientific or otherwise, before I considered a job was worth attempting.

It is clear from this that the crossing was conceived primarily as an adventure –

Sir Edmund Hillary, Dr Vivian Fuchs and Rear Admiral George Dufek (American Task Force Commander) at the South Pole, 19 January 1958

'the last great land journey to be undertaken on earth'. Scientific considerations, however, were to be increasingly important. For it was soon apparent that Fuchs's expedition would coincide with the International Geophysical Year.

The International Geophysical Year (IGY for short) has been described as 'the most significant peaceful activity of mankind since the Renaissance'. And if this sounds a somewhat high-flown claim, the fact is that from July 1957 to July 1958, some 30,000 scientists from sixty-six countries were engaged in research at more than 1,000 stations throughout the world; and that at the end of the year the scientists pooled their findings, *in toto* and without reservation, for the benefit of mankind. Antarctica was recognized as a magnificent natural laboratory for this geophysical research, and more than sixty stations were set up close to or inside the Circle. The studies carried out included meteorology, magnetism, oceanography and (in particular) glaciology; and it was in connection with the last of these that Fuchs's scientific programme took on a new importance. By the time his expedition got under way, it was no longer enough for him to cross the continent; he found himself committed, as part of the British contribution to the IGY, to making regular seismic shots and gravity readings along every few miles of his route.

Fuchs's plan involved three separate phases: establishing a winter base at the head of the Weddell Sea (leader Ken Blaiklock); laying food and fuel depots from the Ross Sea as far as possible towards the Pole (leader Edmund Hillary); and finally the actual crossing of the continent by Sno-cat and Weasel (leader Vivian Fuchs).

Phase One started on 14 November 1955 when the expedition sailed from London in the *Theron*, a small but robust vessel specially designed for work in the ice. A couple of days before Christmas, at the approaches to the Weddell Sea, the members of the expedition met their first adversary, the consolidated pack. And almost at once they came near to suffering the fate of the *Endurance*. In spite of their steel hull, their reconnaissance aircraft and their 1,300 hp engines they became frozen in. It was a frustrating experience. For week after week the *Theron* drifted this way and that at the mercy of current and wind, her crew hacking at the ice with picks, shovels and explosive charges, while her captain tried unsuccessfully to force a way through.

It is impossible [Fuchs wrote in his diary] to describe adequately this butting of the ice. The ship runs up through the crowded brash, forcing three or four-foot-thick plates of ice, many yards in extent, beneath her keel, or up-ending them alongside her hull. Then with a shuddering bump the bow rises on a floe – up and up we seem to go – when suddenly she subsides, and cracks go shooting across the ice. Other times she hangs there with her bows up, and we have to go astern to try once more. Over and over the process is repeated, while the ship jars, twists and shudders till one feels she will fall apart.

Fuchs was attempting to pioneer a direct route to the head of the Weddell Sea; but the way was blocked, and he was fortunate in mid-January to be able to force his way east into the conventional sea lanes which had been followed by Filchner and Shackleton. Here the floes were broken by ice-free leads, and progress was resumed. As soon as the coastal ice cliffs appeared over the horizon, Fuchs and Blaiklock took off in their Auster in the hope of sighting a suitable landing place from the air. They were disappointed. The one harbour that might have offered a safe anchorage, Halley Bay, was seen to be hemmed in to landward by glaciers and crevasses which would have precluded a subsequent advance on the Pole. Fuchs was in a dilemma. For the *Theron* had spent so long in the Weddell Sea that the brief Antarctic summer was already drawing to a close, and the vessel would soon have to be homeward bound. He decided to lie up beside a tongue of ice that looked as if it would be strong enough to support the weight of equipment and stores, and had reasonable access to the hinterland. Unloading started on 30 January.

Progress was slow. It was found that the tractors, which should have been first ashore, had been stowed at the bottom of the hold. This did not seem particularly serious at the time. But on 1 February, Gerald Bowman tells us, the wind backed and increased in fury:

Soon a full-scale blizzard was blowing from the north. The sea was whipped up, and great waves began crashing and breaking over the ice shelf which formed the landing-stage. It had been impossible [without tractors] to keep the landing area clear of stores, and piles of material were still there when the storm broke. Fuchs called all hands onto the ice shelf, where they toiled, waist-high in freezing water, trying to drag the material to safety. [A great deal of it, however, was damaged.] Meanwhile the *Theron* was being pounded by high seas and was bumping and grinding heavily against the ice edge. Suddenly a great mass of floating ice loomed out of the blizzard and crashed into the vessel's side. Her stern anchors were torn from their cables, her forward moorings parted, and the horrified men on the ice-stage saw their ship whirled away. In seconds she was engulfed in the blizzard.

As she disappeared in the maelstrom of spindrift and spume her captain's shout came faintly over the roar of the storm: 'We'll be back.'

The *Theron* was back, against all odds, in less than an hour, Captain Maro bringing her skilfully alongside the ice shelf, with ropes, rope ladders and scrambling nets draped over her side. Fuchs ordered everyone aboard, and man after man swarmed up the swinging, corkscrewing ropes to the comparative safety of the *Theron*'s deck. The vessel then stood into the centre of the bay to ride out the storm.

Within twenty-four hours the weather cleared and she returned again to the edge of the ice. It was obvious, however, that she would not be able to stay for long; for every day the sea ice was thickening and drawing closer to the shore. Unloading became an emergency. For five days the men worked non-stop, first discharging the cargo, then carrying it from the water's edge to the base camp at Shackleton which had been sited about a mile and a half inland. By the morning of 7 February everything had been unloaded, though rather less than half of it had been carried to base. That afternoon a vast conglomeration of pack ice was seen to be drifting in from the north; it was clear that in a matter of hours the *Theron* would be hemmed in. At 3 p.m., with the water's edge still littered with stores and the base at Shackleton not yet started, let alone completed, orders were given to sail. To quote Hillary:

> The wintering party gathered their gear together and threw it overboard. Farewells were said, last instructions were given, and with almost unseemly haste the *Theron* sailed. As we drew away from the edge of the ice, the men left behind looked a lonely and forlorn group, and I doubt if there was anyone on board who didn't feel that we could have done more for them. Few parties have been deposited in the Antarctic so late in the season with so much to do – a hut to build, vast quantities of stores to haul to base, vehicles to be maintained, dogs to be fed, a meteorological programme to be instigated, radio communications to be established, together with the innumerable tasks that are demanded by the simple fact of living throughout the Antarctic winter. There was so much to do that once the ship had disappeared they must have wondered just where to start.

There were eight men in the wintering party, and their immediate tasks were to move some 300 tons of stores from shore to base, and to build themselves winter quarters. They decided to use their Sno-cat crate as a temporary shelter – and this in fact turned out to be their home for the better part of the winter, since wind,

The Ferguson tractor and 'caboose' in which Sir Edmund Hillary drove to the South Pole

A Sno-cat being checked and loaded before leaving South Ice on Christmas Day

cold and lack of timber was to prevent their building a hut. Moving the stores turned out to be a slow business, with frequent delays due to mechanical trouble with the tractors and appalling weather. They had shifted barely a third when a violent blizzard swept in from the sea; the ice shelf that had looked so solid was split asunder and pounded to fragments, and they lost 300 drums of fuel, all their coal, most of their building timber and seal meat, and a Ferguson tractor.

They knew then that they were in for a long, cold and difficult winter.

Fuchs describes their ordeal:

With the beginning of March the weather deteriorated, blinding drift obliterated everything; conditions which were repeated day after day in the weeks and months to come. Wind was their greatest enemy. Relentless, unremitting wind, driving a torrent of snow like a horizontal waterfall, to fill every nook and cranny, burying everything in its path, and making what would have been bearable temperatures almost impossible to endure. . . . At night they retired to their tents; but comfortable sleep was a rare thing, for the temperature fell to $-45°$ F, and their sleeping bags became heavy with frozen condensation, cracking and creaking as the men crept into them.

It says much for the tenacity and inventiveness of Blaiklock's party that in spite of this inauspicious beginning they were able that winter to complete virtually the whole of their work programme. By the time the main expedition came back the following summer, they had managed, somehow, to erect their main hut, install their radio and electrical equipment, train their dogs, *and* pioneer a route towards the Shackleton Mountains and the Pole.

223

Ken Blaiklock has seldom been given the credit for these achievements that he deserves. His uncomplaining efforts, that winter, in the obscurity of the Weddell Sea, laid the foundations on which Fuchs and Hillary were subsequently to build. Polar exploration has few finer examples of unsung, unselfish teamwork.

The *Theron*, meanwhile, had come within a hairsbreadth of being hemmed in by the ice, an enormous floe drifting alongside the ice shelf only a few minutes after she had cast off. She managed, in the nick of time, to squeeze through the narrowing gap, and after a twelve-hour battle with the massing and steadily thickening pack, broke through to open water. A month later Hillary was back in the New Zealand Alps starting a season of intensive training, while Fuchs was back in London supervising the final preparations for his crossing next year. Both returned, the following summer, to Antarctica.

Hillary's New Zealand party was the first to arrive, nosing into McMurdo Sound on New Year's Day, 1957: eighteen men, sixty dogs, seven tractors and a Beaver reconnaissance aircraft. They found the Americans already established at the head of the Sound – they had built an airstrip there, which they were using to ferry men and supplies to their laboratory at the Pole (the *pièce de résistance* of America's programme for the IGY). Rear Admiral Dufek of the U.S. Navy went out of his way to help the new arrivals, lending them an icebreaker to clear their route to shore and a helicopter to help their reconnaissance. After a couple of flights it was decided to set up a base at Pram Point, on the southwest tip of Ross Island (only a mile or two from the site of Scott's Hut Point), and to ascend the polar plateau by way of the little-known Skelton Glacier. These were shrewd choices and the foundation of the New Zealanders' subsequent success.

To quote Hillary: 'Once I had made these decisions, I wasted no time in swinging the expedition into action.' And 'swinging' and 'action' were appropriate words! Hillary had not been 100 per cent happy with events the previous summer aboard the *Theron*. 'We made some big mistakes', he wrote at the time, 'and had been no more than a whisker from failure.' He had jotted down in his diary some maxims for future guidance:

1. It is better to delay sailing for several days and to have things correctly stowed than to arrive at your destination with immediate necessities at the bottom of the hold.
2. Aerial reconnaissance should be carried out *before* the ship enters heavy ice, as there may not be enough water to get a plane off once the ship is stuck.
3. It is vital that the prime objectives of the expedition be given undivided attention.
4. When unloading, one of the first necessities ashore is some form of shelter and heating.
5. Any equipment unloaded onto sea ice must be dragged away immediately and never left at the mercy of bad weather. It is essential therefore that the first thing off the ship should be a vehicle ready for action.

Now, a year later, he was to put these theories to the test. And everything went like clockwork. Food, equipment and building materials were unloaded swiftly and were hauled post haste to the site of the party's winter quarters – indicative of the speed of operations is the fact that the floor of the prefabricated hut was laid one day and the building completed the next – and to quote Hillary: 'Unloading progressed so satisfactorily and the buildings went up so smoothly that it was soon clear we would be ahead of schedule in our completion of Scott Base. . . . I therefore decided to investigate at once a route to the Polar plateau.'

The Beaver aircraft had already been test-flown, and on 18 January Bill Cranfield and Hillary took off to survey the Skelton Glacier.

Soon [writes the latter] we were flying between the massive peaks which lined the valley and were pleased to note that the lower part of the glacier seemed straightforward and easy, except for crevassing along the sides. About 40 miles up, we came to a much steeper rise. To the left of us was a great ice fall – criss-crossed with crevasses and offering no route for vehicles or dogs. But long snowslopes led out to the right, and although these were peppered with crevasses it looked as if a zig-zag route through them would lead to the fields at the head of the glacier. We flew up through this magnificent area, with its great mountains and spectacular glaciers, and as the route unfolded beneath us our enthusiasm for it grew. It is difficult from an aircraft to judge accurately the steepness of a slope or to locate hidden crevasses, but as far as we could tell the Skelton offered excellent prospects. We reached the glacier névé, and could see in the far distance several gaps in the mountain rim which encircled it. . . . Climbing to 8,000 feet we headed for one of them. As we approached, it opened into a wide and easy ramp sweeping up through the névé and onto the broad expanse of the Polar plateau. What a thrill it was to see this plateau disappearing unbroken to the horizon!

In the course of the next few weeks the New Zealanders completed their winter quarters, pioneered a route by dog team up the Skelton Glacier, and established two well-stocked, well-sited depots, one at the bottom of the glacier and one at the top – spectacular achievements brought about by hard work and careful planning. At the end of February their ship the *Endeavour* sailed for New Zealand; and a few days later a spell of blizzards and intense cold heralded the approach of winter. Hillary withdrew his team to the environs of Scott Base.

It was a well-satisfied group of men who settled down to face the winter. Things had gone well: so well in fact that when Hillary came to plan his programme for the following spring, he decided not only to lay depots across the plateau, but to try also to take his tractors right the way through to the Pole. This idea received little encouragement from the expedition's Executive Committee; but Hillary took the view (rightly or wrongly) that provided he laid all the depots that Fuchs and his crossing party could possibly need, he should be allowed freedom of action to pursue whatever subsidiary objectives he thought fit. Winter was spent in modifying the Ferguson tractors, in making local journeys across the ice shelf, in exercising the dogs, and in eating! A comparison of Hillary's Sunday menu (in 1957) with Andersson's (in 1902) shows how the face of polar exploration had changed. The latter's Sunday fare had consisted of 'porridge, cold seal meat and two cups of coffee'; Hillary's consisted of:

| *Breakfast* : | Cereals and apricots | *Dinner* : | Game Soup |
|---|---|---|---|
| | Bacon and scrambled egg | | Curry entrée |
| | | | Roast beef and Yorkshire pudding |
| *Lunch* : | Tomato purée | | Roast parsnips |
| | Cold roast lamb | | Boiled onions |
| | Mashed potato | | Mashed potatoes |
| | Fruit salad | | Tinned green beans |
| | | | Boiled pudding and custard |

Wine was served on Sundays and birthdays.

Without wishing in any way to denigrate present-day explorers, courage and achievement proceed more easily from a full stomach than from an empty one.

The winter was uneventful. Hillary tells us:

> The most eagerly awaited periods were when the moon was up and the whole world was bathed in silvery light. Our dogs were picketed on the snow in front of the house, and we had them running whenever conditions and light permitted. Going out with the dogs on a crisp moonlight night was an experience to remember . . . and the benefit of keeping them exercised became evident when we began travelling in the spring.

Spring travelling started in earnest on 14 October. That afternoon Hillary and his support party set out for the polar plateau. And at almost exactly the same moment, on the opposite side of Antarctica, Fuchs and his trans-continental party set out from the Weddell Sea.

The passage of Hillary's Ferguson tractors from the coast to the central plateau has few dramatic highlights. It was a hard rather than a spectacular slog: a continual battle to prevent the tractors becoming bogged down or falling into the ubiquitous crevasses. The Americans, Hillary tells us, had looked somewhat askance at the Fergusons which, compared to their own big Sno-cats, looked like toys – 'and rather battered and misused toys at that! They [the Americans] wished us well', Hillary adds, 'but freely expressed the opinion that we wouldn't get more than 50 miles.' The Fergusons, however, surprised everyone by their robustness and reliability, ploughing happily through soft snow and up impossible gradients in a temperature of $-40°$ F. It would be misleading to infer that the ascent of the Skelton was anything other than arduous and hazardous, but in Hillary's book, *No Latitude for Error*, it is the glacier's beauty which stands out more vividly than its dangers.

> [October 18th]
> I looked out on a strangely beautiful scene. To the south the sun was a molten ball of fire on the horizon, and its rays brought into sharp relief the jagged sastrugi and transformed their hills and hollows into a patchwork of flame and shadow. The sky glowed a delicate purple, while the great peaks standing all around us were dressed in crimson robes. We were swimming along in a sea of glorious colour, and for awhile I forgot the cold and the discomfort. We drove on and on through the night. Every now and then, when the cold became too unpleasant, we would stop and warm ourselves with a hot drink, or stamp around to get our circulation going again. . . . [October 28th] Before

(left) Sno-cat *Rock 'n Roll* down a crevasse
(below) Aluminium bridges in position underneath Sno-cat *Able* to enable her to be hauled out of her predicament

long the wind dropped to a whisper, and we entered an area of bright sunlight and superb views. The Skelton névé was like a fairyland. The broad expanses of virgin snow, the lovely blue of the sky, the black rock precipices rimming the basin to the south, and the wonderful peaks of the Western Mountains combined to form a scene that would be hard to surpass. Across the middle of the picture we were drawing two long straight lines as our tractors chugged along.

Three days later Hillary climbed out of the Skelton and onto the plateau. He knew at this moment that the rest of his depot laying would be comparatively easy, that Fuchs's requirements would be met. 'To see our battered vehicles and laden sledges at the Plateau Depot', he wrote, 'seemed the fulfilment of an impossible dream. I don't think that ever before, even on the summit of Everest, had I felt a greater sense of achievement.'

During the next two months the New Zealanders established depots close to the 78th, 80th and 82nd parallels, aircraft, tractors and dogs working in relays to bring up both fuel and food. It was difficult work. There were whiteouts, forced landings and abortive take-offs for the plane; while on several occasions the tractors toppled into crevasses and were only saved from plummeting to unknown depths by their towlines. The supply dumps, however, were built up steadily, pound by pound. By 20 December the New Zealanders had fulfilled, and more than fulfilled, all the depot laying that could possibly be required of them. Fuchs, however, on the opposite side of the continent, was bogged down over 500 miles from the Pole; he was making slow progress; and Hillary decided to push south to meet him.

To start with the going was not too difficult. At the approaches to the Pole, however, the plateau rose to close on 10,000 feet, and the tractors, in the rarefied atmosphere, began to lose power. Then they were held up by an area of crevasses. The delays, however, were no more than temporary; and, building cairns every few hundred yards and marking the snowbridges with flags, Hillary pushed steadily over the plateau. He sighted the American laboratory at the Pole a little after midday on 4 January.

> I turned off my motor for the last time [he writes] and scrambled wearily out of the seat. We were swept away in a confusion of congratulations, photographs and questions, then led off by friendly hands towards the warmth and fresh food of the Polar Station. But before I descended underground I took a last look at our Fergusons. The farm tractors, tilted over like hip-shot horses, looked lonely and neglected, like broken toys cast aside after playtime. There was no doubt about it, our tractor train was a bit of a laugh! Yet the Fergusons had brought us across twelve hundred and fifty miles of snow and ice, crevasse and sastrugi, soft snow and blizzard. They were the first vehicles to drive to the South Pole.

As soon as he had rested, Hillary checked his leader's position. He found that Fuchs, alarmingly behind schedule, was still more than 300 miles from the Pole. Things, he felt, had gone wrong and the Weddell Sea party had little chance of

228    (above) Moon halo (Mt Erebus behind) and a vertical beam, 12 June 1905, by George Marston (Shackleton Expedition)
(below) The coast of Elephant Island on one of the few bright evenings experienced by the men left behind, by George Marston (Shackleton Expedition)
(overleaf) Twin-Otter aircraft on the ice, Adelaide Island, 15 February 1973

completing their crossing before they were caught, quite possibly with fatal consequences, by the advent of winter. He suggested to Fuchs that the crossing was abandoned or at least postponed.

He had reckoned without his leader's tenacity of purpose.

Vivian Fuchs and his party arrived off the coast of Antarctica a couple of days after Hillary. It was, however, 12 January before they reached their base at Shackleton, 1 February before they selected a site (South Ice) for their inland base; and 22 February before the latter could boast any buildings. And if this, compared to the New Zealanders on the opposite side of the continent, seems slow progress, two facts should be borne in mind. Firstly, Fuchs was pioneering new territory whereas Hillary was following in the footsteps of a whole line of explorers such as Borchgrevink, Scott, Amundsen and Shackleton; secondly, the terrain behind the Filchner Ice Shelf is a great deal more difficult than that behind the Ross Ice Shelf. This latter fact had been suspected from reconnaissance flights and probing treks undertaken in the autumn; it was not, however, proved till the following spring, when Fuchs's column of Sno-cats and Weasels set out on their 2,000-mile journey.

Fuchs had allowed twenty days to cover some 260 miles from his sea base at Shackleton to his inland base at South Ice. But he quickly fell behind schedule; for he found his route crisscrossed by crevasses the extent of which had not been apparent from the air. These crevasses were a great problem; for they were often covered by a 'windcrust' of innocent-looking snow which was strong enough to support a man on skis but not a Sno-cat or Weasel. Time and again the vehicles lurched into potholes and teetered on the edge of chasms which disappeared into unknown depths. Fuchs did the only possible thing; he linked his tractors together by 3-inch cables, so that if one fell into a crevasse it could be pulled out by the others. However, to quote his own words, 'Driving roped together presents its problems, for the rope must not be so taut as to restrict the acceleration of the vehicle in front, nor so loose as to be run over and snapped by the vehicle behind. Later we were to acquire considerable skill in "roped" driving but to start with our maximum speed was $3\frac{1}{2}$ mph.'

As the expedition edged south into the Shackleton Mountains, the terrain became more and more difficult. Soon they found themselves in a veritable forest of sastrugi, between which a network of crevasses ran in every conceivable direction – 'it was a place', writes Fuchs, 'with a queer "lost world" atmosphere, as though we had strayed unexpectedly into a region of the moon.' His account of the next few days needs no enlarging on.

Nov. 3rd. The ridge, with its chaotic mass of ice hummocks resembling a ploughed field, was now replaced by an elongated basin about $2\frac{1}{2}$ miles long. Its smooth surface looked easy enough, but we were dismayed to find that tadpole-shaped depressions [a sure indication of crevasses beneath] occurred over the whole area. We covered a bare $\frac{1}{2}$ mile that day. The Weasel broke through twice in 100 yards, and the second time we

Dr Michael Gill, in 1967, was the first man to climb Mt Herschel.

nearly lost it altogether, for it hung precariously lengthwise over a crevasse-bridge which had already broken along one side. It was only possible to pull it out along the length of the bridge, and so certain were we that it was going down that every item was unloaded before the attempt was made. . . . November 6th. We used thin aluminium tubes, six feet long, to probe the layers of snow and ice, and assumed the area safe if resistance was still encountered at the full depth of the thrust. Ice-chisels mounted on long wooden poles were used to test the crevasse-bridges, which reverberated loudly and we called 'boomers'. A hole would be cut in the bridge until it was possible to thrust one's head far enough in to see the width and direction of the crevasse. Hanging down over a bottomless pit, with sloping blue-white sides disappearing into the depths, gave the impression of gazing into deep water; it can also be somewhat alarming when you know you will soon be driving a 3-ton tractor over the abyss! By the evening we had prepared another half-mile of the route, and were bringing forward the vehicles in what seemed to be a relatively trouble-free area, when we were surrounded by a rumbling noise like underground thunder: at the same time there was a shuddering and gentle collapse of the whole snow surface. Suddenly two enormous holes, 30 to 40 feet long and 12 feet wide, appeared on either side of the track just ahead of the vehicles. They stopped. Their vibration had caused the bridge of a crevasse just ahead to fall in, but along the route we had probed it stood firm. David Pratt cautiously led on with his Weasel, but he suddenly plunged through a snow bridge six feet thick, and hung precariously suspended by the very front of his vehicle and by a short length of track at the rear. Had the crevasse been six inches wider he would certainly have fallen headlong down. . . . By midnight, when the 'cat' had pulled him out backward, there was a semi-whiteout and we were very tired, so we camped where we were, surrounded by gaping holes.

Small wonder that it took Fuchs not twenty days but thirty-seven to reach South Ice. Nor did his arrival mark the end of his troubles; for more tractors, more fuel, more equipment and more dog teams and food had to be laboriously assembled before the column could continue its advance on the Pole.

Throughout November supplies were fought through. It was hard, temper-fraying, unspectacular work; the tractors needed frequent maintenance (never once could they be driven in top gear, and the fact that they were 'roped' imposed serious strains on their steering); while the aircraft were hampered by high winds and whiteouts.

The aircraft, in fact, only survived because of the skill of their pilots. David Stratton, Fuchs's second-in-command, describes a typical incident when the plane in which he was flying had to take off in a semi-whiteout from the frozen surface of a lake; the lake was small, and hemmed in by ice ridges and nunataks.

It was soon obvious that we were not going to be able to gain sufficient height to clear the ice ridges at the side of the nunatak, and sure enough we gave the crest a number of heavy glancing blows, then fluttered down into the hollow on the other side. Unfortunately this was neither deep enough nor long enough to allow us to gain flying speed and control, and it became apparent we were bumping and boring into the wind-scoop at the side of the nunatak which had a 200-foot ice wall at the head of it. Gordon

The Crossing Party at the South Pole, 19 January 1958. Fuchs (front row left)

Coal seams in the Theron Mountains which correspond to the main coal horizons of Australia and South Africa

took the only possible course – cut his engine – and we bumped and slithered along the bare ice, running parallel to the rock wall. It seemed to take an interminable time to reduce speed, and as we did so a boulder appeared right ahead. Hard-a-port meant descent on to the rocky scree to our left; hard-a-starboard meant ascending the side of the windscoop. Gordon chose the latter, and as we made a violent lurch up the hill, the tail ski jammed in a meltwater crack and was torn off, bringing us to an abrupt halt, perched precariously like a fly on the wall of the windscoop.

Many times that spring, as supplies were flown south, similar accidents were avoided or minimized by the pilots' skill; and both Fuchs and Hillary agree that the aircrew of the Beaver, Otter and Austers played a major part in the expedition's success.

It was late December before Fuchs was ready to move on. Then, on Christmas Eve, his column of tractors again headed south: four Sno-cats, three Weasels and a Muskeg, with dog teams reconnoitring the trail ahead.

As they approached the polar pleateau, Fuchs describes a typical scene:

January 1st. 30 miles today, but what a labour! The vehicles continually in first or second gear as they lurched over the sastrugi. It was impossible to go round these ice-hard ridges, for they formed a field that extended in all directions. The best that could be done was for each driver to judge the course of his own vehicle, and we often found ourselves scattered a mile or two apart, working and weaving our way among ridges four or five feet high, and trying to keep within reasonable distance of the tracks left by the dogs.

By the New Year, Fuchs had struggled only as far as the 84th parallel, whereas from the opposite side of the continent the New Zealanders were virtually within sight of the Pole. This was partly because of the appalling terrain and partly because of the meticulous care with which Fuchs carried out his seismic traverses. The New Zealanders, in contrast, had far easier terrain and far fewer scientific obligations.

It seemed to Hillary that the crossing would have to be postponed and the tractors left overwinter at the American laboratory. As we have seen, he suggested this in his controversial and much publicized message to Fuchs. The latter, however, in spite of all indications to the contrary, was on the edge of a breakthrough. On 6, 7, and 8 January his tractors averaged more than 30 miles a day as they came for the first time to terrain that was mercifully free of crevasses and sastrugi.

From this moment the crossing of the continent was for Fuchs relatively straight-forward. It was still a long and hard haul; but the terrain held no more surprises, and one thing only could now have jeopardized his success – a prolonged spell of bad weather. This he was spared; and by the morning of Sunday, 19 January the Weddell Sea party was approaching the Pole.

Hillary, who had remained behind to welcome them, describes their arrival.

What an imposing sight they were! The four great Sno-cats gave an impression of enormous power, and the Weasel and dog teams made up an extensive entourage. Every vehicle and sledge had a flag flying as they swept up at high speed to come to a halt beside us. Bunny [Fuchs] jumped out of the leading Sno-cat and we shook hands and exchanged greetings. We drove back to the Pole Station in some disorder but in high spirits.

Fuchs spent five days in the luxury of the U.S. laboratory – with its air-conditioning, hot showers and cinema it seemed, he tells us, like another world. Then, with his tractors overhauled and reloaded and Hillary coming part of the way as guide, he set out on the second stage of his journey. He was not yet halfway across the continent; but from now on he would be traversing ground that was proven and marked, and depots well stocked with food and fuel had been left at strategic intervals along his route.

While aircraft evacuated the bases at Shackleton and South Ice, Fuchs pushed steadily north towards McMurdo Sound. The journey could hardly be described as easy. On one occasion his compasses went wild, and he had to steer by hand-planted flags. On another occasion his leading tractor, 'Rock 'n Roll', went careering round in a circle, out of control with its steering broken. But in spite of these hold-ups Fuchs managed to average 30 miles a day. He descended the Skelton Glacier in less than two days, and by the end of February was fairly racing over the Ross Ice Shelf. The end now was almost literally in sight.

It came in the early afternoon of 2 March 1958 when the Sno-cats thundered in triumph up to the huts of Scott Base. 'Our long journey', wrote Fuchs, 'was over at last. We had travelled 2,158 miles. We had estimated that the journey would take 100 days at an average speed of 20 miles per day. In fact we completed the trip in 99 days at an average of 22 miles a day.' After a slow and laborious start the Trans-Antarctic Expedition had built up to a successful and well-deserved climax. After forty-four years Shackleton's dream had been realized.

FUCHS'S EXPEDITION was in many ways a bridge between old and new; for it combined the nineteenth-century preoccupation with attaining a geographical goal, with the twentieth-century preoccupation with science.

It is easy to understand the purpose of the old type of expedition – every schoolboy can appreciate the motives of Wilkes or Ross, Amundsen or Scott. It is not perhaps so easy to understand the purpose of more recent expeditions. Why, one wonders, should a graduate in psychology deliberately isolate himself in darkness throughout an Antarctic winter? Why should a meteorologist spend eight consecutive years on the bleakest littoral on earth studying molecular emissions from the aurora?

A diver preparing to go through sea ice

R. H. Ragle, the leader of a 'deep-drilling' project at Little America, headquarters of Operation Deep Freeze IV, checks the core brought up from below 500 ft.

The answer lies, I think, in the fact that twentieth-century man believes in the adage that to know all is to understand all. And Antarctica has recently become recognized as an untapped reservoir of knowledge, a unique uncontaminated laboratory from which man can learn not only about his planet but also about himself – the psychologist immured in darkness, for example, is, in the case I am thinking of, a specialist in the treatment of deprived children, studying at first-hand the effects of mental and physical isolation.

This quest for knowledge is in itself more commendable than the old-fashioned quest for land. What raises it to an even higher plane is the fact that the whole vast spectrum of knowledge now brought back from the Antarctic is made available, as a matter of course, to all mankind. This Utopian state of affairs is due partly to the International Geophysical Year and partly to the Antarctic Treaty.

The basic concept of the IGY – that of exchanging scientific information between the nations – is hardly new. Pythagoras or Galileo, for example, would have been horrified at the suggestion that his work might be exclusive to any particular country. On the other hand the spirit of nationalism has been so strong in recent centuries that the idea of pooling data does, to contemporary eyes, have a novel gloss. It was Alexander von Humboldt who, in the early nineteenth century, did most to revive the medieval concept of a commonweal of science; for he managed to persuade the British and Russian governments to set up joint stations all over the world from which to conduct the study of geomagnetism. His lead was followed by the German Gauss, the American Maury and the Austrian Weyprecht; and it was largely due to the pioneering work of these far-sighted scientists that the first International Polar Year was held in 1882. A second Polar Year was celebrated in 1932–33, and the idea of holding a third was mooted soon after World War II by a group of U.S. scientists led by Dr Van Allen; 1957 was suggested as a suitable year, since sunspot activity was then expected to be at a maximum. The task of getting such a scheme started was daunting in the extreme, for the Cold War was at its zenith, and Antarctica itself was bedevilled by conflicting and often bitterly contested territorial claims. It soon became apparent, however, that the scientists of the world were better ambassadors for peace than the politicians; and, to quote H. G. R. King, 'the spirit of mutual trust and co-operation displayed in the early stages of the IGY has characterized the relationships between all nations in Antarctica from that day to this'.

In 1955 a committee was set up to co-ordinate the IGY programme in the Antarctic, its objectives being to avoid duplication of effort, to deploy national resources to the best advantage and to evolve a system for the international dissemination of reports. Twelve nations agreed to set up fifty-five observation posts on or around the continent. Some of these were single huts manned by no more than three or four men; others like the U.S. base at the Pole and the U.S.S.R. base at the Pole of Inaccessibility, were highly sophisticated complexes, with a staff of between twenty and thirty. Before the IGY, only one man (Byrd) had ever wintered in

(above) The American base at Hut Point, McMurdo Sound. Beyond on the runway of the Sound's ice surface are some of the ski-equipped planes attached to Operation Deep Freeze. In the distance Mt Discovery
(left) The helicopter from the icebreaker U.S.S. *Glacier* unloads stores on to the ice.

Antarctica more than a couple of miles from the coast. During the winters of 1957 and 1958, however, as many as ten stations were established deep in the heart of the continent. This, on the physical plane, was a hard-won breakthrough. Hard won because the pioneers of Antarctica, like the pioneers of space, soon discovered that man's body does not adapt easily to a novel environment. In the Russian base at Sovetskaya, for example, the scientists 'suffered headaches, shortness of breath, pounding of the heart and low blood pressure; at night they woke with the feeling that they were choking'; and in their first couple of months at the Pole the majority of the Americans lost more than 28 lb in weight. In spite of these pathological problems, nearly 100 men managed during the IGY to winter, with safety if not with comfort, in the heart of Antarctica. An even greater if less spectacular breakthrough was that many of the most successful stations were completely international. The Antarctic Weather Centre in the Bay of Whales, for example, was set up by American scientists, and was manned by meteorologists from Argentina, Australia, France, New Zealand, South Africa and the U.S.S.R., all of whom worked together in perfect harmony. The explorers at last were beating their swords into ploughshares. Oaks grow from acorns. And King may have an important point when he writes: 'very possibly the better understanding which exists between the Soviet Union and the Western nations today owes something to the personal friendships, the sharing of knowledge and the sharing of hardships [that took place] in the Antarctic.'

It was inconceivable that all this arduous, expensive and meaningful work should suddenly come to an end on 31 December 1958. And indeed before the IGY was even under way a committee had been set up to examine how scientific research in Antarctica might be continued. This committee (SCAR) had one overriding objective: to nurture the seed of international cooperation. It did valuable work.

It recommended the continuation of a wide range of investigations – meteorology, atmospheric radiation, auroral physics, geomagnetism, geology, glaciology, geomorphology, cartography, seismology, vulcanology, oceanography, biology and marine biology; it perfected a system whereby all findings from these sciences were automatically fed back to a number of International Data Centres and thence disseminated throughout the world; it also helped to bring about the climate of goodwill and cooperation that led to the signing a few years later of one of the great documents of modern times: the Antarctic Treaty.

This treaty was ratified on 23 June 1961. It was signed by all the nations who had participated in Antarctica in the IGY, together with Czechoslovakia, Denmark, Poland and the Netherlands. Its basic provisions have been nicely summarized by King:

> 1. Antarctica is to be used for peaceful purposes only. Military personnel may be employed there but only on scientific, essentially peaceful work.
> 2. The freedom of scientific investigation and cooperation which characterized the IGY is to continue.
> 3. All scientific observations are to be made freely available to all, and scientific personnel are to be exchanged.
> 4. All political claims (in particular claims to territory) are frozen for the duration of the Treaty (30 years).
> 5. Nuclear explosions and the tipping of radioactive waste are banned.
> 6. All stations and equipment are open to the inspection of observers appointed by the nations concerned.

Recommendations were also put forward with a view to preserving the continent's unique flora and fauna (i.e. no dogs to run free, no low-flying aircraft). And so long as these provisions and recommendations are adhered to there is every reason to hope that the resources of Antarctica will not, like those of other continents, be exploited haphazardly for the profit of the few but will be used with wisdom for the benefit of all.

This hope is summed up in the words of Admiral Byrd, quoted on the plaque of his memorial which today looks out over McMurdo Sound: 'I am hopeful that Antarctica, in its symbolic robe of white, will shine forth as a continent of peace as nations working together there in the cause of science set an example of international co-operation.' It is heartening to record that these hopes are being realized: that the ideals of the IGY and the Antarctic Treaty are, day by day, being transformed to reality by the scientists of the south.

Antarctica today in fact could be described as a continent of scientists. To give an example of the sort of work these scientists are doing, let us take the field of geology. Ever since man first sighted Antarctica he has been asking himself what it consists of. Is it, as Bellingshausen suggested, 'a continent of ice', or as D'Urville suggested, 'a layer of ice forming a crust over a base of rock'; or, as scientists have more recently suggested, 'two ice-covered land masses divided by a strait'?

The geologists' seismic recordings and radiometer photographs have recently given us the answer. Both seismic and gravity surveys indicate that the rock base of the greater part of Antarctica is continental in structure rather than oceanic; they indicate also that the rocks of the eastern or Gondwana province are very different in origin from those of the western or Andean section. This supports the theory that Antarctica consists in fact of two landmasses which have drifted together comparatively recently in the earth's history. And pictures taken by Very High Resolution Radiometers point to the same conclusion. These Radiometers are mounted in satellites flying some 700 miles above the earth; and the pictures they take indicate very clearly that if the ice cap were to melt, Antarctica would be revealed as an old easterly plateau (with structural affinities to South Africa and Australia) and a new westerly range of half-drowned mountains (a continuation of the Andes), the two landmasses being connected by an isthmus not much wider than Panama.

This geological research is typical of the way in which scientists in Antarctica are today pushing back the frontiers of the unknown. They are advancing knowledge. This quest for knowledge has been an important denominator of all the expeditions that have headed south: the wish to unravel mysteries previously unsolved – the mystery first of Antarctica's existence, then the mystery of its shape and size, and finally in recent years the mystery of its content. And if we wonder why men should have left the comfort of family and home to try to solve problems so far removed from their daily lives, no better answer has ever been given than by Nansen:

> An endless procession passes before us – a procession of struggling, frost-covered figures, some erect and powerful, others weak, bent and dying of hunger, cold or scurvy, but all looking forward into the unknown, all gazing beyond the sunset to where their goal might be found. . . . And what were these men seeking? They were setting out with conscious purpose to explore the unknown. In every part of the world and in every age, this quest for knowledge has driven man forward on the path of evolution. And so long as the human ear can listen for the breaking of waves on an unknown shore, so long as the human eye can try to follow the northern lights over silent snowfields, and so long as human thought can reach out toward distant worlds in space, so long will fascination of the unknown carry man ever forward and upward. When man loses this thirst for knowledge he will no longer be man.

The quest for knowledge is a noble one. And it is fitting that a noble story should end on a note of hope. In the past the knowledge brought back by explorers from other continents was often used for selfish ends – commercial exploitation or national aggrandizement. This, by and large, has been avoided in the Antarctic. It was avoided initially because the explorers found nothing that seemed worth bringing back or quarrelling over, and latterly because of the genuine international rapport that has sprung up among the scientists working there. This is the spirit of cooperation that Byrd dreamed of. And his dream has come true. For Antarctica today does indeed 'shine forth in her symbolic robes of white' as the one small corner of the earth where peace and goodwill among men is not a catchphrase but a reality.

# PRINCIPAL EXPEDITIONS TO THE ANTARCTIC

THERE HAVE BEEN nearly 300 expeditions to the mainland of Antarctica. It has not been possible, alas, in a single volume to do justice to them all; I have had to be selective.

Two criteria were used in making a selection. The expedition had to be interesting in itself, and it had to be of real significance in the context of Antarctic exploration as a whole. It was with deep regret that I had to limit many distinguished explorers – such as Weddell, Biscoe, Filchner and Mawson – to little more than a passing reference. It seemed better, however, to deal fully with a few major expeditions than to gloss superficially over many.

| Date | Nationality | Leader | Ship |
|---|---|---|---|

*c.* A.D. 650   Polynesian   Ui-te-Rangiora   canoe
According to Rarotongan legend, in the seventh century a number of canoes sailed into a place of bitter cold where the sea was covered with *pia* (a white powder) and 'things like great white rocks rose high into the sky'

1675   English   de la Roché
Discovery of South Georgia

1738–9   French   Bouvet   *Aigle*
Discovery of Bouvetøya

1771–2   French   Kerguélen   *Fortune*
Discovery of Kerguélen Islands

1772–5   British   Cook   *Resolution*
Circumnavigated the world in high southern latitude, thus disproving the existence of a temperate Great Southern Continent. First to cross Antarctic Circle. Landed in South Georgia, discovered South Sandwich Islands

1800–1   American   Fanning   *Aspasia*
57,000 fur seals killed; their pelts taken direct to China

1819   British   Smith   *Williams*
Sighted South Shetland Islands in February, revisited and landed on them in October

1819–21   Russian   Bellingshausen   *Vostok*
Circumnavigated Antarctica in a high southern latitude. First to sight mainland, 28 January 1820. Discovered Peter and Alexander Islands. Surveyed South Sandwich Islands

The British base Foxtrot on the Antarctic peninsula is one of the six scientific bases visited by the *John Biscoe*.

| *Date* | *Nationality* | *Leader* | *Ship* |
|---|---|---|---|
| 1819–20 | British | Bransfield | *Williams* |

Roughly surveyed South Shetland Islands. Sighted Antarctic peninsula, 1 February 1820. First to chart a portion of the mainland

| 1820–1 | American | Pendleton | *Frederick* |
|---|---|---|---|

Sealing expedition to South Shetland Islands; the occasion of Palmer's controversial voyage in the shallop *Hero*

| 1820–2 | American | Davis | *Cecilia* |
|---|---|---|---|

First recorded landing on mainland of Antarctica: in Hughes Bay 7 February 1821

| 1821–2 | British/American | Powell | *Dove* |
|---|---|---|---|

Powell and Palmer discover South Orkney Islands

| 1822–4 | British | Weddell | *Jane* |
|---|---|---|---|

Penetrated as far as 74° 15′ S in the Weddell Sea

| 1830–2 | British | Biscoe | *Tula* |
|---|---|---|---|

Close circumnavigation of Antarctica: discovery of Enderby Land, Adelaide and Biscoe Islands

| 1837–40 | French | D'Urville | *Astrolabe* |
|---|---|---|---|

Discovery of Terre Adélie and Wilkes Coast; first big national expedition to land on mainland; first rational assessment of the nature of Antarctica

| 1838–42 | American | Wilkes | *Vincennes* |
|---|---|---|---|

Discovery of Wilkes Land; a large segment of the Antarctic coastline followed and roughly charted

| 1839–43 | British | Ross | *Erebus* |
|---|---|---|---|

First expedition to force a way through the pack ice: discovered and charted 500 miles of new coastline, including the Ice Barrier and the active volcano Mount Erebus

| 1872–6 | British | Nares | *Challenger* |
|---|---|---|---|

Important oceanographical research in Southern Ocean: first steam vessel to cross the Antarctic Circle

| 1873–4 | German | Dallmann | *Grönland* |
|---|---|---|---|

Revival of Antarctic sealing; first charting of Bismarck Strait

| 1892–3 | British | Bruce | *Balaena* |
|---|---|---|---|

Joint whaling/scientific reconnaissance; discovery of Active Sound

| Date | Nationality | Leader | Ship |
|------|-------------|--------|------|
| 1894–5 | Norwegian | Bull | *Antarctic* |

The introduction of the Svend Foyn harpoon gun marks the start of successful Antarctic whaling

| 1897–9 | Belgian | de Gerlache | *Belgica* |

Discovered and mapped Gerlache Strait. The *Belgica* was trapped by pack ice southwest of Alexander Island, and was the first exploring vessel to winter in the Antarctic

| 1898–1900 | British | Borchgrevink | *Southern Cross* |

Surveyed coast of Victoria Land: was the first expedition intentionally to winter (at Cape Adare) on the mainland. Scientific programme

| 1901–3 | German | Drygalski | *Gauss* |

Discovered Kaiser Wilhelm II Land: second vessel to winter in the pack ice

| 1901–4 | Swedish | Nordenskjöld | *Antarctic* |

Mapped part of Antarctic peninsula; spent two winters on Snow Hill Island. Comprehensive scientific programme

| 1901–4 | British | Scott | *Discovery* |

Extensive programme of exploration by land: experiments with travel by motor sledge, man-hauled sledge, ponies and dogs. Comprehensive scientific programme

| 1902–4 | British | Bruce | *Scotia* |

First oceanographical exploration of Weddell Sea; discovered Caird coast

| 1904–5 | Norwegian/ Argentine | Larsen | *Fortuna* |

Established the first whaling station on South Georgia

| 1907–9 | British | Shackleton | *Nimrod* |

Discovered Queen Maud mountains; sledged to within 97 miles of the Pole

| 1908–10 | French | Charcot | *Pourquoi Pas?* |

Charted Alexander Island, discovered Fallières Coast. Comprehensive scientific programme

| 1910–12 | German | Filchner | *Deutschland* |

Discovered Luitpold Coast, and charted south shore of Weddell Sea; discovered Filchner Ice Shelf

| 1910–12 | Norwegian | Amundsen | *Fram* |

First to reach the South Pole, 14 December 1911

| Date | Nationality | Leader | Ship |
|------|-------------|--------|------|
| 1910–13 | British | Scott | *Terra Nova* |

Five men reached the South Pole 17 January 1912 but perished during the return journey. Extensive exploration and scientific research

| | | | |
|------|-------------|--------|------|
| 1911–14 | Australasian | Mawson | *Aurora* |

Discovered and explored King George V Land and Queen Mary Land; sledged to South Magnetic Pole. Extensive scientific investigations. First detailed study of Macquarie Island

| | | | |
|------|-------------|--------|------|
| 1914–16 | British | Shackleton | *Endurance* |

First attempted crossing of Antarctica. *Endurance* crushed by the ice, her crew escaping to Elephant Island. Shackleton sails 800 miles by open boat to South Georgia to organize rescue

| | | | |
|------|-------------|--------|------|
| 1928–9 | British/American | Wilkins | *Hektoria* |

Pioneer air reconnaissance

| | | | |
|------|-------------|--------|------|
| 1928–30 | American | Byrd | *City of New York* |

Extensive air reconnaissance. Discovery of Rockefeller and Edsel Ford Mountains; discovery of Marie Byrd Land. First flight over the South Pole

| | | | |
|------|-------------|--------|------|
| 1929–31 | Australasian | Mawson | *Discovery* |

Discovered MacRobertson Land, Banzare Coast, Princess Elizabeth Land. Fixed boundaries of Australian Antarctic Territory

| | | | |
|------|-------------|--------|------|
| 1933–5 | American | Byrd | *Bear of Oakland* |

Semi-permanent base established at Little America II. Extensive air and sledge reconnaissance. Extensive scientific programme, including seismic soundings to determine position of coast. Advance weather station 100 miles inland manned for seven months

| | | | |
|------|-------------|--------|------|
| 1934–7 | British | Rymill | *Penola* |

Survey of Palmer Archipelago and coast of Antarctic peninsula

| | | | |
|------|-------------|--------|------|
| 1935–6 | American | Ellsworth | *Wyatt Earp* |

First crossing of Antarctica by air

| | | | |
|------|-------------|--------|------|
| 1939–41 | American | Byrd | *North Star* |

Extensive exploration by air. Comprehensive scientific programme

| | | | |
|------|-------------|--------|------|
| 1946–7 | American | Byrd | *Mount Olympus* |

Largest expedition so far attempted: thirteen ships and 4,000 men. Extensive photographic reconnaissance

| | | | |
|------|-------------|--------|------|
| 1947 | Argentine | Garcia | *Patagonia* |

Permanent weather stations established. Photographic reconnaissance by air

| Date | Nationality | Leader | Ship |
|------|-------------|--------|------|
| 1947 | Chilean | Toro | *Iquique* |

Permanent weather stations established. Photographic reconnaissance by seaplane

| | | | |
|------|-------------|--------|------|
| 1948–53 | French | Liotard | *Commandant Charcot* |

Research station established in Terre Adélie. Scientific programme including hydrography, geophysics and biology

| | | | |
|------|-------------|--------|------|
| 1949–52 | British<br>Norwegian<br>Swedish | Giaever | *Norsel* |

First fully international expedition to the Antarctic. Extensive meteorological and glaciological programme

| | | | |
|------|-------------|--------|------|
| 1956–7 | American (IGY) | Dufek | various |

Several stations established both inland and on coast, including 'Amundsen-Scott' base at South Pole. Extensive scientific programme

| | | | |
|------|-------------|--------|------|
| 1956–8 | Russian (IGY) | Treshnikov | various |

Stations established inland near South Geomagnetic Pole and Pole of Inaccessibility. Extensive scientific programme

| | | | |
|------|-------------|--------|------|
| 1955–8 | British (IGY) | Fuchs | various |

First crossing of Antarctica by land. Limited scientific programme

The base by moonlight, Signy Island, South Orkney Islands

# Bibliography

## General Reading
Chief sources:
King, H. G. R. *The Antarctic*. London 1969
Kirwan, L. P. *The White Road*. London 1959
Mill, H. R. *The Siege of the South Pole*. London 1905

Further reading:
Bechervaise, John. *The Far South*. London 1962
Chapman, W. *The Loneliest Continent*. London 1967
Christie, E. W. Hunter. *The Antarctic Problem*. London 1951
Hobbs, W. H. *Explorers of the Antarctic*. New York 1941
Hydrographic Department, London. *The Antarctic Pilot*
Hydrographic Office, Washington D.C. *Sailing Directions for Antarctica*
Ley, W. *The Poles*. London 1966
Quartermain, L. B. *South to the Pole*. London 1967
Skelton, R. A. *Explorers' Maps*. London 1958
Sullivan, W. *Quest for a Continent*. London 1957
Useful articles in: *Antarctic* (New Zealand); *Polar Record*; *Geographical Magazine*; *The Geographical Journal*

## Chapter 1
Chief source:
Burney, J. *History of Voyages and Discoveries in the South Sea*. London 1803–16

Further reading:
Balch, E. S. *Antarctica*. Philadelphia 1902
Brosses, C. de. *Histoire des Navigations aux Terres Australes*. Paris 1756
Dalrymple, A. *An Historical Collection of the Several Voyages and Discoveries in the South Pacific Ocean*. 2 vols. London 1770–1

Hakluyt, R. *The Principal Navigations, Voyages, Traffiques and Discoveries of the English Nation*. Hakluyt Society, Glasgow 1903–5
Kerguélen-Trémarec, Y. J. de. *Relation de deux Voyages dans les Mers Australes et des Indes*. Paris 1782
Mason, A. E. W. *The Life of Francis Drake*. London 1941
Seixas y Lovera, Francisco de. *Descripcion Geographica y Derrotero de la Region Austral Magellanica*. Madrid 1690

## Chapter 2
Chief source:
Beaglehole, J. C. ed. 'The Voyage of the Resolution and Adventure (1772–75) by James Cook', *The Journals of Captain James Cook*. London 1961

Further reading:
Badger, G. M. ed. *Captain Cook, Navigator and Scientist*. Canberra 1970
Carrington, H. *Life of Captain Cook*. London 1967
Forster, George. *A Voyage Round the World*. London 1777
Muir, J. R. *Captain Cook*. London 1939
Sparrman, Anders. *A Voyage Round the World with Captain James Cook in H.M.S. Resolution*. Trans. Averil Mackenzie-Grieve and Huldine V. Beamish. London 1953. (Part 2 only of the original Swedish ed.: *Resa till Goda-Hopps Udden*, etc.)
Villiers, A. *Captain Cook, the Seaman's Seaman*. London 1967

## Chapter 3
Chief sources:
Bonner, W. N. and Laws, R. M. 'Seals and Sealing', *Antarctic Research*. Ed. R. Priestley. London 1964
Stackpole, E. A. *The Voyage of the* Huron *and the* Huntress. Connecticut 1955
Stonehouse, B. *Animals of the Antarctic: Ecology of the Far South*. London 1972

Further reading:
(Attributed to) Bone, T. 'Edward Bransfield's Antarctic Voyage of 1819–20, and the Discovery of the Antarctic Continent', *Polar Record*, 32
Christie, E. W. Hunter. *The Antarctic Problem*. London 1951
Clark, A. Howard. 'The Antarctic Fur-Seal and Sea-Elephant Industries', G. B. Goode, *The Fisheries and Fishery Industries of the United States*, Vol. II, Part 18. Washington D.C. 1887
Fanning, E. *Voyages Round the World*. New York 1833
Gould, T. R. 'The Charting of the South Shetlands, 1819–28', *Mariner's Mirror*, 27
Hinks, A. R. 'On Some Misrepresentations of Antarctic History', *Geographical Journal*, 94
Hobbs, W. H. 'The Discoveries of Antarctica Within the American Sector', *Transactions of the American Philosophical Society*, 31, Part I
King, Judith E. *Seals of the World*. London 1964
Martin, F. *The Hunting of the Silver Fleece*. New York 1946
Palmer, N. B. *Log of the* Hero
Scheffer, V. B. *Seals, Sea Lions and Walruses*. Stanford 1958
Turbott, E. G. *Seals of the Southern Ocean*. Wellington 1952


**Chapter 4**
Chief source:
Debenham, Frank, ed. *The Voyage of Captain Bellingshausen to the Antarctic Seas, 1819–1821*. Trans. E. Bullough and others. London 1945

Further reading:
Andreyev, A. I. *Voyage of the Sloops* Vostok *and* Mirnyi *to the Antarctic* (in Russian). Moscow 1949
Armstrong, Terence. 'Bellingshausen and the Discovery of Antarctica', *Polar Record*, 15, 99

Belov, M. I. *Discovery of the Ice Continent* (in Russian). Leningrad 1963
Nozikov, N. *Russian Voyages Round the World*. Trans. E. and M. Lesser. London 1945
Semantovsky, V. N. *Russian Discoveries in the Antarctic* (in Russian). Moscow 1951


**Chapter 5**
Chief sources:
Dumont d'Urville, S. J. C. *Voyage au Pôle Sud et dans l'Océanie sur les Corvettes l'*Astrolabe *et la* Zelée, etc. Paris 1841–54
*Log of the Ship* Huron *of New Haven,* 1821
Ross, J. C. *A Voyage of Discovery and Research in the Southern and Antarctic Oceans, 1839–1843*. London 1847
Wilkes, Charles. *Narrative of the United States Exploring Expedition, 1838–1842*. Philadelphia 1845

Further reading:
Hooker, J. D. *The Botany of the Antarctic Voyage of H.M.S.* Erebus *and* Terror *in the Years 1839–1843*. London 1847
Mitterling, P. I. *America in Antarctica to 1840*. Urbana 1959
Stackpole, E. A. *The Voyage of the* Huron *and the* Huntress. Connecticut 1955
Vergniol, C. *Dumont d'Urville, 1790–1842*. Paris
Wilkes, Charles. *Defence . . . of . . . C. W. . . . to the charges on which he has been tried* etc. (Pamphlet for presentation in court during the court-martial proceedings.) Probably Washington D.C. 1842


**Chapter 6**
Chief source:
Ommanney, F. D. *Lost Leviathan*. London 1971

Further reading:
Chatterton, E. K. *Whalers and Whaling*. London 1925
Cheever, H. T. *The Whale and his Captors*. London 1852

Fraser, F. C. 'Whales and Whaling', *Antarctic Research*. Ed. R. Priestley. London 1964

Hohman, E. P. *The American Whaleman*. New York 1928

Holdgate, M. W. *Antarctic Ecology*, 2 vols. London 1970

Jenkins, T. *Whales and Modern Whaling*. London 1932

Melville, Herman. *Moby Dick*. 1851

Romarate, J. L. y. *Historia del Illustre Pais Bascongade*. Bilbao 1901

Sanderson. I. T. *Follow the Whale*. London 1958

Turbott, E. G. 'Whales and Whaling in the Southern Ocean', *The Antarctic Today*. Ed. F. A. Simpson. Wellington 1952


### Chapter 7

Chief sources:

Cook, F. A. *Through the First Antarctic Night*. London 1905

Gerlache de Gomery, A. de. *Quinze Mois dans l'Antarctique*. Brussels 1902


Further reading:

Amundsen, Roald. *The South Pole*. Trans. A. G. Chater. London 1912

—— *My Life as an Explorer*. London 1927

Arctowski, H. *Die Antarktischen Eisver-hältnisse*. Gotha 1903

—— Articles in *The Geographical Journal*

Duse, S. A. *Bland Pingviner och Säler*. Stockholm 1905

Expédition Antarctique Belge. *Resultats du Voyages du S.Y.* Belgica *en 1897–98–99*. (Summary of the expedition's scientific work.) Antwerp 1901

Lecointe, G. *Au Pays des Manchots*. 1904


### Chapter 8

Chief source:

Nordenskjöld, O. and Andersson, J. G. *Antarctica*. London 1905


Further reading:

Andersson, J. G. *De Pågående Antarktiska Expeditionerna*. Stockholm 1903

Nordenskjöld, O. 'The Swedish Antarctic Expedition', *Smithsonian Report*. 1903. (Scientific papers relating to the expedition are available in a few geographical libraries.)

Sobral, J. N. *Dos Anos Entre Los Hielos*. Madrid 1911


### Chapter 9

Chief sources:

Amundsen, Roald. *The South Pole*. Trans. A. G. Chater. London 1912

Huxley, L., ed. *Scott's Last Expedition* (Scott's Journals). London 1913


Further reading:

Amundsen, Roald. *My Life as an Explorer*. London 1927

Cherry-Garrard, A. *The Worst Journey in the World*. London 1922

Partridge, B. *Amundsen*. New York 1929

Ponting, H. G. *The Great White South*. London 1921

Seaver, G. *Birdie Bowers of the Antarctic*. London 1937

—— *Edward Wilson of the Antarctic*. London 1937

Scott, R. F. *The Voyage of the* Discovery. London 1905.

Turley, C. *Roald Amundsen, Explorer*. London 1935

Wilson, E. A. *Diary of the* Discovery *Expedition to the Antarctic Regions, 1901–1904*. Ed. Ann Savours. London 1966


### Chapter 10

Chief source:

Byrd, R. E. *Little America*. New York, London 1931


Further reading:

Byrd, R. E. *Discovery*. London 1936

—— *Exploring with Byrd*. New York 1937

—— *Alone*. London 1938

—— Also numerous articles in *National*

*Geographic Magazine* and *Transactions of the American Philosophical Society*

Green, F. *Dick Byrd*. New York, London 1928

## Chapter 11

Chief sources:

Fuchs, Vivian, and Hillary, Edmund. *The Crossing of Antarctica*. London 1957

Shackleton, Ernest. *South*. London 1919

Further reading:

Filchner, W. *Zum sechsten Erdteil: die zweite deutsche Südpolar-Expedition*. Berlin 1923

Fisher, Margery and James. *Shackleton*. London 1957

Hillary, Edmund. *No Latitude for Error*. London 1961

Mill, H. R. *The Life of Sir Ernest Shackleton*. London 1923

Richard, R. W. *The Ross Sea Shore Party, 1914–17*. Cambridge 1965

Shackleton, Ernest. *The Heart of the Antarctic*. London 1911

Wordie, J. R. 'Shackleton's Antarctic Expedition, 1914–1917', *Transactions of the Royal Society of Edinburgh*, Vol. LII (No. 31)

Worsley, F. A. *Endurance: An Epic of Polar Adventure*. London 1931

—— *Shackleton's Boat Journey*. London 1933

## Antarctica Today

Hatterton, T., ed. *Antarctica*. London 1965

Holdgate, M. W., ed. *Biologie Antarctique*. 1964

Schulthess, E. *Antarctica* (a photographic survey). Trans. P. Gorge. London 1961

Simpson, F. A., ed. *The Antarctic Today*. Wellington 1952

Stonehouse, B. *Animals of the Antarctic: Ecology of the Far South*. London 1972

Wilson, E. *Birds of the Antarctic*. Ed. Brian Roberts. London 1967

# Acknowledgments

The Bibliography includes a number of invaluable sources of which grateful use has been made. The author and publishers are especially indebted to the following for permission to quote from their publications:

George Allen & Unwin Ltd (E. W. Hunter Christie *The Antarctic Problem*); The Bodley Head (L. P. Kirwan *The White Road*, Hollis & Carter); Cambridge University Press (J. C. Beaglehole ed. *The Journals of Captain Cook* Vol. II); Cassell & Co. Ltd and John Farquharson Ltd (V. Fuchs and E. Hillary *The Crossing of Antarctica*); Christy & Moore Ltd (F. A. Worsley *Shackleton's Boat Journey*); Doubleday & Co. Inc. (R. Amundsen *My Life as an Explorer*); Eurobook Ltd (B. Stonehouse *Animals of the Antarctic*); John Farquharson Ltd (I. T. Sanderson *Follow the Whale*; D. Stratton *Diary* quoted in Fuchs and Hillary *The Crossing of Antarctica*); Mrs Margery Fisher (*Shackleton*, Barrie & Jenkins); Hakluyt Society (F. Debenham ed. *The Voyage of Captain Bellingshausen to the Antarctic Seas, 1819–1821*); William Heinemann Ltd (H. R. Mill *The Life of Sir Ernest Shackleton*); Hutchinson Ltd and Dodd, Mead & Co. (F. D. Ommanney *Lost Leviathan*); John Murray Ltd (R. Amundsen *The South Pole*); Oxford University Press (L. B. Quartermain *South to the Pole*); G. P. Putnam's Sons (R. E. Byrd *Exploring with Byrd*; R. E. Byrd *Little America*). Thanks are also due to the Trustees of the Estate of Sir Leonard Lucas-Tooth and William Heinemann Ltd (Sir Ernest Shackleton *South*) and Hutchinson Ltd (O. Nordenskjöld and J. G. Andersson *Antarctica*).

Every effort has been made to ascertain the owners of copyright. The publishers apologize for any inadvertent omissions and will be pleased to receive any information that would enable these to be rectified in a future edition.

# Index

The page numbers in italics refer to the illustrations.